BITING THE DUST

MARGARET HORSFIELD

BITING THE DUST
THE JOYS OF HOUSEWORK

FOURTH ESTATE • *London*

For my mother, who shines

First published in Great Britain in 1997 by
Fourth Estate Limited
6 Salem Road
London W2 4BU

Copyright © 1997 by Margaret Horsfield

1 3 5 7 9 10 8 6 4 2

The right of Margaret Horsfield to be identified as the author
of this work has been asserted by her in accordance with the
Copyright, Designs and Patents Act 1988.

A catalogue record for this book is available from the British
Library.

ISBN 1–85702–422–2

Typeset by Palimpsest Book Production Limited,
Polmont, Stirlingshire
Printed in Great Britain by Clays Ltd, St Ives plc,
Bungay, Suffolk.

CONTENTS

ILLUSTRATIONS

The Morning Gossip by George Cruikshank (*Hulton Getty*)

Hannah Cullwick in 1872 (*by permission of the Master and Fellows of Trinity College, Cambridge*)

Florence Nightingale in 1891 (*Hulton Getty*)

Advertisement for Ronuk Polish, 1906 (*The Illustrated London News Picture Library*)

A range of cleaning equipment, c.1915 (*author's collection*)

Maids at a London training centre in 1938 (*Hulton Getty*)

Advertisement for household disinfectant, 1929 (*author's collection*)

An attempt to glamorise toilet cleaning, 1942 (*author's collection*)

Harpic and Lifebuoy advertisements (*Advertising Archive*)

Spring cleaning with a swing: Vim advertisement (*Advertising Archive*)

Glamorous images of household cleaning from the 1950s and 1960s (*Hoover*)

ACKNOWLEDGEMENTS

Other people's stories are the backbone of this book. Many have shared their dark secrets of dirty ovens, glowing accounts of gleaming floors and true confessions of reeking dishcloths. I am most grateful to everyone who has taken the time to talk to me, write to me, and answer my questions about cleaning.

For their invaluable help with research I owe many thanks to Yvonne Hewett, Jean Snedegar and Jean Blackburn. They bravely coped with many strange searches and peculiar requests. Thanks also to everyone who passed on ideas and suggestions and who sent books and articles and magazines my way, particularly Christine Aircy, Peter Buckland, Maria Coffey, Joan Coutu, Elizabeth Cowan, Sandra Gwyn, Mora Kelly, Eleanor Moorhouse, Liza Potvin, Brenda Silsbe, Gail Singer, Diane Stuart, Sarah Thring, Claudette Upton and Mary Wilkie. For helping me to understand more about household germs, I would like to thank Elizabeth Scott.

For inspiration and for childcare I am indebted to my neighbours Cathy Hebb and Bernice Brown. Deirdre Gill, Clea Gelinas, and Megan and Zach Sprout also helped me more than they know.

For financial assistance during the writing of the book, I would like to thank both the Canada Council and the Cultural Services Branch of the Province of British Columbia.

Sandra Gwyn and Yvonne Hewett kindly read parts of the manuscript in its early stages and helped me to keep going. Later, Gordon Elliott provided unstinting editorial assistance, in keeping with the consistent support and kindness he has provided ever since I was sixteen, when he frightened me into writing a better essay for my next assignment.

Thanks to my agent Carol Heaton, for her patience, and to my editor Sally Holloway. Special thanks to Paul Gelinas; this book was his idea and the sketches are all his.

To my mother and my father, as always, many thanks. They have been my most faithful friends.

Finally, my thanks and my love to Emma, who so happily washed walls, wiped the table and cleaned the sink while this book was being written. Long may her enthusiasm last.

I am grateful for permission to quote from the following works: *The Second Sex* by Simone de Beauvoir (reprinted by permission of Jonathan Cape, London, and the Estate of the author); *The Limits of Vision* by Robert Irwin (reprinted by permission of Dedalus Ltd); *Blanche on the Lam* by Barbara Neely (copyright © 1992 by Barbara Neely. Originally published in the United States by St Martin's Press. No part of this material may be reproduced in whole or in part without the express written permission of the author or her agent); *The Sacred and the Feminine* by Kathryn Allen Rabuzzi (courtesy of the author); *Queen of All the Dustballs* by Bill Richardson (reprinted with permission of Polestar Book Publishers Ltd, 1011 Commercial Drive, Vancouver, BC V5L 3X1); *Women and Families: An Oral History 1940–1970* by Elizabeth Roberts (reprinted by permission of Blackwell Publishers, Oxford); *The Diaries of Hannah Cullwick* edited by Liz Stanley (reprinted by permission of Virago Press); *I, Gloria Gold* by Judith Summers, published by William Collins, London, 1988 (reprinted by permission of the author).

PREFACE

Think for a moment of dirt, household dirt. About grease on the top of kitchen cupboards, slime on dishracks, dustballs in corners and sticky messes on floors and countertops. Think of getting rid of this dirt, from your kitchen countertop for example. How often do you wipe it, with what, and why? Or consider cleaning the bathroom sink or the toilet. What do these activities cost, in time and in money, in energy spent on labour, argument or procrastination?

Chances are you have rarely given much conscious thought to household dirt or to the subject of housecleaning. Few of us do. Cleaning has absolutely no *cachet*, unlike other domestic pursuits like cooking, gardening, decorating or child-rearing; as an important part of our daily lives it is loftily disregarded. Such disregard is unjust.

Keeping our homes clean involves a great deal of time and effort; it arouses strong feelings and preferences and prejudices; it conjures up bizarre practices, deeply ingrained beliefs, and decades of powerful conditioning. How we care for our homes, and how we are encouraged to care for them, is a deceptively simple matter. But just lift the corner of the rug, and see what lies underneath.

Examining this ordinary subject of housecleaning reveals a mess of social and commercial pressures; it leads into a minefield of motivations, into an unending source of stories, and into a history that is downright strange. Anyone who cleans – and most of us do to some degree – is part of a long and mixed legacy of others, mostly women, who have cleaned their own homes and who have influenced us in how we clean ours. Maids and mistresses, housewives and home economists, sanitary reformers and feminist critics are all part of this legacy. Their attitudes towards and advice about cleaning are not only entertaining and odd, they provide a kind of social barometer that reflects the changing role of women, the changing economic and social patterns of the last century and a half.

This book is mostly about women, for reasons that will become obvious. In fairness to men, however, a whole chapter has been devoted to them, and they appear elsewhere in the book as well. Most of my attention is directed towards people who do their own housecleaning, though the role of the housecleaner is addressed in Chapter Fifteen – something I could hardly overlook, having been a cleaner myself.

Housecleaning habits and attitudes towards housework come under scrutiny in this book as well as the history of cleaning practices. I should stress that household cleanliness is the subject here, not personal hygiene, though the two can overlap; also that I am interested in domestic settings, not institutions like hospitals or schools or restaurants. I should also clarify that when I speak of housework or of housekeeping, I am using those terms solely in reference to cleaning.

The material used in this book comes from many sources: from magazines and newspapers, domestic advice books, advertisements; from scholarly studies of housework, social histories, home economics texts; from novels, childrens' stories and poetry. Most importantly, I have drawn on over a hundred interviews I have done about housecleaning, not to mention countless conversations with friends, colleagues and strangers. The people who discussed their cleaning habits are a random lot; they live in England, America and Canada, their ages vary considerably, their economic circumstances differ greatly. One characteristic they all share is their frank amazement at how much they had to say about cleaning, once they started. Their talkative enjoyment of the subject has been enormously encouraging; I am in their debt.

No ponderous tome lies ahead, weighted down with sombre analysis and anxious assessment of data. Far from it. Here, simply by paying close and quizzical attention to housecleaning, a common pursuit gains long overdue recognition as protests are heard, advice analysed, stories told. Many voices are raised in this book, many points of view aired, and cleaning house is, I hope, justly celebrated, and given the credit it deserves as an important and revealing activity in our lives.

1

DENIAL AND DEFENCE

COMING CLEAN ABOUT HOUSEWORK

'No one wants to talk about it,' announced Mary. 'Everyone sounds so defensive.' Mary had promised that several of her friends were going to gather for a convivial chat about cleaning, and I was planning to join them. 'We're up against some real denial here. They're all saying they never clean, but I know these women, and they spend *hours* cleaning, one way or another. What's going on?'

Denial and defence again: a familiar pattern. Here, yet again, women were shying away from talking about the Cinderella skills of housecleaning, and yet again making me feel that the subject was not worthy of attention. The protestations were the usual ones. 'What is there to say?' 'I hardly ever clean – you should *see* my place!' 'You want to know something about cleaning? Don't come to my house.'

This would be a temporary hiccup. Once the ice was broken with this or any other group of women, the discussion would become lively. Cleaning stories are like fishing stories: once the talk starts flying, each person has a bigger and better tale to tell. This group was no exception when we finally met.

You should meet my sister-in-law – I'm not joking, she doesn't let my brother or my nephew stand up to pee. They have to sit down because she says if they stand up and spray all over the place she'll leave. And the amazing thing is that they do sit down – and they are trained to wipe the shower curtain, never to eat in the living room, to clean the tub – the place is spotless.

How would you deal with a house guest who insisted on washing all the floors? I felt ridiculous. She did it twice in one week – and the floor really wasn't all that dirty, or I didn't think it was. And I'm pretty sure she cleaned the toilet a few times, too.

She died in that house last year, and I swear she hadn't cleaned it since her husband died in 1975. It was unbelievable – all those cats everywhere, and the stink of cigarette smoke, and everything on the walls discoloured, and that good china all furry with dust. She always offered us a cup of tea out of her good cups, and it was horrible, trying not to drink it, or to eat anything, or to touch anything. The towels in the bathroom were grey with dirt. It scared me.

I always loved the Dick and Jane story books when I was in school. Our own house was such a mess, and I wanted to live in that dream world of clean white houses where everything was perfect. And that's what I aimed for when I got married – I really did.

Don't talk to me about the stove – just don't mention it. My mother refuses point blank to cook at my place; she says the stove is just too dirty. It's not all that bad – I reckon most of the dirt gets burned off. And I have no problem about the oven – I just don't ever look in with the light on.

The voices merge into a babble of anecdotes of what we do and don't do, how we feel, what we buy, how we act. There is a rich vein of story here, a lot of strong feeling, often an active sense of the ridiculous. Yet in telling these stories few of us pause to think about what we are really saying about ourselves and our homes and our expectations. We are not in the habit of analysing how we clean and why.

How could this be otherwise? Housecleaning is not something

we have ever been encouraged to think about. It is not a public achievement like getting the vote, or a social skill like cooking; it cannot brag of a long, well-documented history; it has not been rescued and restored to dignity by feminist historians. It is a daily activity that occupies men and women – but mostly women – the world over. It is tiring, it is never done, it often goes unnoticed, and it is largely thankless. Many of us would rather not do it but we must, however badly and however patchily; some of us pay other people to do it, some of us try to turn a blind eye to it altogether, some of us do it in slightly mad outbursts. Few if any of us are able to ignore it completely, though some of us may try.

I tried to ignore it. For years on end cleaning was the last thing on my mind. There were infinitely better things to do, out there slaying giants in the working world; making radio programmes and writing articles and books. Preoccupation with domestic concerns was beneath me, and the last thing I would have cared to admit. Like many women I vaguely believed that expressing interest in such menial matters would somehow be a betrayal of the sisterhood: after all, our feminist forebears did not chain themselves to railings to empower us to keep our houses bright and clean.

When the idea for this book arose, I was horrified. The idea was not mine. It came from a friend who knows me well and has seen me in action both at work and at home. Tired of listening to my complaints about the Dead Sea Scrolls – I was then working on a radio programme on the subject – he looked at me in exasperation and said that it was high time I worked on something closer to my heart, something I understood and was naturally good at – like cleaning the house. The argument that ensued was long and lively. How dare he diminish me that way, how dare he suggest cleaning house was all I was good for. This was not what he meant, he argued, just that I was always cleaning; it was my way of procrastinating, of venting my anger, of clearing my mind, of making myself feel better; it was something I had strong opinions about, so why not turn my mind towards a subject that was part of my life, part of *everyone's* life.

A likely story. I fumed for days, but the annoying idea stuck. I began to consider the time and energy I spend cleaning, the effort involved, and the complete lack of thought I had ever given it. I began to talk to others about it, asking them about their housecleaning habits, and immediately ran into strangely mixed attitudes. Response was almost always guarded. 'Why are you asking me this?' one woman said, suspiciously. The responses were interesting.

To come clean about how we clean and why we clean is more of a challenge than it first appears. Many people try to shrug it off, describing their cleaning habits as a series of disorganised swipes with a cloth, disclaiming any particular interest in the subject. But just try asking people how often they clean their toilets, and witness the response. A silence, a laugh, a moment to think, a quick calculation of how they might be judged; then from some the admission that they have no idea, from others a litany of germ-killing frenzy, from still others a defiant confession of monthly encounters with a toilet brush.

Of course there are those for whom cleaning is a matter of considerable pride, but they rarely discuss it. Clipped phrases are common, such as 'I do like the sink to be nice and clean' or 'It's just not nice when grease is splattered all over the stove' or 'It's nice to give things a good going over'. From contented cleaners, the word 'nice' pops up again and again, leaving the impression of cleaning as a peculiarly private and inarticulate pleasure, which leaves a happy although temporary glow.

When cleaning is under discussion, the apologisers are without number. I have lost count of the people who have apologised for the state of their homes. This experience is not unique to me. Mary Ellen Pinkham, who is hailed as 'America's number one household authority' on the dustjacket of her book *Mary Ellen's Clean House* (1993), writes crisply that 'There isn't a house I go into where my hostess doesn't apologise for how the place looks (and most of the time it looks pretty good)'. Familiar territory: I too have so often apologised or made excuses about my own home – and still do. As I write this, large dustballs lurk under the beds in the house, spider webs are festooned in many corners, you could write your name in the dust on the bookshelves, the bathroom is just tolerable and the kitchen sink is full of dishes. My mother, who raised me to perform much more adequately, is not impressed when she visits.

Those of us brought up in the 1950s and 60s and coming of age in the brave new world of feminist thinking witnessed the pressures on our mothers to have a whiter-than-white household. Many of us have tried to resist the pattern of our housebound, houseproud mothers. We strode forth into the world determined to have minds above ring-around-the-collar and waxy yellow buildup on our floors. Yet we are far from immune to these early influences and, while perhaps wishing to put such conditioning behind us, when we get down to specifics it becomes blindingly evident that we have not escaped scot free. Rueful confessions always emerge of strong feelings about the kitchen sink or the toilet; about white socks or children's school clothes; about dust on mirrors or grease on glasses or stained coffee mugs or – my own particular horror of horrors – dirty dishcloths.

Such admissions we often make reluctantly. Ever since Betty Friedan's powerful and stinging analysis in *The Feminine Mystique* (1963), cleaning house has become an activity for which no politically correct woman in her right mind would dare show much enthusiasm. In Friedan's view it is a ghastly legacy. She shows how advertisers have manipulated women into taking ridiculously exaggerated pride and interest in such ordinary activities as washing dishes and floors. She shows how women who know better clean more than is necessary and buy products that they do not need for tasks that are superfluous. She quotes marketing reports that are merciless in targeting the needs and weaknesses of their intended victims, reports that openly declare how they intend to capitalise on the housewife's 'guilt over the hidden dirt'. The marketeers puff women up with pride and self-importance for doing what is, to Friedan, unfulfilling and unchallenging work that any dim-witted fool can do in probably half the time.

In the face of this condemnation, how many women would now dare be caught waxing a floor and enjoying the shine? Being honest about taking mild pleasure in the simple ordinariness of such activities can be strangely difficult. I remember once biting my tongue with embarrassment when, without pausing to think, I asked a neighbour how she managed to keep her floors so shiny. Even though curious to know – it was a dazzling floor – I was appalled to hear myself talking like a bad television advertisement. A similar moment arose when a friend asked me how my baby's cloth nappies remained so white; instead of feeling pleased that someone had noticed this minor achievement, I felt profoundly silly. We were both professional women who should have minds above such concerns. Admitting an interest might mean revealing myself as a mere housewife, a poor sap at the mercy of every advertiser, every advice book, every cleaning product, a helpless and stupid rabbit caught in the glare of strong headlights.

Yet this kind of reaction is nonsensical. I know perfectly well that I do not have a mind above cleaning and that few people do, no matter what they say. Most of us are down among the mops and brooms and dishcloths, however resentfully, however inefficiently or spasmodically. If anyone persistently denies any interest in, involvement with or concern about cleaning, only three conclusions are possible. They are lying, or flamboyantly eccentric, or they hire someone else to do all the work.

The truth is there are a lot of clean – or at least clean-ish – homes out there, and a great deal of time and effort and money goes into keeping them that way. Many people wash floors and clean bathtubs; many not only buy but read books of household advice; many sincerely worry about how to kill germs in the toilet or on kitchen countertops. Why pretend that such concerns have disappeared just because they display 'a bourgeois lack of cool', as the narrator says about cleaning in Margaret Atwood's novel *Cat's Eye* (1988)? Housecleaning may be derided as an uncool, unliberated preoccupation, but it continues to be done, it continues to be a time-consuming and important part of many everyday lives. We are not as free, and perhaps can never be as free from 'the dusty drudgery' as some might like to imagine.

This fact does not bother me because, despite my apologies about cleaning, despite many years of ignoring it, I genuinely like cleaning. I always have, ever since those Saturday mornings when my mother paid me two dollars to wax floors and do the laundry and clean the bathrooms. The luminous patterns I made on the linoleum with the electric floor polisher, the comforting chug of the old wringer washer, the gleam of sinks and taps when I had finished – all of these pleased me. My later experiences as a cleaner and chambermaid only reinforced these feelings.

What *does* bother me about housecleaning, and what is so intriguing about it, is the low esteem so persistently granted it. This low esteem is longstanding: 'Such work has generally been done by vulgar people, and in a vulgar way', wrote the domestic adviser Catharine Beecher in *A Treatise on Domestic Economy For the Use of Young Ladies at Home and At School* published in 1841. She, along with many others, was fired with determination to enhance and improve the image of 'such work'. Her success has been, at best, limited. In many quarters, cleaning is still seen as the 'least desirable of labours' involving all that is 'basest and foulest'.

Yet paradoxically, cleaning house is also a way in which women can assert their moral, familial and domestic worth. Keeping a place clean is a way of declaring one's superior values and standards; a way of setting oneself and one's surroundings apart from the chaos and dirt of the outside world; a way of shoring up self-esteem. 'I feel *so* good about myself when the house is clean,' one woman said. 'I feel the house is a better place for me and for my family, and the credit for that is all mine, and everyone knows it.' For this woman, doing battle with dirt is an act of conscious virtue, and achieving that virtuous glow far outweighs any negative notions about cleaning as a lowly occupation.

When cleaning is under consideration, a rich array of attitudes and actions quickly become evident. And every attitude, every action, every belief about cleaning is open to question and criticism, every term used invites scrutiny. Clean, for instance:

What *is* clean? Or what *is* dirt? Such questions leave most of us scratching our heads and giving up after thirty seconds, but they provide a meaty challenge to social theorists. Mary Douglas's magnificent book on pollution and taboo, *Purity and Danger* (1966), is helpful here: 'Our idea of dirt is compounded of two things, care for hygiene and respect for conventions. The rules of hygiene change, of course, with changes in our state of knowledge. As for the conventional side of dirt-avoidance, these rules can be set aside for the sake of friendship.' Then follows a quotation from *Far From the Madding Crowd* in which the shepherd Gabriel is offered a clean cup to drink from and he refuses it, to the approbation of his fellow-labourers. 'I never fuss', he says, 'about dirt in its pure state, and when I know what sort it is. I wouldn't think of giving such trouble to neighbours in washing up when there's so much work to be done in the world already.' In accepting the communal cup, Gabriel is at one with his fellows; to insist on something separate, cleaner and special would have been a social *faux pas* on a par with asking a hostess at a party if you could please have a chair free of cat-hair. As it is, Gabriel is hailed as a 'nice unparticular man'.

Mary Douglas's point here is that both the conventional definitions of dirt and the hygienic definitions of dirt are non-absolute. They change with social circumstance and with scientific knowledge. Think, for instance, of the different standards of cleanliness we accept when travelling or camping, compared to the standards of everyday life. Think also of how easily our notions of hygiene sway: our cleaning habits can change overnight because of an increased fear of salmonella, for instance, or dust mites; because someone is sick in the house; because we have read a scary article about how dishcloths spread germs. Yet while our boundaries and definitions are open to change, they are contained within an underlying (and largely unarticulated) sense of order.

Dirt is essentially *disorder*, Mary Douglas stresses. Sociologists define dirt as 'matter out of place' within a pattern that is perceived as normal and ordered, suited to our own world view. Very young children make this sense of order abundantly clear. They notice dirt acutely: on their hands, on their clothes, in their homes, and they often want to get rid of it, not because it is bad, but because it was not in that particular place earlier and it offends their sense of how things ought to be. How many mothers have had to respond to their toddlers' outraged shouts of 'Dirty, Mum' by patiently wiping a sticky hand or toy with a grubby tissue. Nothing is rendered much cleaner by such action, but a juvenile sense of what is right and proper is restored.

Children see dirt that many an adult would happily ignore. 'This sink very dirty,' declared a visiting tot, gazing at my bathroom washbasin. He was apparently offended by a few blobs of toothpaste. 'I wash it.' And he did, for twenty-five minutes of uninterrupted concentration. My own young daughter had a passion for washing walls for about six months around the time of her second birthday. 'Dirty,' she would announce firmly, glaring at some small speck or other, and taking a cloth she would slop water over whatever wall she was allowed near. This fixation was entirely hers and because I never, ever wash walls, she was not copying me. 'Fluff,' she would also declare disapprovingly whenever she rolled under the bed. 'Mum get it.' Her disapproval of dirt and fluff and the degree to which it bothered her intrigued me: the way she seemed to sense that something – the speck of dirt or the fluff – did not belong there.

'Where there is dirt there is system,' writes Mary Douglas. 'Shoes are not dirty in themselves, but it is dirty to place them on the dining-table; food is not dirty in itself, but it is dirty to leave cooking utensils in the bedroom, or food bespattered on clothing.' Thus in many households cat-hair on every chair is the norm, in others, unthinkable; in some, coffee-stained mugs or a hairbrush on the breadboard never raise an eyebrow, in others they are embarrassing evidence of dirt and disorder. No absolute rules apply to all people, because all people order their lives differently. As a result, definitions of dirt and of cleanliness vary hugely, something that is obvious when people talk about their household standards. What one person perceives as absolutely essential – say, disinfecting the toilet daily – will strike another person as just plain foolish. These two people may share similar educational backgrounds and similar economic status, but they have entirely different notions about the level of cleanliness that is 'needed' around the house.

Having talked to and interviewed many people about cleanliness, and having read countless books of household advice, I have learned to watch with interest for the terms 'need' and 'necessary'. They crop up all the time. One woman explained at length why she needed to sweep the hall and kitchen three times daily. Another cheerfully said she saw no need ever to wash windows because it rained so much in her part of the world. 'Buy a heavily patterned carpet,' volunteered another. 'They hardly ever need vacuuming.' Purveyors of professional domestic advice are full of 'necessary' admonitions. 'Even "no-wax" floors need a dressing or finish'; 'The washing of walls and paint needs fifteen hours twice a year'; 'The desire for cleanliness must end up becoming a real *need*.'

For every one of us the definition of what is 'necessary' is different, just as it is with our personal hygiene, our eating habits or in our social lives. One never lacks outside interference and advice in any of these areas; someone is always there, waiting to tell us what is 'necessary'. When these outside agencies win too much power and influence, the result can be alienating and tragic; we then suspend our own judgement, our confidence erodes. We buy foolishly, we listen credulously, we behave ridiculously. From a rational perspective, housecleaning seems to have led women to indulge in punishing excesses.

Cleaning is not, however, a rational process. To spend hours as so many women have done in whitening doorsteps, dusting walls, vacuuming lampshades, polishing kitchen grates or waxing floors does *not* make sense. On a strictly rational level, the health and welfare of a household clearly does not depend on such activities. And such behaviour cannot be dismissed as a regrettable feature of our unliberated past; to this day, countless people in the western world indulge in comparably daft excesses. Is it really necessary for us to wash clothes as often as we do, or to change the sheets at least once a week? And among the women I have talked to, is it necessary for Ruth to disinfect her children's toys regularly? Is it necessary for JoAnne to keep her fridge so clean that she will do it at midnight so that she can go to work the next day with a clear conscience? Is it necessary for my neighbour to wash her bathroom floor daily? Habit comes into play here, soothing social rituals, psychological games, diehard beliefs – all of these. Yes, but necessity?

Trying to understand housecleaning in terms of some absolute standard of 'need' is as futile as trying to impose absolute definitions of what is 'clean' or 'dirty'. No such standards or definitions exist. Once this fact is accepted, the whole exercise of examining cleaning habits becomes much more interesting. Because cleaning then becomes a personal, not an impersonal activity, having nothing to do with the pursuit of a disembodied ideal and everything to do with how we define ourselves and our surroundings. We are forced to ask what is really going on when we are cleaning, and we are forced to look at our own behaviour. How we clean our homes reflects many forms of social conditioning; it is part of a long legacy of how other people in other eras cleaned their homes. It is often part of how we express ourselves and exert ourselves: its daily ordinariness speaks volumes about us.

There is no escaping this conditioning. Even if we decide *not* to clean, *not* to bother about keeping our homes and our possessions clean, we are still open to the same scrutiny. Some of us have the means, the know-how, the ability, to keep our homes and our possessions clean, yet we let it all moulder away. Clothes lie in damp and dirty heaps for weeks on end; new stoves become encrusted with baked-on dirt; damaging amounts of dust creep into the computer keyboard. Call it what you will – carelessness? oversight? sloppiness? – such behaviour is also connected to an expectation of built-in obsolescence.

Our consumer-oriented western world reassures us that if we choose not to care, not to clean, everything can be put to rights because of an unconscious expectation that if something is too dirty, too spoiled by lack of care, we can replace it. In other words, indifference to dirt is now often a mark not of poverty, but of affluence. 'When I was so depressed after the baby was born,' said one woman, 'I just couldn't do the laundry. It lay there for weeks and weeks, and some fascinating thick mould grew over the wet baby clothes. I remember thinking "Oh well, I'll just buy some more".'

After her kayak trip around the world, travel writer Maria Coffey was forced to rethink her attitudes about cleaning and tending her possessions. She and her husband Dag found themselves in their double kayak on the remote stretches of the flood plain of the Ganges in northern India; they spent time in desperately poor villages along Lake Malawi; time and again they were face to face with the most basic poverty, staying in huts with people who owned virtually nothing.

'I never expected this to happen,' Maria has said, 'but the trip changed the way I feel about keeping house. The women in India would take such pride in keeping their huts swept. Their little collection of cups and plates would be so carefully cleaned and stored in the rafters of the house. They would take a palm leaf and brush the dirt floor every day and they would trace intricate patterns to decorate the dust on the ground outside the door. They have so little and they take such care of it, and I came back to our house and couldn't get over how much we have and how little we really care for it. Now I do try a bit more, not just to keep things clean, but to care for what we have. And cleaning is part of that.'

A young married woman echoes these comments, although in a very different context. Danielle and Bill have only been married for one year but already her nerves are rubbed raw on the subject of housecleaning. Living in a newly purchased house, and both holding full-time jobs, Danielle is aghast at Bill's persistent disregard for housework. Not only does he take no pride in the home, he seems completely indifferent to mess and dirt and disorder.

'It's disrespectful,' says Danielle. 'Not only to me, because he expects me to do all the work, it's disrespectful to the house, to our things, to our shared space. Everything gets spoiled, unless I step in, because he just doesn't care. He thinks it's beneath him to care.'

Perhaps being like Bill, one of those who truly do not seem to care about their surroundings, is liberating. What, after all, would happen if we simply stopped cleaning and stopped caring and let everything alone? The inimitable Quentin Crisp is reassuring on that point: 'After the first four years the dirt doesn't get any worse.'

In a moment of languid decisiveness, Crisp claims that he simply gave up cleaning. 'On the Third Programme, I was given a chance to deliver this message of hope to a drudging world . . . I doubt if my words were heard by many inveterate dusters and sweepers or if the conventual rigours of *Woman's Hour* were subsequently relaxed, but we must not mourn.' He explains what lies behind his stance: 'I decided . . . that I would never become a thrall to rituals of domesticity', recalling with horror how half his mother's life was engulfed in such rituals. With modest pride he announced that 'squalor became my natural setting. I felt it was only by a series of unfortunate accidents that till now I had always lived in the captivity of hygiene.'

To express such lordly dismissal of hygiene, of dust, of germs; to be able to sweep such concerns aside with a grand gesture is gloriously anarchic, a showy, antisocial, attention-catching posture to adopt. Attitudes towards cleaning involve many strange posturings: avid, martyred, dismissive, defensive. We can be just as self-righteous in how we deny any interest in cleaning as we are in having – or in the quest to have – a clean home. On examination, either attitude is a bit silly.

Cleaning is – with all due respect to Quentin Crisp – a basic part of our lives, a necessary, ordinary and telling activity. Neither our be-all nor our end-all, it is none the less a real concern, a serious consideration in our lives and it presents us unceasingly with trivial rounds of common tasks. A vast amount of social conditioning has determined our attitudes towards cleaning. Looking more closely at this conditioning can be revealing, aggravating and richly entertaining.

2

DIRTY WORK AFOOT

DIFFERING ATTITUDES TOWARDS DIRT

'Why, the whole place is *clean*!' says one of the dwarfs in Walt Disney's *Snow White*. He is horrified. The dwarfs have returned to find that Snow White has cleaned their home from top to bottom. Warily they look around, noting that all their cobwebs have gone, their dishes are done, their floors have been swept and the windows washed. 'There's dirty work afoot!' growls another of them crossly.

An apt phrase to illustrate the contrary nature of our responses to the subject of household cleanliness. On the one hand, Snow White blithely singing 'Whistle While You Work' as she effortlessly flaps away cobwebs from the dwarfs' home, confident she is doing the right thing for everyone concerned, happy in her work, virtuous beyond reckoning. On the other hand, the ungrateful dwarfs, suspicious of the cleanliness and of the intrusion into their world that it implies.

In many varied ways dirt is often preferred over cleanliness, even relished; cleanliness, in turn, often seems a highly suspect quality. Nothing is clear or straightforward here. Dirty work can be afoot in more than one way when the subject of cleanliness is under examination. With such a complicated array of motives and methods and attitudes at play, this is not surprising.

Let us turn first of all to dirt, which often seems so much more *fun* than cleanliness. Cleanliness imposes limits and laws that are often uncongenial and constricting; dirt is free-spirited and teeming with life. This notion is abundantly evident in children's stories, both in terms of personal hygiene and domestic surroundings. Nothing is more appealing than a bit of dirt and preferably some cheerful chaos thrown in.

In the Canadian children's story *The Bears We Know* (1989), three mysterious bears live in a house where anything goes. No one tells them what to do: they jump up and down on the furniture until they break it, they stay up late and sleep as long as they want, they smoke cigars, eat strange and wondrous food, and of course their house is magnificently dirty. They make sure it stays that way. 'When it looks too clean, the bears bring in buckets of sawdust and throw it around.' The children in this story deeply approve of the bears.

In another children's story, *The Mother Market* (1966), two motherless children go to a special market in search of someone to look after them. They are desperate to get rid of their housekeeper, a terrible creature called 'The Gloom' whose main concern is keeping everything and everyone clean. She smells of bleach and has a picture of Louis Pasteur hanging on her wall; she starches and irons everything; she forbids any mess whatsoever. Humourless, rigid and restrictive, she typifies all that is most negative about people who pursue cleanliness and order. Thankfully, the children are able to find a proper mother at the market.

The bears, with their delight in dirt and disorder, stand at the opposite end of the spectrum from 'The Gloom'. They stand for what Mary Douglas refers to in *Purity and Danger* as a world view that is 'dirt-affirming' rather than 'dirt-rejecting'. Such a world view finds many forms of expression. Douglas provides details of primitive societies which celebrate dirt as something powerful and creative, although dangerous, where dirt stands for what she calls 'creative formlessness'. On a more mundane level, many of us may feel this way about our own special places, about our offices or kitchens or bedrooms: our mess and clutter and dirt are peculiarly ours and must not be disturbed by outsiders.

This disorder is part of our image and necessary to our

productivity; it is something that must remain beyond the reach of orderly impulses. 'Too much cleanliness is an enemy to creation, to speculative thought.' So says the troublesome priest Parablane in Robertson Davies's *The Rebel Angels* (1981), summing up what many have struggled to express when they find themselves falling victim to cleanliness. Henry, in Arnold Bennett's *Riceyman Steps* (1923), is simply horrified when his new wife has his home professionally cleaned: 'He could not like the cleanliness. He had been robbed of something. And the place had lost its look of home; it was bare, inhospitable, and he was a stranger in it.'

Works of fiction often look askance at cleanliness. Enthusiastic cleaners are repeatedly given short shrift. They are at least laughed at, occasionally humbled, often scorned, sometimes even killed off. Fictional heroines who enjoy cleaning are frequently the targets of innuendo. Their mental health may be questioned, or their sexuality, or both. In Alice Munro's story 'Friend of my Youth' (1990), the energetic Flora habitually does a rigorous spring cleaning in her Ontario farmhouse:

> [Flora] carried all the furniture out of one room after another so that she could scrub the woodwork and varnish the floors. She washed every dish and glass that was sitting in the cupboards supposedly clean already. She scalded every pot and spoon. . . . The cleanliness was devastating. My mother slept now on sheets that had been bleached and starched and that gave her a rash . . . Flora's hands were raw. But her disposition remained topnotch.

Flora is cheerful, capable and kind; yet seen through the eyes of the narrator of the story Flora is undeniably peculiar. Earlier in her life she had lost out on an opportunity to marry a good man, not once but twice. The narrator implies that Flora is not only slightly dotty, she is probably sexually cold. There is little direct evidence for this, but Flora's housewifely efficiency clearly counts against her. Such hearty enthusiasm for the mop and broom is unsexy.

Gloria Gold is another such. In *I, Gloria Gold* (1988), a novel by Judith Summers, the unfortunate Gloria spends a vast amount of her life cleaning, only to be shunned by almost everyone in the novel. Her mother, a free-spirited eccentric who wonders how she ever bred such a daughter, declares:

> 'Five minutes in your house is enough to drive me mad. It's like being in a museum. I don't know how Morry stands it – everything stinking of bleach and draped in dust sheets! . . . I've never known anyone so obsessed by germs. You're running a house, not an intensive care unit.'

When Gloria, much offended, replies that she simply takes pride in her housework, her mother sighs and asks how *anyone* can take pride in scrubbing a floor. But by the end of the novel, Gloria has come around. She is transformed into a woman who is wiser and kinder and more lovable and sexier. Unsurprisingly, she has had a luscious love affair in her journey to self-knowledge, and now has a dirtier house. All that fresh sex has helped her to see the error of her ways and to give up her impassioned housecleaning.

After all, 'The healthy young woman will hardly be attracted by so gloomy a vice', as Simone de Beauvoir puts it in her discussion of housework in *The Second Sex* (1952). She writes with horror of meticulous and orderly households with their limitless tasks that women pursue 'in a state of distraction and mental vacancy' that offer them a flight from themselves: 'And this flight may often have a sexual tinge. It is noteworthy that the rage for cleanliness is highest in Holland, where the women are cold, and in puritanical civilisations, which oppose an ideal of neatness and purity to the joys of the flesh.' De Beauvoir does not cite her sources for her damning comment about Dutch women, perhaps just as well. But her assumption that cleanliness is the enemy of sensuality is common and widespread. She looks south to warmer climes: 'If the Mediterranean Midi lives in a state of joyous filth, it is not only because water is scarce there: love of the flesh and its animality is conducive to toleration of human odour, dirt, and even vermin.'

No one wants to be labelled sexually cold, but if 'love of the flesh' necessarily involves 'joyous filth' and possibly even entails toleration of vermin as an added attraction, many of us would still be virgins. As a Canadian, brought up in a cold climate in a clean house in a puritanical society, I am only too relieved that Simone de Beauvoir did not deign to write about Canadian women. She prefers to expend her energy venting a great deal of anger about the general awfulness of having to clean house at all:

> Few tasks are more like the torture of Sisyphus than housework, with its endless repetition: the clean becomes soiled, the soiled is made clean, over and over, day after day. The housewife wears herself out marking time: she makes nothing, simply perpetuates the present. She never senses conquest of a positive Good but rather indefinite struggle against a negative Evil.

Such Sisyphean labour has an entirely 'negative basis' according to de Beauvoir. Even in the most privileged households there is no possible victory in the battle against dirt and dust and disorder which will always buoyantly return. So one finds no fulfilment here, no life-giving joy; many women find only the servility of maintaining the status quo of a household, doing work that few notice and fewer still appreciate. And that way, unsurprisingly, madness lies.

Robert Irwin, in his bizarre novel *The Limits of Vision* (1986), uses the manic housecleaning of his protagonist Marcia as a way of illustrating her desperate need for contact with other people, and as a focus for her crazed energies. Marcia is quite mad. Alone within the confines of her home she invents personalities with whom she discusses housecleaning in a series of frenetic, nightmarish conversations. As she becomes ever more drawn into her own tangled fantasies, she is both repelled and mesmerised by the intricacies of cleaning and the structure of dirt. She finds herself entirely at odds with her neighbours, women who want to talk of other matters:

> Steph is going on about the feminist exhibition, Griselda and Mary are talking about the new vicar, and the rest are listening to Rosemary being solemn about her bloody novel.

Stuff her novel. Isn't her housework enough for her? It's all so false. In God's name why don't we, why can't we talk about housework? That's all we ever do all day long so it must be important. It is always in our thoughts. We must talk about it then. I am screwing up my courage to say so.

For these visitors, Marcia puts on a feverish display of washing dishes, describing the process in thrilling detail, eulogising about how the dishes shine. She realises that her friends all think she is hysterical, perhaps having a breakdown. Rapturous effusions about washing dishes are not socially acceptable. Marcia persists: 'Be honest. Haven't you even enjoyed racing drops of water, like these two running down the plate here?' Her bemused friends leave, with Marcia sure she is the only honest one in the group. Giving rein to her free-wheeling fantasies about cleaning, about germs, and mould and fungus and dust mites, about the Hoover and the laundry washing powder sends Maria spinning out of control, yet she never loses her ability to express cunningly observed details of household lore: how dust dances in a beam of sunlight, how it settles on the wall in a 'thin vibrant matting', how dishwashing liquid curls so beautifully into the water. She is a character for whom it is difficult to have any real liking. Anyone so completely mad about cleaning is unlikely to be appealing; Marcia proves the point.

In *The Second Sex* Simone de Beauvoir presents a kind of fierce and terrible version of Marcia. This person is listed in the index of the book as 'Housekeeper, maniac'. De Beauvoir depicts an exaggerated, tragi-comic creature who indulges in an orgy of excess around the house; she takes to the broom as others do to drink, creating a home so neat and clean no one can live in it:

> When any living being enters her house, her eye gleams with a wicked light: 'Wipe your feet, don't tear the place apart, leave that alone!' She wishes those of her household would hardly breathe; everything means more thankless work for her. She shuts out the sunlight, for along with that come insects, germs, and dust . . . She becomes bitter

and disagreeable and hostile to all that lives: the end is sometimes murder.

Without a doubt, de Beauvoir wants the housekeeper to be the murder victim, not the murderer. That seems the only possible solution, given the scenario outlined above. How else could one deal with such a person other than to put her out of her misery, and thereby stop her wreaking havoc in the lives of others.

In the whodunnit *Death of a Perfect Wife* (1989), author M.C. Beaton comes to the same conclusion. Here we meet Trixie, the perfect – and perfectly awful – housewife who exerts a dastardly influence on the doctor's wife Angela, a vague and pleasant character renowned for her bad housekeeping and her love of reading: 'Trixie worked. Her hands flew here and there. She was amazingly competent. Grease disappeared, surfaces began to gleam . . . It was all magic to Angela, who felt she was watching a sort of Mary Poppins at work.' Angela is enthralled. She has not been at ease in her own sloppy household:

> Often she thought of getting down to it and giving the place a thoroughly good clean, but a grey depression would settle on her. For relaxation she once enjoyed reading women's magazines but now she could not even bear to look at one, the glossy pictures of perfect kitchens and fresh net curtains making her feel desperately inadequate.

With Trixie to help, Angela sets things straight. Her husband is not amused. 'Dr Brodie sniffed the air suspiciously when he came home that night. Everything seemed to smell of furniture polish and disinfectant.' It gets worse. Raffles the cat, who once walked happily over the dinner-table licking the dishes, is now shut out of the house. 'Why the sudden fear of pollution by Raffles?' asks the doctor. Because, according to Trixie, cats are a menace, their hair goes everywhere and they are 'full of germs'.

Within a short time, the doctor has decided he wants a divorce, but in the nick of time some kind soul conveniently murders Trixie. Shaken by all that has transpired, Angela thankfully reverts to her former messy ways. The last scene in which she appears features Raffles the cat back on the dining-table, resting his chin happily on the cheese dish, while the doctor beams with pleasure at the restoration of his wife, who once again embraces dirt and disorder in a manner, it is implied, well suited to a creative and intelligent person of reasonable social standing.

The same message comes through in Josephine Tey's *The Franchise Affair* (1948). In this novel Marion Sharpe and her mother are living in a large ungainly house in genteel poverty, unable to afford good domestic help. 'Just a girl from the farm who comes in once a week and does the rough cleaning,' says Marion dismissively. When a series of bizarre events leads them to seek help from the local solicitor Robert Blair, their ill-kept home is subject to his scrutiny. Accustomed to the elegant standards of his aunt's home where he lives, Robert is at first taken aback and then helplessly charmed by the Sharpes' domestic priorities. When he sits down to lunch he notices all the details: 'It was a cherrywood table, very pleasant in grain but sadly needing polishing. The wine glasses, on the other hand, were polished to a diamond brilliance. (How like Marion, he thought, to concentrate on the thing that mattered and to ignore mere appearance.)'

'I am not a house-proud woman,' announces Marion. 'I loathe domesticity.' Robert's fascination with her increases with every such pronouncement: to him she is a gypsy, a free spirit, someone free of all the conventions of domesticity that he has previously taken for granted. Dreaming of rescuing Marion from her surroundings leads Robert to speculate about her domestic needs: 'Where he would take her he did not quite know . . . It would have to be a place where there was nothing to polish and nothing to carry and practically everything was done by pressing a button. He could not see Marion spending her old age in service to some pieces of mahogany.'

To spend time polishing tables is plainly beneath Marion. Such trivial pursuits are only suited to Robert's aunt, that kindly soul who has cared for him year after year: '"Robert," said Aunt Lin coming in pink and indignant, "did you know that you left the fish on the hall table and it has soaked through to the mahogany."'

Transformed as he is by his association with Marion, the formerly fastidious Robert couldn't care less. Poor Aunt Lin is left behind in the dust; years of polishing all for nothing. Robert turns his back on her and follows Marion into the unknown.

Such material fuels the argument that cleanliness is simply not attractive. A picture builds up in which the lawless freedom of a dirty house appears infinitely preferable and more admirable than the limiting conventions of cleanliness. To admire those who flaunt or who are supremely indifferent to prevailing social standards and expectations is a common reaction, of course. Hence the enduring attraction of the engaging villain who gets away with breaking laws, and the appeal of the devil-may-care libertine.

Yet for some of us, our 'dirt-affirming' tendencies can go no further than a rather wary, sometimes rather wistful admiration. To have the courage to act according to these dirt-affirming tendencies is another matter altogether. So although often we may wish we could be less concerned about cleaning, the truth is we feel constricted by household chores even if we fail to do them. No freedom is to be gained by following Quentin Crisp's advice and refusing to do any cleaning; many of us would be aware of dirt all the time and at some point we would simply have to go at it. However much we may try to turn a blind eye, in the long run we fail to do so. All I am capable of is a nervous admiration of the anarchy of others who have more nerve.

Many women feel the same. Christine, whose own house is kept in apple-pie order, sums this attitude up neatly in describing the habits of an old friend: 'This woman is amazingly filthy – her bathtub is scary. I once took a scrubber and some false teeth cleaner when she asked me to tea, and when she was out in the garden for a few minutes I rushed to the sink and cleaned some of her mugs because I was too frightened to drink out of them. I never told her I did that. But she is such an impressive, energetic person, and so unapologetic. I think a lot of us really admire her for having the courage to ignore cleaning so completely. She makes me feel extremely mundane and conventional, but all the same, I know her standards wouldn't work for me – I couldn't cope. I must have clean mugs in my house. I can't help it.'

The unctuous piety that has long been associated with cleanliness makes matters even more difficult. Those of us who feel we must have clean mugs or dishcloths or floors or toilets cannot embrace the cheerful dirtiness of our freer friends and neighbours, yet we do not wish to align ourselves with the hard-line moral superiority so often associated with cleanliness. Nineteenth-century books of domestic advice are full of this moral superiority, such as the following outpouring from the *Encyclopedia of Domestic Economy*, published in 1844:

> Cleanliness . . . has moral as well as physical advantages, personal as well as domestic; hence its claims on our approbation and daily observance. It evinces an absence of slothfulness; for without activity and exertion, cleanliness cannot be practised: it is an emblem, if not a characteristic, of purity of thought and propriety of conduct.

More of the same follows, with cleanliness trumpeted in ever more exalted terms. 'Cleanliness is an unequivocal good; and accordingly we find that it confers a species of rank on all its votaries' and 'We delight to see the supremacy of cleanliness, its victory over dirt and smoke'.

Smug and self-righteous in tone as such statements are, they invite any right-thinking modern person to disown them completely. Yet to deny that cleanliness has lost its edge over dirt in the home is pointless. Both socially and morally, cleanliness remains a must.

Few people care to admit that they pass judgement about cleanliness, but most will confess that they have their limits. Some have an extremely low threshold. One woman told me that if her white socks get dirty in walking across someone else's floors, she thinks she is in a really dirty house. Many of us have floors that would not pass such an inspection. At the other extreme is an acquaintance who is by my standards utterly indifferent to dirt. His dishcloths and cutlery should be handled with tongs and his kitchen floor is positively agricultural, but in describing old friends of his he sounded outraged. 'They live in stomach-turning squalor,' he announced. 'I definitely couldn't stay there overnight; I'd catch something from the sheets. The whole place sort of festers. I don't know how they can stand it.' Knowing the state of *his* sheets, I decided never, ever to go to visit these people myself.

Not many women or men in the western world could walk into an exceptionally filthy place without feeling shocked, whether or not they care to admit it. This reaction of shock operates on many levels at once: because the place is probably a danger to health, because its blatant filth is anti-social, and because, perhaps unconsciously, we perceive that filth to be morally questionable. Something seems profoundly wrong when dirt spirals rampantly out of control, when it makes conditions intolerable. Comments and questions loaded with moral overtones rise unbidden to our lips: 'What's the matter with this person?' 'How can they live like this?' 'I wouldn't let my dog stay here.'

'I've only once seen a place that I'd call absolutely filthy,' says Lorna. 'It shocked me senseless. Three birds were in a disgusting cage in the main room; there was birdshit everywhere and feathers all over everything. You could have grown a garden on the floor; it was hard to know if there was a carpet or not. All the sheets were grey with dirt. The cobwebs were so thick you could have made a ball out of them, and you literally couldn't see through the dirt on the windows. The worst was the smell, and thinking people really lived like this. But they seemed quite content, the old couple who lived there, and neighbours told me it had been that way for years. It made me feel a bit sick, partly because I'd known their daughter at school and we jeered at her all the time for being dirty. Now I saw why and I felt terrible for her because we had been so cruel, and terrible for them, because being dirty like that meant no one ever visited them. I burst into tears when I left.'

In graphic detail Ella remembers looking after some children when she was a teenager in a house that was unutterably awful. 'I've never seen anything like it since. Everything was sticky and yellow with dirt and nicotine; the whole place stank of urine; there were mouse droppings all over the stove and kitchen counters; the toilet lid was so encrusted it wouldn't move up and down; the fridge was just oozing with stinking old food; there were filthy clothes and dishes everywhere. It was grotesque. I didn't want to sit down or touch anything. I kept wondering what was wrong with these people: they weren't really poor or anything, but the place was unbelievable.'

There is something peculiarly mesmerising about such stories. Extremes of filth may make us gulp and shudder, but they rivet our attention. For the most part they evince powerfully negative reactions which, whether we like it or not, place us in the same camp as earlier moralists like those writers of the *Encyclopedia of Domestic Economy*, even though the terms used in such homilies may seem entirely foreign. However life-affirming and attractive the cheerful anarchy of a bit of dirt may be, when we are faced with extremes, cleanliness looks intensely attractive.

Far from exuding a sense of creative disorder, or giving rise to a barely contained shudder, dirt also excites in some people a perverse fascination. To be in contact with, to have knowledge of dirt in its muckier manifestations, is somehow dangerous and exciting, like the deliberate violation of a taboo. Expressions of this type of fascination are not often found in relation to housecleaning, but some sources give inklings of it.

'I have hardly ever met wi' a *servant* yet who wasn't ashamed o' dirty work & who wouldn't be glad to get out of it for something they think is *better*.' This was a low moment for Hannah Cullwick in her journal of 1863. Over a century later, in 1984, Hannah's journal was edited and published as *The Diaries of Hannah Cullwick, Victorian Maidservant*. Normally, Hannah writes with relish about getting her hands into the muck and mire of the trade. Nothing is too dirty or too hard for her to tackle. She takes pleasure in the most menial of jobs and Victorian households had plenty of them to offer, everything from blacking boots and polishing knives to cleaning the fire grates.

In the 1860s and 1870s Hannah wrote her journal in short episodes which she posted regularly to Arthur Munby, Victorian gentleman and educated man of letters. Munby had a strange and secretive obsession with lower-class women and he asked Hannah to provide him with accounts of her daily life as a servant. He wanted to know in detail all about its dirtier aspects. Perhaps for Munby's gratification, perhaps because she really believed it, Hannah states time and again how she takes pleasure in the lowly status of her work. At one point she describes how a lady of the household stood over her as she worked and kicked Hannah with her foot while showing her how to do something. 'I dare say she thought I *sh'd* feel hurt & vex'd with her but I didn't. I was glad she thought me humble enough without kicking again.' At another of her places of employment when Hannah had a kitchenmaid working under her she was uncomfortable, claiming she did not feel 'fit' to have a position above another person; she wanted to do the washing up and the roughest work herself.

Something odd is at work here. Hannah's unequalled ability to describe a Victorian housemaid's work as an insider to the trade cannot be questioned; her laconic and informative descriptions of her day-to-day work are extraordinary. Yet her attitudes towards her social position and towards dirt itself, while being highly memorable, make uncomfortable reading. Certainly her awareness of social status and niceties is acute, particularly in relation to Munby, but also respective degrees of dirt and cleanliness. She peppers her descriptions of the relationship between them with startling reminders of her 'lowness' and dirtiness and his cleaner superiority.

For years Hannah wore a chain and padlock under her dress to mark her as Munby's slave; when she visited him she would black her face with oil and lead; she regularly washed his feet and she always called him Massa. By any understanding they were a strange couple. They first met in 1854 and after a courtship – if it can be called that – of eighteen years, they married, but even then kept the relationship largely secret. They lived apart for most of their thirty-six years of married life, and they each left diaries destined to puzzle and intrigue future generations.

Hannah's insistence on her own ability to embrace dirtiness is entirely out of the ordinary. She describes blacking grates and polishing fire irons with her bare hands, sweeping chimneys when stark naked, and licking Munby's boots when cleaning them. She claims that Munby taught her to love the low and dirty work that was her lot. 'I think different about it now a good deal than I did ten years ago 'fore I knew Massa. He has taught me, though it's been difficult to learn thoroughly, the beauty in being nothing but a common drudge & to bear being despised by others what don't have to work the same way.'

To believe that Hannah protests too much about how she revels in her dirty and lowly work is tempting, but her engaging pride in her strong physique – she was a large woman – and in her ability to do hard, dirty physical labour has a ring of truth about it. She was a powerful personality, often at odds with her 'Massa', and well able to stand up for herself at work when she chose to. Far from showing a poor and resentful victim caught in a treadmill of domestic drudgery and victimised by a gentleman of breeding, her diaries reveal a woman who chose to stay where she was and to do the work she did. Despite her bad days, Hannah genuinely seems to have enjoyed cleaning the houses in which she worked. Her relish for handling dirt, for dirtying her face, her hands and her whole body, clearly filled some need – psychological, sexual or pathological – that she shared with Munby, and it also seems to have helped her enormously. Without flinching, she sets to, revels in the lowest of low tasks, accepts and even welcomes the hard work and the dirt.

In households of the Victorian age smaller than those described by Hannah Cullwick, the lady or ladies of the house occasionally lent a hand with some of the cleaning. Not the rough and dirty cleaning, but the more genteel tasks, particularly dusting. Charlotte Bronte's Jane Eyre, formerly a mere waif and stray, becomes an equal of the two pleasant and unaffected ladies of Moor House. This middle-class establishment has no pretensions, boasting only one devoted servant, another Hannah. Just before Christmas, Jane indulges in an outburst of enthusiastic housecleaning. This does her image no harm at all, perhaps because it comes near the end of the novel when she is well established as an independent free-thinking heroine. Besides, she does not *habitually* clean house, or even think about it. Her spurt of housecleaning comes as a bit of a diversion for her: 'My first aim will be to *clean down* (do you comprehend the full force of the expression?) – to *clean down* Moor House from chamber to cellar; my next to rub it up with beeswax, oil and an indefinite number of cloths, till it glitters again.'

She makes this announcement to her cold-blooded cousin St John Rivers, going on to describe eagerly all the other housewifely duties she will perform in making the house ready for Christmas. His response is characteristically chilly, ending with the hope that she will 'look a little higher than domestic endearments and household joys'. She counters that these pursuits are 'The best thing the world has!' St John is unimpressed. Jane knows that he is repelled by the notion of what he calls 'housemaid's work', finding it 'at once sordid and trivial'. She cannot agree.

> Happy at Moor House I was, and hard I worked; and so did Hannah; she was charmed to see how jovial I could be amidst the bustle of a house turned topsy-turvy – how I could brush, and dust, and clean, and cook . . . it was delightful by degrees to invoke order from the chaos ourselves had made.

Jane sounds alarmingly like Flora Poste from Stella Gibbons's *Cold Comfort Farm* (1938) here, busily and cheerfully transforming a household to her liking. But Flora's aims are far more radical. When she takes it upon herself to improve her Starkadder relatives' gloomy farm and transform all its peculiar inmates, she first tries to clean it up a bit. The filthy kitchen with smoke-blackened walls, the dirty windows, the soiled lace curtains all grate on her nerves, as do the curtains in her own room, hanging heavy with dirt. She decides to have them washed. 'Wash them?' snaps Mrs Beetle, the lady who comes and 'does'. 'I never thought I'd live to hear of anyone up at Cold Comfort wanting a bit of washing done.' Before long Flora has rearranged not only the domestic habits of everyone at the farm, but their love lives, their careers, their futures. Cleaning things is an important initial stage of Flora's radical reorganisation of the farm, for 'curtains must be washed and life generally tidied up before anyone could even begin to think of enjoying it'.

Worth noting is that both Flora and Jane Eyre have help in doing the dirty work they undertake; they have Mrs Beetle and Hannah respectively. Walt Disney's Snow White, too, has help, a host of friendly forest animals lend a hand in cleaning the dwarfs' home. In all cases, this help makes their status as heroines easier to uphold; their hands are dirty only for a short time, and by choice, and they have willing underlings to do their bidding. In all cases, too, these characters go on to marry the prince of their choice, and probably never sully their hands with such concerns again.

The belief that housecleaning is not work fit for ladies (or for women with a mind to higher and better things) has endured for a long time in the face of many efforts to change it. Even now that belief strongly influences our attitudes towards cleaning. However democratic and liberated we may be, however self-sufficient and capable of doing all our own work around the house, we are not immune to such entrenched ways of thinking. Given half a chance, cleaning is probably the first domestic task that most of us would pass on to someone else if we could, and amongst the last occupations we would willingly embrace.

3

MOTHERS AND MENTORS

THE INFLUENCE OF MOTHERS ON HOW WE CLEAN

We all have voices in our heads that haunt us and inform our behaviour, voices we cannot get rid of that influence how we behave and how we feel about even the most ordinary things. For many of us, from time to time, these voices speak of cleanliness and provide an immediate and direct impact on our actions and attitudes, try as we may to resist them.

The catchy promises of advertisements resound in our heads for decades: Ajax, that 'cleans like a white tornado'; laundry powder promising a white 'whiter-than-white', a clean 'cleaner-than-clean'. The founder of Methodism, John Wesley, is there too, though we may not recognise him; his is the voice declaiming that 'Cleanliness is next to godliness'. Our teachers might also be there: one woman described how she can never clean the toilet without hearing the ringing instructions of her large-bosomed domestic science teacher: 'Now girls, remember – flush, brush, flush!' Strange snippets of half-remembered advice on household matters may also rise unbidden to mind. In *The I Hate to Housekeep Book* (1962) domestic advice writer Peg Bracken has a couple of memorable suggestions about how to avoid cleaning up before a party: give the party *while* you are remodelling the house, she says, or use dim candlelight everywhere.

But the most powerful voices of all are those of our mothers and our grandmothers. I hear mine all the time, stalwart and persistent, telling me what to do around the house. 'Just arrange the flowers nicely, dear, and no one notices the dust,' was my maternal grandmother's oft repeated dictum. And when reaching for the dishwashing liquid I hear my other grandmother's confident assertion that 'Soap powder gets dishes much cleaner than detergent'. From the same battered tin she always used, she would add a gritty spoonful of soap to the dishwater, quite undeterred by complaints about how it didn't lather and was hard to rinse off. Born as she was in 1891, detergent remained for her a new invention and not to be trusted. 'I've always used soap, dear.'

The most dominant voice of all is, of course, that of my mother. 'The first thing anyone notices is front steps and the porch. You must sweep them every day.' 'Hang it on the line in the sun and you'll kill all the germs.' 'Don't leave a sloppy mess on the counter.' So on and on. Other women recall their mothers' pithy criticisms of less-than-perfect housekeeping: 'a lick-and-a-dab cleaning', 'slopdolly housekeeping', and 'she's just not trying'.

Maternal influence, so powerful and so close to the heart, is arguably the most important influence in our lives. On the subject of cleanliness, as on so many others, our mothers' voices make themselves heard for the rest of our days, and mothers' expectations and habits intrude on our own. Writing this book has involved speaking to over a hundred women aged between twenty-five and seventy-five, many of whose mothers are still alive. Almost without exception, these women agreed that their mothers' standards and practices have dogged them throughout their adult lives, even if the mothers' standards are angrily rejected or studiously ignored.

The smells, the rituals, the sounds, the sensations of cleaning house are, for many of us, the stuff of powerful childhood memories. When the narrator in Marguerite Duras's novel *The Lover* (1984) writes of scrubbing a wooden floor in her youth her memories are vivid and intense: 'The whole house smells nice, with the delicious smell of wet earth after a storm, enough to make you wild with delight, especially when it's mixed with the other, the smell of yellow soap, of purity, of respectability, of clean linen, of whiteness, of our mother.' Never mind that this cleaning is set in Vietnam in the 1930s, the experience is universal; the mother ordering this cleaning, the daughter unwittingly transfixed by the busy, confident process. The purposeful energy of this housecleaning still charms the narrator, though her mother was mad and cruel and is long since dead. Such cleaning provided a moment of normality, of simplicity: 'She'll have the house scrubbed from top to bottom, to clean it through, scour it out, freshen it up, she says.' Here, fleetingly, were sanity and order, both for mother and daughter.

In my own experience, everything connected with cleaning goes back to my most sane and ordered mother. I grew up in an extremely clean house. 'Just look at your mum's toaster,' a boyfriend once said in awe. 'I've never seen anything shine like that. What does she *do* to it?' 'God knows,' I remember saying impatiently. 'My mother shines everything.' I was in my twenties at the time and cleaning was the last thing on my mind.

My mother's house glows. Her housecleaning agenda is power-ful, unyielding, and full of the highest expectations. It sweeps all before, including my own earlier indifference and my own better judgement when she comes for a visit, or perhaps I should say when she comes for an inspection. Then I am impelled into a panic attack of housework. I clean what I normally ignore. Recently I polished the cutlery, waxed the one wooden chair, dusted the tops of doors, and scraped grease from the chrome knobs on the stove. Why? Because my mother makes me feel like a lazy slut, though she would never say anything of the kind. But I know she suffers, often loudly, if a house is dirty. Such suffering makes me wince.

Of the women I have interviewed, most agree that the person they clean up for especially is their mother, or perhaps their mother-in-law. Women tell repeatedly of cleaning for their mothers' visits, abjectly wiping away at floors and stoves and toilets until midnight on the night before the plane or train gets in. 'There I was, nine and a half months pregnant,' Janice remembers, 'up on a chair scrubbing inside the kitchen cupboards before she arrived. I went into labour that night.'

'It's like giving her a gift,' says Claire of her mother. 'I don't have the heart to inflict a dirty house on her, even though I don't want to keep up the same standards she did. But I know she'll notice everything, so when she comes to visit I whip around the house like mad.'

There are exceptions. 'Not me. I will *not* do anything special if my mother comes, or my mother-in-law. I'm beyond caring about what they think,' declares Marie. With two children under the age of four, she works from home and practises a highly developed form of selective perception. 'I've learned not to *see* the dirty dishes, but I'll always pick up magazines and toys and sort out my papers.' For about a year after the birth of her first child Marie's entire, five-foot-long kitchen counter was usually covered with dirty dishes. 'If my mother came over I would just throw towels over them so we didn't have to see them. I'd do that much to keep her happy. But I never washed them.'

Stories abound of visiting mothers who can bear their daughter's homes no longer and simply take over the cleaning. 'I am sorry, Kath, but I just can't cook anything on your stove until I've cleaned it. I don't know how you can bear it,' declared one mother to her 40-year-old daughter. 'She cleaned house until an hour before she had to leave for the airport,' muttered Kath resentfully. '*And* she has a weak heart. But I just couldn't stop her. This cleaning seemed to satisfy some need in her, or perhaps she somehow had to stamp herself on my home.'

'Once my mother was staying and I caught her bleaching my sink and my washing-up bowl,' Christine remembers. 'I said, "I know you think I'm an absolute slob" and the pause was just *too* long before she replied, "Oh, no, no, no! You just don't have the time, do you?".' Mothers like Christine's and mine earnestly try to understand their daughters' lower standards. 'Of course I was home all the time, so I just kept on top of things,' my mother once said to me. She was sweeping *my* front steps at the time. 'I wasn't trying to do two things at once like you.' Bravely continuing, she looked around and added, 'And it's not so bad here, it's just surface dirt.'

Although my standards are not nearly so high as my mother's, hers never let me be. Finding myself with broom in hand, sweeping the front steps, I feel her approval radiating towards me from a great distance. Kathryn Allen Rabuzzi, in her book *The Sacred and the Feminine: Towards a Theology of Housework* (1982), defines this kind of cleaning as 'ritual enactment', actions inherited that we perpetuate despite ourselves. She writes of her own experience of housework: 'catching myself repeating what was presumably a characteristic gesture or attitude of my mother, I have the eerie feeling I *am* my mother'. She goes on:

> The ritual enactment of housekeeping typically links its performer back in time to the company of female ancestors . . . To do a task precisely as you observed or were taught by your mother or grandmother is to experience a portion of what they each once did . . . The ritual enactment of housework thus helps provide continuity from one generation of women to another. Consequently, although housework as it is generally practised is a solitary occupation, some sense of community is provided by the *method* of doing, when that method reflects the performance of earlier women.

Despite such elevated thoughts, repeating the patterns and practices of our mothers can be a most disheartening experience, particularly if we did not like them in the first place. 'Sometimes I look around this place and think "What a mess". It looks just like my mother's house did and I don't want it to be like that. I didn't like it was I was growing up and I don't like it now,' says Bernice in dismay. 'Piles of stuff everywhere, nothing put away, dirt everywhere. I'm just like my mother – even worse – but oddly enough my sisters are all so different.'

Bernice's two elder sisters, who left home determined *not* to repeat their mother's patterns, are much more houseproud than Bernice. 'I think it's because my two elder sisters were a lot older than the rest of us. They were eight and ten when I was born. They had to play mother, and they just got tired of having to deal with the mess, and decided their own homes were going to be better. And they really *worked* to make that happen. Just remembering our mother's house is enough to send my eldest sister straight to the vacuum cleaner.'

'It amazes me,' volunteered another woman on this same subject, 'how three children from the same house and the same mother can be so different in their approach to cleanliness. I drove my sister crazy; her half of the room was always spotless and she would nag me about things like dust under the bed when she was only eight or nine years old. And our brother was and still is a *total* slob. I'm just average around the house now, like my mother, and my sister's place is immaculate.'

Her sister commented on this, rather tensely. 'My mother never kept house the way I wanted. I had friends whose houses were all white and shiny, like storybook homes. *That's* what I wanted. When I was very little I heard my mother saying that someone's floor was so clean you could eat off it, and I remember thinking our floors weren't like that but when I grew up that was what I wanted. I didn't want my house to be like hers at all. And it isn't.'

Resisting, or trying to resist, a mother's influence can be hard work, but many women succeed. 'What would my mother say about this place if she could see it?' Jane pondered for a moment. 'She'd probably tell me to take a flame thrower to it; that was her comment on places that were beyond redemption. I honestly don't think I could get her inside the door, she'd be so horrified. It's just that the way we live is so completely different from anything she knew, with both of us working and no time to tidy up, and three kids throwing their food around. I won't even try to keep house like she did. If she were still alive, I think I'd have to put her up in a hotel if she came to visit.'

Jane's mother was a legendary housekeeper, even in the brand new suburb near Toronto where they lived in their immaculate 1950s bungalow, a setting where housecleaning was something of a blood sport, so competitive were the women of the neighbourhood. Even with three children in the house, this woman changed all the sheets every second day, washing them and ironing them. Her kitchen floor was dark linoleum tile, polished daily to such a shine that when Jane was little she and her sisters would sit on the floor combing their hair, using the floor as a mirror.

'I think my mother became so houseproud because there was nothing else she could control or achieve,' says Jane. 'She didn't have a job, she didn't finish school, she didn't have much confidence. For years and years she just kept house for my dad and my sisters and me. She wanted my dad to come home to a perfect house, and as kids we kept messing it up. She worked all the time to control mess and dirt – and us.'

Jane's mother typifies the cleaner-than-clean suburban housewife of postwar North America, that stereotyped, polished and coiffed creature featured in 1950s sitcoms like *Leave It to Beaver* and *Father Knows Best.* 'By 1945 the American home and the American housewife had achieved the position they would enjoy in the post World War II era as the loveliest, best smelling, most sanitary houses and women in the world. Almost magically, the homes were spotless without marring the beauty of the women responsible for them. Such magic was sure to be short-lived,' according to Phyllis Palmer in *Domesticity and Dirt* (1989).

She is quite right: the magic of spotless suburban America soon came under the severe scrutiny of critics like Betty Friedan, who set out to debunk the myth of the happy-stay-at-home housewife in *The Feminine Mystique.* Friedan saw postwar American women as enslaved practitioners of unnecessary domestic chores, poor fools hoodwinked into thinking their occupation was worthwhile. '. . . vacuuming the living room floor – with or without makeup – is not work that takes enough thought or energy to challenge any woman's full capacity.'

'My mother,' says Rachel, a woman of twenty-four, 'grew up in a home that was straight out of *The Feminine Mystique.* My grandmother had all the new gadgets and gizmos, and she was a stay-at-home super-houseproud wife and mother. My mother remembers with horror all the cleaning Gran did – every week she waxed the Venetian blinds, and every day she polished the stainless steel sink with some special polish. Stuff like that. Mum couldn't get away from it fast enough. Her place has always been a disaster.' In turn, Rachel has rejected her mother's standards;

her home is immaculate. 'Ironic, isn't it? I'm more like Gran than my mother is. My mum says I'm a throwback to the 50s and I'm just doing it just to spite her.'

Homes like that of Rachel's grandmother were – and are – by no means solely a North American phenomenon. My travels throughout Britain and in Germany, Holland, Iceland, Eastern Europe and Scandinavia have taken me into countless homes in which the standards of cleanliness easily equal and sometimes outstrip the self-styled, postwar North American model. Such pursuit of high domestic ideals can be found almost anywhere in the world, although it may be less self-conscious than in America.

Kerstin was brought up in Germany in the 1960s. She now lives in New York at a safe distance from her mother. 'I've never been in a home in the States that can equal my mother's,' she says. 'There is a special word in German, *Putzteufel*, it means the cleaning devil and there's also *Putzfimmel* which means a chronic frenzy of cleaning. These sum up my mother. Her home is always like a sterile showroom: you honestly can't believe anyone really lives there. I have never, ever, seen any dust in it.'

Growing up in such a house was a nightmare for Kerstin. 'I was fourteen before I even dared ask if I could try to bake a cake. I knew she'd say no, and she did: the kitchen would get messed up. So I learned to bake in my friend's home, her mother didn't mind. To this day I've never cooked in my mother's kitchen, and I'm nearly forty.'

On Kerstin's last visit to Germany she was drying the dishes and some water dripped – just a few spots – on the shiny kitchen floor. Knowing her mother had noticed and was biting her lip, Kerstin tried to make amends by taking the dishcloth from the sink to mop up the water. Her mother whipped the cloth away. 'No, no, no – not with that cloth – use the floor cloth. You *know* we don't use the dishcloth on the floor.' A peculiarly painful moment for them both. 'My mother was almost shaking,' says Kerstin. 'She was *trying* not to mind, but she just couldn't bear it and she *had* to stop me.' Kerstin emerged from this experience feeling, for the first time, sorry for her mother rather than being seethingly annoyed with her. 'She sees me living so differently, she knows I really don't share her standards, and I think she knows I find her anxieties a bit pathetic. Seeing how I don't care about or even notice what bothers her so much shakes her confidence, I think.'

Cleanliness has long been an abundantly confident, often smug virtue, well conscious of its own worth and not easily shaken. It rarely stands alone but goes hand in hand with a host of other often quellingly self-righteous qualities. In Robertson Davies's *Fifth Business* (1970), Dunstan Ramsay, the narrator, describes his family as the 'better sort' living in the small Canadian village of Deptford. The Ramsays thought well of themselves and were not surprised that the majority of Deptford people looked up to them: 'they looked to us, the Ramsays, for common sense, prudence, and right opinions on virtually everything. Cleanliness, for example. My mother was clean – oh, but she was clean! Our privy set the sanitary tone of the village.' Maintaining this 'temple of hygiene' and a rigidly clean home was only one way Mrs Ramsay expressed her unforgivingly high standards; another was dominating her children. An extremely able and efficient woman of 'furious rectitude', she is almost a caricature of the ferocious type of mother who *would* keep a mercilessly clean home as a means of defining herself and declaring her worth to her family and her neighbours.

The housecleaning habits of such characters can seem infinitely strange; equally so the habits of our own mothers and grandmothers. To look back and proclaim the error of these women's ways is easy; to dismiss much of their housecleaning as unenlightened make-work projects is certainly tempting. Keeping things white, making things shine, chasing dirt that no one else perceives or cares about have been the preoccupations of many women for many generations. It may be tempting to think we know better, that the only real requirement is to keep a home free of disease and reasonably free of smells and messes. Tempting, but untrue; our domestic landscape is far more complex than that, as our mothers and grandmothers – and theirs before them – well knew.

Take, for instance, the tradition of whitening doorsteps in working-class areas in the north of England. In *Women and Families: An Oral History 1940–1970* (1995), Elizabeth Roberts pays close attention to this ritual. She takes us to the grim little streets of terraced houses in Lancaster and Barrow-in-Furness early in the twentieth century. Here, as in so many other areas, generations of women whitened their doorsteps daily with a soft white stone, rubbing it on the freshly scrubbed and damp front steps and sometimes even on the flagstones of the courtyard. A light colour wash was the result, creamy or white when it dried; a ludicrously impractical finish that withstood neither rain nor footsteps. The whole process of whitening doorsteps was irrational, time-consuming and laborious, but the practice persisted in some areas of England until long after the Second World War. Roberts quotes a woman who tried to buck this tradition following her marriage in 1954: 'I got married and I said, "I'm not going to spend my life scrubbing front steps." It's absolutely ridiculous and I refused to do it.' Her mother was so ashamed that she came herself and did her daughter's steps. 'She wouldn't let the neighbours see that I had a front step that hadn't been done. So then I had to do it myself, to stop my mother coming and doing it, and I was very resentful.'

Elizabeth Roberts's interviews suggest that this practice had little to do with cleanliness or hygiene; it was a social statement, a declaration of self-respect, of moral worth, in areas that were often both poor and dirty. Roberts also asserts that the social value of this work was considerable. Women could chat with each other as they worked on their front steps; the work was an amiable, regular and important part of the life of a street. It was also an effective means of checking up on people; neighbours would know something was wrong in the house if a woman had not done this outward and visible task.

The staunch determination of these working-class women to put on a good face is clear in everything about their domestic lives. 'In those days, we had Nottingham lace curtains, they were full-length, beautiful lace, and the ends were scalloped . . . Now all those had to be washed by hand, and then they were all starched . . . it was who could have the nicest curtains. They were really houseproud, you know . . . I remember coming home and thinking, Mummy's put up clean curtains, they used to look so lovely.'

Even when hygiene could be said to be involved, pride continued to play its dominant part. One of Roberts's interviewees recalls the competitiveness of all the mothers, each of whom tried to have the whitest table top, and the whitest toilet seat, both of which were wooden and required real effort with washing soda and a scrubbing brush. 'The toilets [were] outside in the yard. They had a long board across with a hole in the middle, and that had to be scrubbed snow white. [The women] used to pride themselves, they were really clean.'

We need not look to such outdated practices to see how pride and self-worth are entangled with the processes of cleaning. Think of the habit of leaving a house spotless for the next inhabitants. When my family was moving out of our much-loved home, my mother was still cleaning the empty and echoing house as the movers were packing up all our belongings and carrying them out to the van; although exhausted she was determined to leave the house in good order for the next owners. She washed and waxed floors and dusted mouldings and cleaned cupboards until she nearly dropped. As an act of common courtesy what she was doing made sense – up to a point – and I was helping as best I could. I had not appreciated, however, that she meant to leave the house in a near antiseptic and entirely dust-free state. Clearly no one was going to move into this house in which she had taken such pride and find any dirt whatsoever. Seeing her growing more and more tired, I insisted on finishing the work so that she could leave and have a rest. She agreed, but not without issuing a long list of utterly mad instructions. I was to clean all the kitchen shelves, none of which had a speck of dirt that I could see; I was to wash the windows, I was to dust the tops of the doors, and what I remember most clearly was her insistence that I vacuum the shelves of a built-in cupboard in her bedroom.

'Yes, yes,' I said, and bundled her out of the door. Then

I stood looking up at that ceiling-high bedroom cupboard. Narrow, awkward-to-reach and deep, its upper shelves were only accessible by standing on a chair, balancing the vacuum cleaner on one hip and poking the nozzle blindly into the recesses of the cupboard. At least that is what I should have done to comply with my mother's wishes. Instead, I sat down with a cup of coffee and a detective story. When the appropriate amount of time had lapsed, I took a damp cloth to one or two kitchen shelves, ignored the doortops and windows, turned my back on that ridiculous bedroom cupboard, packed up all the cleaning tools, locked the door, and went to join my mother. Such was my farewell to the family home.

'How did you manage with the cupboard?' asked my mother. I complained how difficult holding the vacuum and reaching the back of the cupboard had been. She relaxed visibly. 'Thank you,' she said, with real gratitude in her voice.

Having since owned and left two different homes of my own, I now sympathise more with my mother. Before leaving these places, I too cleaned frantically, far, far more than had I been staying. Leaving a home of your own, I discovered, was stressful. On each occasion everything seemed out of my control; I was losing beloved homes and going into the unknown. To say goodbye, to imprint myself on the places for one last time, to calm myself, to show the incoming owners my true worth, I cleaned. Scouring dark corners and reaching into cupboards never touched before, I wryly concluded that the last laugh was not mine, after all, but my mother's.

'STOP ME – I'M BECOMING MY MOTHER' declared a fridge magnet in a home I recently visited. Much more than housecleaning is addressed in such a pithy comment, but cleaning is part of the picture. As self-styled crusaders against dirt, defenders of family health, killers of germs, setters of standards, mothers can be unbearable; at once tyrants and martyrs. There is so much to do, it is so little appreciated, it is so essential, no one helps: so go the common complaints and the arguments.

And yet, a word for the defence. Nothing forces a woman to reconsider her stand on housecleaning more than having a child.

First come the months and years of nappies, the endless washing, and the visions of germs prancing madly all over the place; then the child spends what seems an eternity eating anything within reach: dirt, old food from the floor, used tissues, bugs in the garden, fermented dog food. Then comes the sharing of toys with other children, invariably infected with horrible diseases, then school and keeping school clothes presentable. The continuous parade of muddy feet through the house never stops, and eternally there is laundry, laundry and more laundry, spills and stickiness and the volcanic explosions of untidiness and dirt and mess that make up life with children. Along with all this comes the sense of responsibility for *doing* something about it, trying to keep the tidal wave of dirt at bay, and also the accompanying burden of domestic guilt for never doing enough, never really being on top of it all. Only the very strong-minded can withstand the pressure.

'How will you sterilise your nappies?' said a friend to me sternly when I was eight months pregnant and had just revealed to her that I planned to use cloth nappies for the baby. This was my first child, I was invincibly ignorant. Surely the days of boiling nappies were over? Couldn't I just wash them in hot water, maybe after soaking them in something? I vaguely remembered hearing that a solution of vinegar and water would do the trick. My friend was horrified. Within three minutes I heard about all the brand-name nappy soaking substances that were on the market; two brands were recommended, and I learned in exhaustive detail just what I should do with them.

What became clear to me very quickly was that my status as a mother was definitely on the line in that conversation. Good mothers did this kind of task properly, my friend implied, and *properly* meant buying lots of substances to kill germs, purify, sanitise, deodorise and brighten not only the baby's nappies, but the baby's clothes, surroundings, possessions, its very self. And all for the baby's own good, to keep the little creature free from harm and danger. I already felt inadequate and guilty and the baby was not yet even born.

Ignoring all advice and deciding to use vinegar and water to soak the nappies took a while; refusing to disinfect the toys as I had been instructed took even longer. I started off soaking the toys in a disinfectant solution now and again, only to be told by a neighbour that the disinfectant I was using was no good. Why, I have no idea. And why I believed her I have no idea. But I did and I was sufficiently intimidated to try another germ-killing offensive. I boiled them, only to discover that when you boil nice colourful plastic toys to kill germs some of them lose their colour and turn a funny shade of dishwater grey. Some even melt. This was ridiculous. I decided not to bother. Reaching that conclusion took a certain amount of nerve, for I was discovering that peace of mind is hard to come by in this motherhood business.

Other mothers can be so very intimidating. 'How do you clean the nappy pail?' Somehow I just knew that rinsing it with just a swoosh of hot water was not the right answer. 'You always wash the nappies separately, don't you?' 'Is your hot water wash really hot enough to kill germs?' 'What do you use to disinfect the carpet if the baby pees on it?' 'You don't let her near the cat food, do you?'

Mothers speak so firmly of their various domestic convictions; of the importance of separate towels, of never sharing toothmugs in the bathroom, of *never* using the teatowel to dry your hands, that finding slime on the inside of sink plugs is so disgusting, of how when a child has wet the bed, all the bedding must go immediately into the washer with disinfectant. When my neighbour told me about disinfecting all her doorknobs and light switches and telephones in the house when her daughter had 'flu, I didn't have the nerve to admit I have never disinfected a doorknob, light switch or telephone in my life. Worse, I wasn't even sure how to do it. I remained silent. I am easily thrown by what mothers say.

Think of the imposing brigade of mothers who so confidently assert their right *not* to clean, in the name of spending 'quality time' with the family. Not for them, this daft business of scrubbing a house clean. They can be remorseless bullies to those of us who are less enlightened. Sue is a leading proponent of quality time for the family. On one occasion she arrived at my house at the end of a difficult day, and as she walked in I was ignoring my child's clamorous demands for attention and stoically washing the dishes. 'Don't you think her needs are more important than the dishes?' she asked disapprovingly, looking at my scarlet-faced and bellowing daughter lying on the kitchen floor kicking her heels. At that moment, definitely not. As the valiant survivor of a day with a toddler, after all the tantrums and demands of the previous hours, doing the dishes seemed like a blissful escape. Yet Sue made it clear I should be on the floor playing yet another game of 'let's pretend', or skipping around the apple tree, letting the house go to hell.

Coming from her this was strange, because I knew full well that her own insistence on shoes-off-at-the-door and never-eat-in-the-living-room routines led to unending power struggles with her husband and children, despite all the quality time they spent together. She was no more immune than I to the need to impose a bit of order on chaos, she simply expressed it differently. So we were left in a state of mutual incomprehension, quietly disapproving of each other. Mothers are complicated, competitive creatures.

Yet there are mothers who are glowing role models to their daughters. Frances, a mother of four, part-time teacher and full-time graduate student, is the eldest of twelve and she speaks of her mother with warm admiration. Yes, the children all had to work around the house; yes, they had to apply paste wax to the hardwood floors by hand every Saturday and wash the windows and clean their own rooms and keep the bathroom sink respectable; and yes, her mother was often overcome by the chaos and dirt and heaps of laundry. 'But you know what she did? She took time off every afternoon. She went to lie down and she *read*. Hermann Hesse, Melville, Thackeray, Dickens; she read every day, no matter what was going on. We knew that those books and her time alone were every bit as important to her as the house. And I am eternally grateful for that example – because I can now read and forget about the house with a clear conscience, and if my mother comes to visit I don't feel any pressure at all.'

Jennifer's mother was not at all like that, but Jennifer speaks of her with similar admiration. 'She cleaned every day, Monday till Friday, until noon. And she loved it. For her it was meticulous, orderly and peaceful. She would save up special jobs that she really liked – dusting special ornaments or washing all the good china in the cabinet – and doing those jobs was like a little treat. She made such an art of it – and of ironing the pillowcases just so, and polishing the bedside tables for visitors. There was a kind of grace in it.'

Coming to understand our mothers and why they behave as they do – or as they did – around the house is partly just a function of getting older. 'My mother waged an unending war to keep our house clean, despite my dad. I used to get so exasperated with her, and tell her "Leave it". Now I know she couldn't. I can't either.' So says Eileen. 'I remember how she tried and tried to get my sister and me to do things like wipe down the tiles on the bathroom wall after showering. Now I realise why and I hear myself telling my own children the same thing. It's not that I clean her way – she did the toilet every day, and I only do it when it looks dirty – but I have much more sympathy for her.'

To have more sympathy for our mothers, to come to see their household patterns more clearly, is one step towards understanding how domestic history has unfolded and how it continues to unfold in our own lives. But if we are to have any real understanding of the forces that shaped our mothers' and grandmothers' housecleaning habits we need more background, more sense of the implacable continuity of domestic history. The habits of our mothers and grandmothers, like ours, are connected to earlier ones, and these earlier patterns and habits take us back to the turn of the twentieth century and even earlier, when the powerful conditioning of 'the housewife' really began.

HAPPY AND GLORIOUS

THE IMPOSSIBLE IMAGE OF THE HOUSEWIFE

How can I tell her?
By her cellar, –
Cleanly shelves and whitened walls.
I can guess her
By her dresser,
By the back staircase and halls,
And with pleasure
Take her measure
By the way she keeps her brooms;
Or the peeping
At the keeping
Of her back and unseen rooms.
By her kitchen's air of neatness,
And its general completeness.
Where in cleanliness and sweetness
The rose of order blooms.

This improving bit of doggerel appeared in the *American Kitchen Magazine* in 1899, when the housewifely arts were being raised to new heights and heaped with new honour and glory. In its prim, self-satisfied way, this verse pretty much sums up the domestic ideals coming into their own as the twentieth century dawned.

Here she is. The happy and gloriously contented housewife who produces the cleanliness and sweetness in which 'the rose of order' can bloom; here she is, the unreal genie who over a hundred years ago popped out of a bottle and has haunted women ever since.

Here we have a happy housewife running her home efficiently, probably aware of the latest developments in sanitation and plumbing, well versed in how to prevent disease, eager to hearken to the latest advice from the new home economics movement, and increasingly able to run her home without full-time domestic help. This glorified superwoman of her time merrily trilled the 'Happy Housewife's Song':

> The grime and dust I sweep all away,
> My mind no trouble can borrow,
> For deadly disease, which lurks therein,
> Is routed today, for tomorrow.

To dismiss such jolly little rhymes as mere trivia is easy enough, but they carry a message of domestic virtue that has been lasting and potent. Advertisers and household advice books have impressed on us for decade after decade that women who clean well and efficiently are self-respecting superwomen with sparkling, spotless, and happy homes, and that they are women of superior moral stature. Whether or not we believe this message is almost immaterial: it has endured.

'Happy Housecleaning!' announces the advertisement for the Wizard Triangle Mop in 1914, telling a grateful world how 'housecleaning loses all its old-time drudgery and discomfort' with this invention guaranteed to 'make it all easier and happier'. 'Cinderella Wouldn't Know the Old Place Now' declares an ad for Masonite Presdwood Products, a new kitchen surface product. 'Once a drab scene of drudgery, the kitchen in the modern home is a cheerful room of distinctive beauty . . . with conveniences and equipment that save steps, save space and save money.' And from the *Ladies' Home Journal*, one of the many little ditties advertising Sapolio:

The belle of Spotless town you see
Who shines in bright society.
Her mind is broad. Her waist is slim.
Her pots and pans are never dim.
She has the cents to make a show
By polishing with Sapolio.

How did all this hyperbole arise? The evolution of the improbable figure of the gloriously clean housewife has a long and tangled history. The age-old insistence on purity common to so many religions lies beneath the surface here; the notion of attaining the spiritual cleanliness so repeatedly referred to in the Bible; the ideas and practices associated with the washing away of sin. The cry of the psalmist still echoes: 'Wash me clean of my guilt, purify me from my sin.' (*Psalm 51*) 'Blot out all mine iniquities. Create in me a clean heart.' (*Psalm 52*) This desire for a clean, pure heart – a clear conscience if you will – can translate into the struggle against dirt and the pursuit of a clean home. In polishing the mirrors or keeping the rugs spotless we are, at least sometimes and at least in part, declaring the cleanliness of our own selves, making ourselves unassailable.

As the apron-clad housewife swabs her floor with a pungent solution of Mr Muscle or Spic-and-Span she is not, in any obvious sense, on a quest for religious purity, or driven by the urge to be cleansed of her sins. Far from it. Most of the time she just wants a clean floor because the cat got sick, or the soup which boiled over last week is still sticky underfoot. Yet as she drives out the dirt she may unconsciously be re-establishing order and safety; eliminating the bad, making herself feel better about her own home and her own self in it. That her home might be seen as blemished, dirty, or out of control is, for innumerable women, a disturbing, even a profoundly upsetting, notion.

Yet although some of the influences that combined to create the image of the happy, cleaner-than-thou housewife can be traced back a long way indeed, such ancient influences, while possibly powerful, are indirect; they work largely on a subconscious level. Women in charge of ordinary households were not as a rule consciously preoccupied with cleanliness until well into the nineteenth century, either in North America or in Britain. In pre-industrial society, their homes were simpler places, more sparsely furnished and equipped and therefore easier to tend. Earthen or stone floors were kept clean with sand which was either used as a scrubbing agent or left on the floor to absorb grease and dirt. Homes had fewer and smaller windows, carpets were a luxury for the rich, as was crockery, and even soap.

With the economic growth that accompanied industrial expansion, more goods came into the home: more iron, more implements, more decorations, more carpets, more glass, more fabric, and also more coal to spread dust over everything. As Caroline Davidson points out in *A Woman's Work Is Never Done: A History of Housework in the British Isles 1650–1950* (1982), the growth in Britain's iron trade alone accounts for an incalculable amount of previously unnecessary housecleaning because of 'the phenomenal increase in the number and size of iron grates and ranges in Britain, all of which needed regular black-leading to look presentable'. She also points out how the increased trade in the Staffordshire potteries led to the practice of washing dishes regularly; previously the few communal plates of pewter or wood were used and then cleaned with a swish of cold water before being rubbed clean with bread or straw. Mass-produced washing soda boosted commercial soap production in Britain, and by the middle of the nineteenth century the high tax on soap had been removed. With more soap readily available to more people, laundry became an ever more demanding chore, because soap, unlike many earlier laundry methods, required hot water, which in turn required more fuel and more effort.

So as affluence increased higher standards of cleanliness began to be pursued and housework grew ever harder and more demanding for women. More and more were able to employ others to help them, and a romantic adulation of the 'woman of the house' became widespread. To have an 'idle' wife who did not need to join the unruly mob of wage-earners and could afford a servant or two became a benchmark of the newly emerging middle class. Going and gone were the pre-industrial days of equal productivity, working side-by-side at shared ventures with the man of the house. Cottage industries in which women had participated so successfully were edged out of existence by large factories. Men were drawn into the new industries and factories and although many women and even children had to join them, the signal of social and economic success came when women could stay at home. Therefore in the best of all possible worlds it evolved that the men's sphere was outside the domestic circle and in the world of commerce and industry and production; an active, outwardly bound, dynamic sphere, while women were inside providing support and order and all the creature comforts of home.

Given the changes in industrial production, the work performed at home also altered greatly. The availability of cheap cottons from the mills, of commercially produced clothing and soap and candles and butter meant that many domestic chores gradually became obsolete in the nineteenth century. As this productive work in the home decreased, 'housework' increased. In *For Her Own Good: 150 Years of Experts' Advice to Women* (1978), Barbara Ehrenreich and Deirdre English describe the priorities of domestic activity before the industrial revolution: 'the pressures of home production left very little time for the tasks which we would recognize today as housework. By all accounts pre-industrial revolution women were sloppy housekeepers by today's standards. Instead of the daily cleaning or the weekly cleaning, there was the *spring* cleaning.'

In the industrial age, women tied to the home became ever more assiduous about their 'housework'; they also became consumers of goods rather than producers. Their domestic role had, of necessity, to be redefined, even reinvented. Domestic advice books reflect this process brilliantly. Although books of household lore had existed for centuries, they began to show up in numbers from the early to mid-nineteenth century. Many influential household books appeared both in America and in England, written usually – although not always – by women who were spurred on by their genuine concern for the changes affecting the home. Full of earnest exhortations, usually in tiny print and bristling with 'receipts' and 'maxims' of every description, from how to stuff a goose to how to make a mustard poultice to how to make silver polish, these books either address the mistress of the household or, in a manner both improving and stately, they inform servants of their duties and how to perform them. These books were not generally aimed at a one-woman household, but they were setting the tone and the standards for what was to come later.

Advice about cleaning is strewn unpredictably through the early publications addressing household management and domestic economy. Often these books are affably disorganised, with tips about blacking boots or cleaning mirrors (with gin and a silk handkerchief, if you please) appearing without rhyme or reason alongside suggestions about the best ways to make summer pudding or store winter vegetables. 'Receipts' for lethal-sounding cleaning compounds are a common feature. The ingredients for these often sound like the incantations before a witch's cauldron: dried fowl's dung, ox's gall and purified bullock's blood, not to mention gum-dragon, fig-blue, and treacle. Those few are all mentioned by the inimitable Mrs Isabella Beeton.

'Nothing lovelier can be found, In Woman, than to study household good.' This quotation from Milton on one of his more pompous days graces the title page of Mrs Beeton. Her book first appeared in monthly instalments in *The Englishwoman's Domestic Magazine*, between 1859 and 1861, and later enlarged editions extend to well over a thousand pages. Mrs Beeton addresses an established English household with several servants, evidently a fine institution in her view. She is remarkable for her thoroughness and for her unapologetic relish for an era and a type of household that have long since gone the way of the dodo bird.

When Mrs Beeton discusses cleanliness, she is characteristically firm and clear: 'Cleanliness is . . . indispensable to health, and must be studied both in regard to the person and the house, and all that it contains.' Expectations are high, to put it mildly. For the housemaid, 'perfect cleanliness and order' is the object, and without a qualm Mrs Beeton sets out a detailed schedule of daily work that sounds like unremitting slave labour. Up with the birds, the housemaid was to clean and polish the grates, lay the fires, dust and polish the furniture in the main rooms of the house, sweep these rooms as well as the stairs and halls, clean the steps, and lay the table for breakfast, all before the family came down to eat.

Of that slightly more elevated creature, the lady's maid, Mrs Beeton says, 'There can be no allowance made for the slightest approach to uncleanliness or want of order.' To the lady's maid fell the task of keeping the mistress's room clean, the daily round of emptying the slops from the washbasins, putting out fresh water, sweeping the carpet with damp tea leaves, dusting, bedmaking. The care of her mistress's clothes is also the lady's maid's responsibility. She must know all the intricate tricks of her trade; how to dust her mistress's bonnet with a light feather plume; how to clean kid boots with a cloth soaked in milk, how to wash lace collars.

The American advice books of the nineteenth century tend to be more down-to-earth than the British, and quite early on are addressing the one-woman household, or at least one woman with only a *little* help. Mrs B.C. Howard, who wrote *Fifty Years in a Maryland Kitchen* in 1873, is utterly practical and thorough throughout, and she appears to speak as one who has done it all herself. She certainly could never be accused of suggesting the easy way out. A barrage of cleaning tips appear in her book, all of them advocating fiercely hard work, and make no mistake, there is a clear assumption here that such hard work helps the housewife attain a morally higher plane.

'To Clean White Walls' sounds like a straightforward under-taking, but Mrs Howard soon disabuses us of any such idea. You must take:

> One pound of Fuller's earth, half a block of white soap, half a pound of whiting and half a pound of soda. Mix it all well together, and put to it half a gallon of water, enough to make a soft paste. Having brushed the walls well, apply the paste with a brush, and then wash it off with soda and water. To half a bucket of water, a tea-cupful of soda.

By my reckoning, this process of making the paste, applying and removing it, would take more time than it would to repaint an entire room.

Mrs Howard also provides graphic instructions to the American housewife about making soft soap:

> Allow sixteen pounds of grease and potash, each, for a barrel of soap. The grease should be good, neither mouldy nor wormy. The potash should be the color of pumice stone . . . Cut up the grease into pieces of one or two ounces, and put it into a tight barrel with the potash. Then pour in two pailsfuls of either rain or spring water . . . Add a pailful of soft water every day until the barrel is half full, stirring it well every day . . . It is best to keep it three or four months before using.

Her zealous descriptions of boiling up solutions of lye 'strong enough to bear an egg', of grating potatoes to obtain starch for muslin, of scrubbing carpets with a solution of ox-gall and water all combine to give an impression of tireless energy and initiative, of a woman who was a combination of Granny Clampitt of the *Beverly Hillbillies* and Marilla Cuthbert in *Anne of Green Gables*.

But the doyenne, the model, of all American domestic writers is a woman who combines both the down-home practicality of Mrs Howard and the educated sensibility of Mrs Becton: Catharine Beecher. The first edition of her book preceded both of theirs by a number of years. In 1841 Mrs Beecher wrote her *Treatise on Domestic Economy, for the Use of Young Ladies at Home and at School*, an enormously popular work that was revised and reprinted frequently during the two decades that followed. Here and in her later works, Beecher establishes herself as the first of many who set out to redefine the work of women in the house.

Housework becomes, in Beecher's estimation, an honourable and serious profession, one which requires training and specialist knowledge, one which embraces 'high responsibilities'. Home, in her world view, is where women should be, and where women should work in an organised, sane, and progressive fashion. A constant theme running throughout her many writings is the self-respect of the housewife. She insists repeatedly that 'a woman who has charge of a large household should regard her duties as dignified, important, and difficult'. Included amongst these duties is reconsidering how best to use space in a home. Beecher favours smaller houses: 'Every room in a house adds to the expense involved in finishing and furnishing it, and to the amount of labor spent in sweeping, dusting, cleaning floors, paint, and windows, and taking care of, and repairing its furniture.' Above all, Catharine Beecher calls for system and order in keeping a house. No detail is too small for her attention, and her well thought-out ideas about organising kitchen space, about the design, size and location of cupboards and work areas were highly influential.

Addressing an American audience to whom running water and decent drains and reliable heating were luxuries, an audience in raw cities with muddy streets, in isolated towns and in rural cabins, Beecher displays cool common sense about cleanliness. She does not ask the impossible. Suellen Hoy, in *Chasing Dirt: The American Pursuit of Cleanliness* (1995), points out how the very term 'clean' is reserved by Beecher for things that can be made white – for laundry, or walls: she knew better than to insist that a floor be clean enough to eat from. In *The American Woman's Home*, which Beecher wrote jointly with her sister Harriet Beecher Stowe in 1869, she advises her readers to 'form all plans and arrangements in consistency with the means at command, and the character of those around . . . [A woman] must aim at just as much as she can probably attain, and no more; and thus she will usually escape much temptation, and much of the irritation of disappointment.'

The decades following Beecher's *Treatise on Domestic Economy* saw major sanitary reforms taking effect in America, and these years also saw the establishment of a public health system and the beginning of the home economics movement, all of which enormously influenced the cleanliness of individual households. Mrs Beecher was amongst the first of the domestic crusaders who set out to take the new complexities of housework seriously, and to call for this work to be recognised as a serious and 'professional' calling. Many more followed, urgently demanding the study of 'household science' in schools and at home. Household advice books in both America and Britain encouraged women to take their domestic role seriously; to think highly of themselves: 'It may safely be said that the mistress of a family is called upon to exercise an amount of skill and learning in her daily routine such as is demanded of few men,' declares *Spon's Household Manual*, published in London in 1887.

Some potent image-making was at work here. A loftier image was manufactured for even the most ordinary housewife struggling in a difficult setting with few conveniences at her command. Most domestic advice writers actively encouraged the virtuous moral glow presumed to accompany the 'profession' of housewifery. Pious expressions of the sanctity of home life became increasingly popular throughout the nineteenth century, hailing womankind as the domestic embodiment of all virtue, 'the antithesis of economic man'. Described by Catharine Beecher in elegant and flourishing language as the one in charge of the 'sacred ministries of the family state', the woman of the house was suffused with a radiant and romantic light.

Popular sentiments abound about revering the family home and the woman within it. Her duty was to safeguard a haven from the rigours of the outside world where social change and industrial development were creating such an uncertain mêlée. Organised and knowledgeable, this woman was expected to be the fount of all domestic wisdom, conversant with all sorts of special subjects: architecture, plumbing, hygiene, horticulture, drains, cookery and – of course – cleanliness. She stood apart from the unseemly bustle of the outside, workaday world, proudly and serenely in charge of her own sphere and buoyed up by romantic notions about her role.

So it began: the birth of an image, the creation of housework as an idealised profession. Decade after decade this 'sexual romanticism' has persisted, often expressed in eye-popping superlatives. 'It is because I feel woman is of such enormous importance, as queen of her own home, that I want to see her do it regally,' declares an article in *The Gentlewoman and Modern Life* in February 1926. Such effusions were common. Never mind that any such puffed up declaration about being queen of the house or the sacred preserver of familial bliss is, as most of us know, all too soon deflated by a brief encounter with greasy dishwater or soiled nappies or any other of the tough jobs around a house.

There is no question that any woman who cleaned house faced a huge amount of work during the decades of forging the cleaner-than-thou happy housewife image. Try to picture life in 1860 in large cities in either Britain or America. The streets were filthy, the sewers and drains disgusting, coal or wood fires burned in every home, devastating epidemics of cholera and typhoid were common. But thirty years later, by 1890, the scene had changed: the streets were cleaner, sewers and water supplies had improved greatly, gas was installed in at least some homes, experiments with electricity in the home were underway, epidemic disease was under better control. And thirty years still further on, by 1920, changes were even more marked: the motor car was making its mark, there were fewer animals and less filth in the streets, electricity and running water and indoor plumbing were becoming commonplace, labour-saving appliances were available, and fashions in domestic design had changed beyond recognition. By this time the middle-class household was being hailed in women's magazines, in advice manuals and in advertisements as a glorified one-woman show.

The housewife who was left on her own with all, or most, of the work to do became a praiseworthy creature; her social standing was intact despite having to do housework. To any right-thinking woman, the tasks around the home should by now have become a mere doddle anyway. Domestic advisers and advertisers had been telling her for decades that 'work' was not the right word for these tasks; that housework, correctly pursued, is not really *work* at all. With the right attitude, the right equipment and the right materials, the modern woman-around-the-house should not be reduced to anything as lowly as *work*. As the authors of *The House and Home* plainly stated in 1896: 'The daily care of a house, if reduced to a system and accepted as a pleasant and imperative duty, never burdens a rightly balanced woman.'

Many domestic advice books advocated that through proper 'efficiency' or 'scientific management' the home should run smoothly and with minimal effort. As Mrs S.A. Barnett states in *The Making of the Home* (undated), if the lady of the house exhausts herself in an unseemly fashion, the exhausted lady then 'totters on her throne, and is only prevented by the love, faith, and patience of her family, from falling down to the level of house-cleaner'. She should not be tired, she should not be a mere overworked housecleaner. Her job is to be a ladylike homemaker: with all the new advice and devices available to her this should be perfectly possible, with little effort on her part.

'Just like Play' declares an advertisement for O-Cedar Mop Polish in 1913. 'Dusting, cleaning and polishing hardwood floors with the O-Cedar Mop Polish is but little more than play. You dust, clean and polish all at one time.' Advertisers consistently promised – as they still do – that their product would ease the workload, provide free time, allow a life of more ease. Such claims became ever more extravagant once electricity and labour-saving devices entered the home. As Adrian Forty states in his wide-ranging study of advertising, *Objects of Desire* (1986), the idea was that 'machines could turn housework from laborious drudgery into a few minutes' pleasure'.

Adrian Forty points out the absurdity and the 'gross self-deception' in all this encouragement to think of housework as something *other* than work. According to Forty this claim comes from many directions, most obviously from advertisers, but also through 'a whole set of ideologies' about housework and how it is done. He catalogues some of these: how doing housework has variously been described as an expression of self-sacrificing love for the family, an expression of moral purity, an indication of social standing, a dignified scientific profession – as anything but real *work*. To convince women that housework was not the lowly and undignified drudgery of earlier times, housework took on loftier names – domestic science, housecraft, home economics – but the obvious truth is that it remained *housework*. The happy and glorious housewife was not supposed to know this.

Here we have the beginnings of what in the 1960s Betty Friedan was to call 'the feminine mystique'. In *Chasing Dirt*, Suellen Hoy makes the point that by the 1920s in America, the web of this mystique was already drawn tightly around women. Even the most cursory glance through women's magazines shows that well before the Depression, advertisers lavishly idealised the woman who ran a happy and sparkling home. Helping to establish this powerful image were the domestic reformers and home economists who in their many books and articles repeatedly insisted that a woman could find great happiness and satisfaction in the pursuit of household perfection, and what's more it was her duty to do so, in order to protect the health and well-being of her family.

Thus the stage of the twentieth-century household was set, the players were in place and progressing cheerfully up the primrose path of cleanliness. Dirt was being chased and vanquished in ever new and better ways. For the formerly beleaguered housewife, life should now be much easier with all this expert help, all these appliances, all these shining privileges. But no. Higher standards and scientific knowledge and new attitudes led, in the end, only to more work for mother.

5

MAIDS AND LADIES

THE NINETEENTH-CENTURY HOUSEMAID
AT WORK

Before examining the peculiar paradoxes of household cleanliness that arose as the twentieth century advanced, attention is due to that much-discussed creature, the housemaid. Hers were the hands required to do so much more cleaning as standards rose. Hers was the labour enabling several decades of middle-class women to distance themselves from the ever-increasing demands of the household. Without her, domestic developments in the late nineteenth and early twentieth centuries would have been entirely different.

'Clean'd away,' writes Hannah Cullwick, 'clean'd away'. Time and again she repeats this phrase as she describes her daily round of work as a Victorian housemaid. For all she refers to herself as an 'unletter'd drudge' Hannah was an exceptional diarist and a remarkable housemaid. Almost every night, month after month, year after year, through the 1860s and 1870s she recorded her day's activities.

> Opened the shutters & lighted the kitchen fire. Shook my sooty things in the dusthole & emptied the soot there. Swept & dusted the rooms & the hall. Laid the hearth & got breakfast up. Clean'd 2 pairs of boots. Made the beds & emptied the slops. Clean'd & wash'd the breakfast things

up. Clean'd the plate; clean'd the knives and got dinner
up. Clean'd away. Clean'd the kitchen up . . . Clean'd the
steps and flags on my knees & scour'd the tables. Scrubb'd
the flags around the house & clean'd the window sills . . .
Clean'd the privy & passage & scullery floor on my knees.

Nothing makes me appreciate my own domestic lot more than
reading Hannah's diaries. Nothing makes me realise more
acutely how much artificial gloss exists in the costume-drama
fascination for the upstairs-downstairs lives of nineteenth-
century servants. Millions of girls and women worked at
jobs like Hannah's. According to census reports in Britain,
by 1891 roughly one in eight females over the age of ten was
in service, and with women aged between fifteen and twenty
the number rose to one in three. Great numbers of these girls
and women spent most of their waking hours cleaning other
people's homes.

Maids and the ladies who employed them are part of the long
legacy of women who have contributed to our own attitudes
towards household matters. They lived and worked in domestic
settings that may seem infinitely strange to us, but which are not
so very distant in time. The way Hannah Cullwick cleaned and
was expected to clean reflects the experience and expectations of
women of my great-grandmothers' and even my grandmothers'
generations, and her voice still radiates with life and energy in
telling of her daily rounds. However much our own circumstances
may differ from hers, at least some of what she says still speaks
to us vividly, and it serves to make us realise sharply how much
domestic life has been transformed.

Hannah Cullwick is a first-rate witness, providing a unique
account of housecleaning in Victorian homes. She is mercilessly
matter-of-fact in describing how she cleans, how long her hours
are and the often grim nature of her working conditions. The
sheer amount of hard work is breathtaking:

Lighted the fires & clean'd the hearths. Clean'd 2 pair of
boots. Swept and dusted the rooms. Laid the cloth & took
the breakfast up. Clean'd away after and wash'd up the

things. Put the linen ready for the wash. Wash'd up the
dishes & clean'd the knives. Fill'd the scuttles & made the
fires up. Got the dinner ready. Clean'd the things away after
& clean'd the hearths . . .

In one of Hannah's situations, she had five fireplaces to do every
morning, and the dining room and study and the halls and steps
and the lady's maid's room and all the lower ground floor – most
of this before breakfast. She writes not only of her daily routines,
but recalls her early days in service, starting at the age of eight.
As a girl her jobs varied from house to house; at one she would
be cleaning the 'bright long halls', the next job would find her
amongst the endless pots and pans and kettles, at the next she
would be tending the boots and cleaning the nurseries of eight
children, carrying all the water up and down stairs for their baths
and the coal for the nursery fires.

The interest generated by Hannah's diaries is often dominated
by attempts to analyse the relationship between her and her
'Massa', that strange gentleman Edward Munby, for whom she
wrote her daily journal. As a result, scant attention has been paid
to Hannah's ability to describe her daily work; a task that is far
from easy to do. For most of us, nothing could be less alluring
than describing our own housecleaning, yet day after day, with
gusto and in great detail, Hannah took pen in hand and recorded
her day's work.

In her terse manner, Hannah often radiates a real enjoyment for her work. She balked at nothing; no job was too
hard. She revelled in the strength of her hands, her ability to
beat carpets and black grates and scrub floors, especially on
those glad days when the family would be out for the day.
Then she could sing as she worked, and clean upstairs in
her dirty clothes without offending the ladies of the household. She describes one particular day when the family had
departed as 'first-rate chance for me to get some cleaning
done'. She sets to avidly, tackling boots, grates, halls, dining
room, mats, windows, steps, broom closet, passages, potato
hole, shelves, back cellar, knives, dishes, as well as preparing

and clearing up meals. That day was apparently one of Hannah's happier ones.

Hannah's assessment of her various employers is both pithy and sharp. In 1864 she changed jobs in order to be near 'Massa', and found herself working for one Mrs Bishop, who was 'vulgar' and emphatically *not* a lady. Hannah felt she was 'lowering herself to the very bottom of service', and she knew that here she would have to work 'hard and low'. In this job, Hannah rarely emerged from the low underground kitchen except to shake the mats and clean the steps in the morning; her only chance to breathe fresh air. The kitchen was dark and very dirty, inches of thick mud lay under the tables and in the passages and stairs. Hannah was pleased to be allowed to clean upstairs and the leaded windows outside. With her face and hands grimed, she felt she had become as poor and dirty as any common drudge in the street.

Hannah did not last long with Mrs Bishop; she was clearly happier in better households. Yet even in better homes with more affable company, Hannah's lot was a thankless one. When she lived with a Miss Henderson and her sister, Hannah was once asked to clean thoroughly the whole house at a time when they were away. She was given only two weeks to do this and little extra help. There were four storeys, at least fifteen large rooms as well as landings, hallways, front and back stairs and two indoor water closets. Cleaning this house completely included organising men to whitewash the kitchen, the scullery and the dining room ceiling; the men also cleaned the walls in the dining room. Apart from that, Hannah and 'the boy' did the rest. All the nailed down carpets had to be taken up and beaten; all the draperies had to be removed, and either washed or beaten. Hannah started at six every morning and often worked to midnight by gaslight, but the job was impossibly large. The lady's maid, seeing this, told Hannah she was working herself to death, but in her diary Hannah stoutly claims she is doing this to please herself, though she ruefully adds that 'the Missis' probably will 'never know one half o'the dirt I'd clean'd away nor what labour it'd took to make things straight as they was, let alone the tipping and pulling and lifting there'd bin with all the carpets'.

Predictably, 'the Missis' is less than grateful for Hannah's labour, telling Hannah she is surprised everything is not more thoroughly done. Hannah is hurt and defends herself, saying that she had worked hard to do this much, but it would take two months to do the house really properly. Tiredly she writes in her diary that 'it must be 'cause they didn't know what a house was like with all the carpets up & only one to clean. She said no more, but left me feeling quite sick with disappointment.'

Hannah rarely complains about her work, but occasionally she heaves a heartfelt sigh: 'Got up & come down to the wretched looking kitchen & I felt so sick & bad from so much dirt and hard work.'

The work of these girls and women was invariably hard, dirty and exhausting, beginning at five or six in the morning when they rose to struggle with the kitchen fire. Once the grates were cleared, the cast-iron kitchen ranges had to be dusted and black-leaded; this meant breaking off a piece of black lead from a solid block, mixing it with water and applying the inky solution with a round-headed brush to every part of the range, letting it dry and then rubbing it until it shined with a polishing brush or a leather. Some stoves had bright and shiny steel areas which had to be polished with rottenstone and sweet-oil, fiercely rubbed on with a soft leather. Then the kitchen fires were lit, the kettles boiled, and other work could begin. The coal fires in the main downstairs rooms came first, then dusting and sweeping carpets with damp tea leaves or sand, cleaning the downstairs halls and landings, and finally upstairs, to the unlovely messes left behind in the bedrooms.

Imagine how unpleasant it must have been to deal with chamberpots and slop pails in every bedroom; how tiring and how messy to carry slops downstairs day after day and clean water upstairs. 'Some poor girl's got to go up and down, up and down, and be tired out,' remarks Ann, in *Kipps* (1905), by H.G. Wells, '. . . and no water upstairs anywhere – every drop got to be carried! It's 'ouses like this wear girls out. It's 'aving 'ouses built by men, I believe, makes all the work and trouble.' The work upstairs involved yet more fires, more grates to be blacked, more fenders and fire irons polished, and candle grease to clean up. Then downstairs to clean the lamp chimneys blackened with soot, to polish the steel knives and scour the wooden tables and clean the drains and sinks and scrub the floors on hands and knees. While scrubbing the maids' long skirts would be draggled with water and their legs cold and wet.

The housemaids in larger houses were equipped with a remarkable kit of materials and brushes to go about their work. According to Mrs Florence Caddy in her book *Household Organization* (1877), a housemaid should have at the ready: 'black lead, red, if liked, blue starch (a very little lasts a year), matches, hammers, pincers and nails, carpet tacks, and a riser, emery cloth, Turks'-head, feather brush, mattresses and other brushes, lamp-wicks, haberdashery. She will want one or two dozen dusters well softened, three to six chamber-cloths, two hearth cloths, from two to six dust-sheets, one ironing blanket, plate leather if she does the plate, twelve glass-cloths, twelve teacloths marked pantry, a window rubber, lamp cloths and sponges.'

Housemaids were faced with a particularly stubborn form of dirt in nineteenth-century households with coal-burning fireplaces. Robert Roberts, in his *Guide For Butlers and Household Staff* (1827), launches into a revealing outburst about different types of coal. He much prefers hard coal because it is *clean*; the superior dust from hard anthracite meets his approval for it is 'light and fine ... clean and pure, and easily dislodged from the mantel-piece and furniture, without leaving the least trace of its presence'. But the dust from softer coals leaves greasy smears; burn these coals and 'your clothes are smutted – your flesh begrimed – your furniture dirtied – your walls blackened ... I say nothing ... of those globules of pure greasy black in the shape of *pollywogs* that go sailing around the room'. Roberts describes how soot settles in streaky seams along the walls, how it stains the carpet, ruins books and papers, and how it highlights cobwebs by outlining them in black. He adds in an injured tone that without this soft coal soot the same cobwebs 'might otherwise have hung undisturbed for months or years'.

If popular literature is to be believed, no housemaid worth her salt would or could overlook a cobweb. Women's magazines and household advice books frequently carried improving little homilies explaining the duties of the housemaid. An anonymous 'lady' produced a book called *Common Sense For Housemaids* in 1853:

> A really good housemaid should never be able to be alone in a room with a table or a chair without giving it a good rub, or, if the room is occupied, without wishing to do so. Tables and chairs should be to her objects of deep interest; after her own family and the family of her mistress, they should claim the next place in her affections.

Pages later, the cleaning of the room draws to a happy conclusion: 'The housemaid may now look round with modest triumph, and exclaim, *Sublime*: a drawing-room in perfect order, *how lovely it is!*'

A far more sensible booklet, undated and by an unknown author, is *The Housemaid*. Addressed to the mistresses of large households, this booklet advises ladies how to instruct and inspire a housemaid in the arts of housecleaning. Room by room, problem by problem, *The Housemaid* provides extremely detailed descriptions of cleaning, with particular attention to the problems of central London. In the estimation of this booklet, the housemaid is a valued servant, an attitude that is notably exceptional in such publications. Her well-being is repeatedly considered; she should be provided with a mat to kneel on when she is scrubbing the floor; she should not be allowed to clean the outside of windows because of the danger of falling; she is assumed to share her mistress's dislike of dirt, and to share the eager desire to vanquish it. She is assumed to be entirely conscientious and thorough and perfectly pious to boot, a young girl to whom the sound of the church bell 'comes like music to her ear'.

Whoever wrote *The Housemaid* really *liked* cleaning, for there is a lively relish to the writing. Imagine, for example, doing the windows in a narrow London street. First you dust them carefully with one of your many brushes. 'Then some Spanish white is smeared on the pane, and washed off with a wet woollen rag . . . Each pane is finished with a clean, dry cloth; and should be left so transparent as that every brick of the opposite houses, and every fleece of cloud in the sky, may be seen as distinctly as if there were no glass in the frames.' Or polishing the mirrors: 'the glass of the mirror should be washed with pure water and a soft woollen, dried with a clean cloth, and finally polished with a silk handkerchief . . . rubbing with a silk handkerchief clears away the last dimness and makes the mirror as bright as the light.'

Contemporary magazines and advice manuals often reveal in a painful light the attitudes of mistresses towards their domestic servants. Extraordinary expectations and ideas abound:

> In choosing a servant, see that the applicant's head extends back some distance behind the ears. This portion of the head is known as the 'domestic region' and where it is not well developed, a servant is likely to be unsteady and dissatisfied. See also that the bump of firmness on the apex of the head rises well above the region of self-esteen, directly behind it. Otherwise the servant may prove insubordinate, independent, and altogether unpleasant.

This little gem appeared in *The American Kitchen Magazine* in 1899. A few pages later, perhaps unsurprisingly, an advertisement appears for the American Institute of Phrenology.

Mrs Mary Eliza Haweis, in *The Art of Housekeeping*, expends a vast amount of ink and energy advising employers how to judge and deal with their servants. Writing in London in 1889, she does not mince her words. Servants, she says, are 'no more like the gentry than dogs are like cats'. Compared to her gentle readers, 'they are quite different flesh and blood', and anyone who thinks or acts otherwise is clearly a fool. She does not blame the servants for their shortcomings; most servants were 'imperfectly brought up at home' and trained haphazardly. It is the mistress's duty to see that she takes control of the situation and makes herself clear to these people. 'Keep as few servants as you possibly can . . . Give every servant plenty to do, and see that it is done; give them meat only twice a day, and no beer . . . for drinks, water, lemonade (which is cheap enough), or the American fashion of tea.'

Mrs Haweis is coolly calculating about the labour she can expect from her servants. 'How much work can a healthy young servant undertake?' she asks, and concludes that a single housemaid can reasonably take charge of a house of 'twelve, thirteen or even fourteen' rooms, cleaning one (and sometimes two) each morning, on a fortnightly rotation, 'and yet there will be time for her to dress by one o'clock', when presumably she must help serve the family dinner. Mrs Haweis means a *thorough* cleaning: a complete turning out of the room in question, and she also means that this cleaning will follow the housemaid's normal early morning rituals of cleaning all the grates, sweeping halls and stairs, cleaning the doorstep, dusting main rooms, etc.

This recommendation of a fortnightly cleaning of rooms is not usual. Weekly cleaning was the norm, but Mrs Haweis begs to disagree:

> As a rule, a room turned out every week is *not* very thoroughly done, the maid often argues, 'it will be done again in a few days'. When a room has to last a fortnight, every piece of furniture must be shifted out, the corners must be seriously tackled, else the housemaid is sadly disgraced in ten or eleven days by the accumulations of dust. It must be remembered that a fair-sized room takes fully three hours to clean properly, and the housemaid must not begin later than ten on such a morning.

The process of cleaning these rooms would begin with removing or covering all the ornaments; covering furniture with dust sheets, sweeping, allowing the dust to settle for half an hour during which 'the housemaid will make time to run down for her "lunch" of bread and cheese and glass of – let us hope *not* beer'. She would then return to wash or polish ornaments, beeswax the furniture, rub the floors, and finally to dust. After all of this the mistress 'should peep at corners, high shelves etc. *herself*.

Such painfully pompous advice to employers is common fare, and advice aimed directly at housemaids is yet more grating in tone. Mrs George Cupples, in her 'Talks on Home Management' in the 'Magazine for Young Women', *The Home Friend*, in 1882 typically advises servants how to bustle about their work and learn the complexities of a household. Housemaids are told to rise early, tidy themselves and 'compose your mind in prayer and read a chapter'. That was to be the last quiet moment of the servant girl's day.

Off the girl then goes to tend to the fires and to get breakfast ready. Mrs Cupples regales her readers with the story of an exemplary servant called Maggie who worked with a smile and hearty good will all day long, doing all the work for a full household of five people. 'She rose at six o'clock, attended to her kitchen fire, cleaned out the dining room well, filled the coal-box, swept the stairs and lobby, washed the front steps, cleaned the bell, black-leaded the scraper and dusted the lobby.' All this before breakfast. After shaking the mats, Maggie ran upstairs to put on her 'nice print dress', and came down to do a cooked breakfast for the family. While they ate, she got the slop-pail, and off upstairs again to do the bedrooms, emptying the slops from the washbasins, making the beds, and doing her own room.

Mrs Cupples makes much of the fact that the ladies of the household helped Maggie, often even doing their own beds, 'so that all Maggie had to do . . . was to empty the slops, fill the ewers and bottles and clean it out thoroughly'. The ladies also assisted in cleaning the silver, the glasses, and dusting the drawing room, as well as helping with the cooking every day, using materials which Maggie would leave out for them. Maggie considers herself most fortunate, according to Mrs Cupples, declaring her work a positive pleasure. Her work continues all day long, through three meals and tea, with extra effort required on washday when she receives some outside help from the washerwoman.

Such Utopian notions of a perfect servant represent the triumph of optimism over experience. The young girls who normally worked as housemaids were inexperienced and under-paid, overworked and unappreciated and often lonely and far from home into the bargain. No wonder they enjoyed the reputation of being unreliable and flighty; they must have hoped continually to find a better situation. As a steady, older, hard worker well able to stand up for herself and content with her lot, Hannah Cullwick was the exception not the rule. More often than not, young girls entered service with reluctance, desperate for employment because their families needed help. Some found work in the grand and gracious houses beloved of costume dramas and romantic novelists; most were confined to smaller homes belonging to the newly enriched industrial middle classes, working for mistresses who were, according to Mrs Beeton, 'just a step above [the maid] in the social scale; and although the class contains many excellent, kind-hearted women, it also contains some very rough specimens of the feminine gender'. In such homes, the maid-of-all-work not only did the work of several servants – cook, housemaid, kitchenmaid – she frequently had to suffer a mistress who for the first time in her life had the leisure and the means to employ a servant and delighted in her new-found power to bully the unfortunate underling.

As junior servants in larger households, housemaids had more strictly specified cleaning work, but gained little in the bargain. Frequently they were badgered by other staff, worked long and thankless hours, and enjoyed almost no time to themselves. Housemaids did not enjoy any status in the hierarchical world of Victorian servants; the only ones with less were the kitchenmaid or the scullery maid.

The pecking order below-stairs in large households was com-plex, as one American lady discovered during her stay in London in the 1840s, when she was informed that her own maid would not take tea with a housemaid or a footman.

'The division of labour,' she wrote, 'or rather ceremonies, between the butler and the footman I have now mastered, I believe in some degree, but that between the *upper* and the *under* housemaid is still a profound mystery to me, though the upper has explained to me for the twentieth time that she did only "the top of the work".' (quoted in Huggett, *Life Below Stairs*)

When a house was large enough to merit more than one housemaid, the upper housemaids took charge of the appearance of the room: curtains, covers, ornaments, plants and flowers. Under housemaids, as might be expected, did the hard work of floors and fires and carpets.

As the nineteenth century drew to a close, articles in women's magazines and household advice books increasingly addressed the 'servant problem', both in America and in Britain. As new options opened out for them in industry and commerce, girls began to turn away from domestic work. Employers were not amused. Peevish and repetitive, the complaints were loud about the type of help available, the cost of help, the expectations of servants, the reliability of servants. American writers are particularly critical of their Irish maidservants, accusing them of laziness and dirtiness. In England, the general lack of gratitude of the servant class is a favourite theme.

Grudging admissions began to appear that it was possible to use a daily charwoman instead of a live-in housemaid, but this option was not highly regarded. Despite all the grief servants could cause their mistresses, due to breakages, losses and general indolence – evils much discussed by the ladies of the day – it was still preferable to have house-servants than that even more mistrusted figure, the charwoman. Besides, having servants had the added benefit of conferring status upon a home. Mrs Haweis, never at a loss for dispensing breathtakingly awful advice, tackles the problem of hiring a charwoman:

Unless you are happy enough to know a trim, honest widow, who does a little charing to supplement her income, and does not live by it, better do without the charwoman. She is more irresponsible than a house-servant, and less easy to supervise. She breaks, and leaves the blame on others. She not seldom brings in diseases, and carries away soap and candle-ends, and odd tea-cups . . . and she is always the most costly servant in the establishment.

If a charwoman *must* be had, her wages, according to Mrs Haweis, should be two shillings per day and her food, or two shillings and sixpence without her food. Her hours are seven to seven.

Given such biliously ill-natured employers as Mrs Haweis, it seems amazing that the era of easily available domestic help lasted as long as it did. Injured outpourings about the servant problem continued to appear in books and magazines for decades, well into the twentieth century. Eventually the penny dropped, and employers were forced to realise that potential servant girls had other and better options. Such realisation led to rueful comments like this, from *The Gentlewoman and Modern Life*, in 1926:

Unfortunately, the ordinary maid is still looked down upon by the majority, not, perhaps, in so many words, but the old prejudice still lives in people's minds, a most unfortunate heritage from the 'old-fashioned' days. Nurses, waitresses, laundry and factory hands all have raised their status by various methods of improved conditions; now is the time to improve the resident domestic.

To attract maidservants and to keep girls happy who were already in service, employers began to offer everything from easier hours and better working conditions to attractive uniforms. Earnest promises of greater respect for domestic help became commonplace. Training was also offered to attract servant girls to their 'profession'. One of the main objectives in the early days of the domestic science movement in Britain, as with the home economics movement in America, was to train girls properly before they entered domestic service: to school them to think of their work as a calling in which they could justly take pride.

The emphasis placed on training girls for this profession led to many overblown articles in magazines and newspapers extolling the virtues of educating domestic help. In August 1899, an article in the *Baltimore Sun* tells how eighty-five students of domestic economy, all of them girls, cleaned their school as a graduation exercise. Marks were assigned for this, just as for laboratory work.

> From top to bottom of the big building they have cleaned it as in all its history it was never cleaned before. They have scrubbed walls, windows and floors, dusted books, chairs, desks and stools, purified every corner, routed every cobweb and spider . . . in many of the corridors graceful young ladies, mounted high in the air, were seen waving above them a feathery duster or a damp rag. There would be a rakish looking cap on the maiden's head, and her hair would be in a state of collapse, but she didn't care a rap for that – she was a domestic economist.

Largely unmoved by the lofty descriptions of domestic economy as a calling, as the twentieth century advanced girls increasingly chose to seek employment in the wider worlds of industry and commerce. They were not fooled. Whatever anyone tried to tell them, they knew that taking care of a house involved a lot of hard and thankless work. After the First World War, the numbers of domestic servants in both America and Britain declined steeply and steadily.

In America, the employment of domestic help was never the enormous industry it was in Britain. In *The American Woman's Home* (1869), Catharine Beecher speaks with pride of a 'universal rejection of domestic service in all classes of American society', contrasting this favourably to England where a 'distinct serving class' existed. Although Catharine Beecher almost certainly overstates her case in arguing for Americans' 'universal rejection' of a serving class, she voices a genuine unease on this subject, an unease shared by many Americans who were fighting slavery in the Southern States. Certainly Beecher herself, and her sister Harriet Beecher Stowe, co-author of *The American*

Woman's Home and author of *Uncle Tom's Cabin*, held strong views about any type of servitude claiming that:

> The condition of domestic service . . . retains about it something of the influences from feudal times, and from the near presence of slavery in the neighbouring States. All English literature of the world describes domestic service in the old feudal spirit and with the old feudal language, which regarded the master as belonging to a privileged class and the servant to an inferior one. There is not a play, not a poem, not a novel, not a history that does not present this view.

Not all gentlewomen in the New World felt critical of the old roles of mistress and maid, though. Far from it. Newly arrived, many women yearned desperately for a supply of 'girls' ready to do domestic work, and these good ladies were nonplussed by the recalcitrant attitudes they encountered. When a local lass arrived at the door to visit Mrs Susannah Moodie at her new, rough home in Canada, Mrs Moodie assumed the girl had come to offer her services. 'How!' responded the creature. 'I hope you don't take me for a help. I'd have you to know that I'm as good a lady as yourself.' Mrs Moodie's horror at such an unthinkable comment was only matched by her misery at having to do her own housework, year after year, and never finding the grateful and biddable servant of her dreams.

Florence Stanton breathed more privileged air than the likes of Mrs Moodie. Well placed in American society, she could afford to have 'proper' servants who knew their place. Untroubled by Catharine Beecher's democratic ideals, Mrs Stanton favoured a full complement of servants in every well-run home. Her book, *The Practical Housekeeper and Cyclopedia of Domestic Economy* (1898), radiates a daft and random charm. Double-columned, closely printed, replete with 'Five Thousand Practical Receipts and Maxims' as well as two hundred engravings, the book even features a dreamily beautiful picture of Mrs Stanton. She looks about nineteen years old, her dress ripples with lace, her hair curls winsomely about her forehead and she holds a feather quill pen. Florence Stanton gives the impression of being an engaging dilettante, possessed of no particular domestic aim other than maintaining the status quo peculiar to a well-off household in urban America at the turn of the century. Her scattered instructions about cleaning do little more than direct the housemaid in her daily duties, recommending that she rise at 5:30 a.m., do all the regular cleaning described by Hannah Cullwick in a big household and even more, including daily brass polishing, filling the kitchen boiler with water, and three times a week washing all the bedroom floors.

Mrs Stanton bemoans the fact that in America servants are more difficult to find than in England. In a fine English household there are – or so she believes – far more servants than in an American home of equivalent wealth and social standing. She evidently judges the status of a home by the number and efficiency of its servants. Yet writing in this vein near the dawn of the twentieth century, Mrs Stanton was rapidly becoming an anomaly. Such attitudes as hers were not to survive much longer, particularly in America.

The reliance on servants to do the dirty household work was generally more widespread and lasted much longer in Britain than in America. Interesting consequences resulted. A much repeated observation amongst social historians is how the dependence on cheap domestic labour in Britain dramatically delayed the advance of domestic technology. For example, the slow acceptance of central heating in Britain is directly connected with the ready availability of cheap labour. With so many girls trained to clean, set, and light the countless and inefficient open coal fires, it seemed extravagant luxury to install costly heating systems to replace the services of the maids. The same argument applies to the installation of both gas and electricity in British homes; with inexpensive help to clean lamp chimneys and to cope with inefficient kitchen ranges, why go to all the expense of installing new-fangled systems? Not until domestic help, male and female, was siphoned off by the challenges, the tragedies, and the new work opportunities provided by the First World War did British householders begin to accept that new ways and systems of running the home must be embraced, however reluctantly.

As it slowly became apparent that the 'servant problem' was not going to be easily resolved, a new tone began to be sounded. Ladies who were left to fend for themselves in their own households began to write about the challenge of it all, sounding game and plucky as they stepped forth to face the jolly challenges of do-it-yourself housekeeping. 'I am Glad my Servant Left', rejoices an article in the *Ladies' Home Journal* in 1918. 'My maid left to go into Munitions work . . . and I'm glad she's gone!' The article goes on to explain that now her maid has left, the lady of the house has bought all sorts of exciting new equipment to help her do the housework properly; the thrills of owning a vacuum cleaner, a dishwasher and a washing machine are now hers. Helpful books appeared around this time with titles like *First Aid to the Servantless* (1913), and *The Servantless House* (1920), invariably encouraging the purchase of electrical appliances and the efficient reorganisation of the household.

Despite such dogged optimism, the appeal endured of being able to employ servants. A full page ad in *Woman* in 1937 still harps on the theme that every British woman truly wants a maid. 'I've just got a maid at fourpence a day!' declares the happy lady of the house. 'Tireless workers who never need afternoons off or evenings out. To describe them in one simple word – Hoovers . . . It *beats* the grit from carpets just as they lie – it *sweeps* up fluff and animal hairs – it *suctions* away every trace of dust.' Nearly twenty years later, an advertisement in *Good Housekeeping* still assumes a maid is present in the middle-class household: a woman in evening clothes is on the telephone saying 'Come to dinner on Sunday'. She pauses to listen before replying, '*Whose* night out? No, she's left . . . we bought a Dishmaster instead.' The telephone conversation continues with cheery chat about how having a dishwashing machine has transformed the domestic life of the household, now no longer in need of the maid.

The exchange of maids for machinery in the household probably rarely occurred. According to Adrian Forty in *Objects of Desire*, this notion was more a fantasy of advertisers than a reality. Vacuum cleaners were indeed called such 'servant' names as the Daisy or the Betty Anne, but this myth of a 'mechanical servant' only existed to feed the social illusions of people who never employed a servant in the first place. In the early days of labour-saving devices, appliances were bought in the hope of attracting and keeping a maid in the house. Advertisements repeatedly reflect this hope.

'Now you have a parlourmaid,
The next thing is to keep her
What you must do is banish brooms
And get a Eubank Sweeper.'

Similarly, a 1911 advertisement for the Vortex Suction Cleaner shows the parlourmaid turning towards the lady of the house and graciously conceding: 'Now you've this, m'am, I'll stay.' But a new era had arrived, and such advertisements were fighting a rearguard action. Not for a houseful of sweepers or suction cleaners would those maids have stayed for ever.

6

PUBLIC CONCERN

THE IMPACT OF SANITARY REFORM

Because of the dirt and overcrowding and disease that predominated in most cities, by the middle of the nineteenth century cleanliness had become a more public and more urgent issue than ever before. This urgency was well merited. Living as we now do in the western world in cities with fairly clean streets, with decent drains, sewers and rubbish collection, the harrowing sanitary conditions of earlier times are unimaginable. Yet if the increasing desire for cleanliness and the popular moralising about cleanliness that arose in the nineteenth century are to make any sense at all, we must try to understand their context.

Strict notions about cleanliness arose at least partly in response to the alarmingly dirty conditions out of doors. Every foot that touched the pavement or the sidewalk could be tainted with manure or sewage; the hem of every long dress was in danger of being dragged through stinking messes, the smells were beyond description, the water supplies unreliable. If we had to deal with such conditions on a daily basis we, like many of our forebears, might be driven to the conclusion that no effort is too great to attain a clean home and we too might be harshly and openly critical of those failing to attain decent standards.

A new and intense kind of urban poverty had been spawned by the growth of industry; increased dirt and overcrowding followed the victorious captains of industry as they planted their factories in city after city. Housing was limited, amenities were minimal, work was often brutal, yet still the workers came and as urban population densities increased, living conditions worsened. In America these problems were even more acute because of the crowds of immigrants arriving in the rough new cities that often lacked the most basic infrastructure. On both sides of the Atlantic overcrowded slums were the order of the day; poorly organised sanitation and water supplies, wretched drains, streets filled with garbage and manure and scavenging animals and waste of all sorts. In the face of such filth, pious preaching about keeping oneself and one's home clean was simply farcical. Much more was required.

Into this breach stepped the sanitary reformers, precursors of the public health movement. One of the earliest and best known of these in mid-nineteenth-century Britain was Edwin Chadwick. A tireless agitator, Chadwick cared not one whit about being offensive. Starting in the 1830s, ceaselessly and belligerently, year after year, he pushed his ideas about waste disposal and city cleansing in front of government authorities. Chadwick advocated centrally controlled systems for sewerage and city cleansing, an idea that meant radical reorganisation. At that time, London was a chaos of many small local boards taking responsibility in a patchy and inefficient manner for city cleansing and sewerage as well as for paving and lighting. With each board in London and in every other city keen to protect its authority, and the overall policy of government reluctant to impose regulations upon free enterprise, Chadwick faced a huge struggle in his wish to centralise these services.

In 1842 Chadwick's *Report on the Sanitary Conditions of the Labouring Population of Great Britain* appeared, based on surveys of conditions in different areas of the country. Chadwick's report drew on first-hand investigations by medical officers from many of the poorer working areas in England. A dismal picture emerges of workers' dwellings as overcrowded and vile places, with inadequate water supplies, with overflowing privies and cesspools reeking outside the door, with 'heaps of filth' nearby that included everything from human excrement to dead animals.

'Foul and putrid' streets and courtyards, and 'open, deep, black, and stagnant' ditches and sewers, full of 'obnoxious effluvia' are described in rich and rolling language on page after page.

While such conditions were more widespread in large urban centres, smaller towns were far from immune to this pervasive filth. The Provost of Inverness wistfully writes that 'Inverness is a nice town, situated in a most beautiful country, and with every facility for cleanliness and comfort', but goes on to admit that few houses in the town have so much as a privy, and that there are virtually no public privies. 'Hence there is not a street, lane, or approach . . . that is not disgustingly defiled at all times, so much as to render the whole place an absolute nuisance.' Plenty of water is available, he argues; available 'by little trouble', but the population does not avail itself of this, and therefore 'MUCH filth in-doors and out of doors *must* be their portion'.

From the East End of London one of Chadwick's closest collaborators, Dr Southwood Smith, reports that the 'streets, courts, alleys and houses in which fever first breaks out . . . are invariably those in the immediate neighbourhood of uncovered sewers, stagnant ditches and ponds, gutters always full of putre-fying matter, nightmen's yards, and privies, the soil of which lies openly exposed and is seldom or never removed'. Southwood Smith mercilessly details an East End of stinking alleys deep in filth, disgusting courtyards, and disease-ridden slums, where no one with any pride could live or survive. He tells of one young woman doing her best against the tide of filth:

A short time ago I was standing in one of the streets branching off Rosemary Lane, looking at a stream of abomination that was flowing down from a court into the open gutter of Blue Anchor Yard. This poisoned stream was flowing close to a house, at the door of which there stood a woman with ruddy cheeks, neatly clothed. 'Five times this day,' she said to me, 'I have swept this place, but you see the state it is in again.' Her whole appearance indicated she was a newcomer; in a few days she would give up her hopeless attempt to keep the place clean, and if she remain there she must necessarily sink into the state of squalor and filth so general among her neighbours.

Water was available for urban slum dwellers from communal sources in the streets or courtyards, sometimes at a considerable distance from the home, or down many flights of stairs. 'I cannot say', reports one officer from Whitechapel, 'whether it is the actual scarcity of water, or their reluctance to fetch it, but the effect is a scarcity of water.' On visiting the rooms of the slum-dwellers, this officer found 'only a very scanty supply of water in their tubs. When they are washing, the smell of the dirt mixed with the soap is the most offensive of all the smells I have to encounter. They merely pass dirty linen through very dirty water. The smell of the linen itself, when so washed, is very offensive.'

Every large city had comparable stories from similar slums. Liverpool was the worst of all, known as the unhealthiest place in England, with an average life expectancy in 1843 of nineteen years. One of the medical officers from Liverpool who gave evidence to Chadwick's report describes how sixty-three cases of typhoid had occurred recently in one courtyard that contained only twelve houses. On visiting this courtyard he 'found the whole court inundated with filthy fluid which had oozed through the walls from two adjoining ashpits and which had no means of escape . . . having no drain'. No escape from the smell was possible, nor from the sight of gutters filled with 'noxious matter'. Vast dumps of 'night soil', ash, rotting vegetable matter, foul straw, and offal from slaughterhouses accumulated in the streets, removed irregularly and infrequently by street cleaners. Dungheaps of alarming proportions accumulated in all cities; a medical officer from Greenock reports on one that was 'a hundred cubic yards of impure filth', overtopping and oozing through a twelve foot wall on to the street, attracting swarms of flies.

In a society where most thinking people lived in great fear of the danger of bad air, the smell and supposed fumes from all this material was tantamount to a death sentence. Such air was believed to be the chief source of contagion. As Chadwick wrote in 1842, 'the various forms of epidemic, endemic, and other disease [are] caused, or aggravated, or propagated chiefly amongst the labouring classes by atmospheric impurities produced by decomposing animal and vegetable substances, by damp and filth, and close and overcrowded dwellings'. The many medical officers who contributed to Chadwick's report tirelessly repeat their beliefs about how disease spreads: through polluted water, open sewers, overcrowding, and most insistently of all, through bad air.

This concern for bad air and 'atmospheric impurities' arose from the dominant 'miasma' theory of disease. This theory goes far to explain the concern for ventilation and pure air and odour-free drains that is expressed by so many medical authorities of the nineteenth century, and that appears so repeatedly in household advice manuals. Notions about miasma were vague and ill-defined, maintaining that 'noxious exhalations' and bad air were the agents of disease; that infection was spread in this bad air; that its cause was animal and vegetable refuse, and that their smells not only carried disease, they *were* the disease.

Because of the prevailing fear of impure air, many sanitary reformers emphasised clean air and ventilation above all else in their campaigns for cleaner cities. This preoccupation was widely shared by many authorities, including Florence Nightingale who harped ceaselessly on the theme of household ventilation. In her *Notes on Nursing* (1859), she lists five essential features for a healthy home: pure air, pure water, efficient drainage, cleanliness, and light. Her dominant concern for ventilation allows that ventilation is futile in filthy conditions: 'Without cleanliness, within and without your house, ventilation is comparatively useless . . . You cannot have the air of the house pure with dung-heaps under the windows. These are common all over London.'

For better-off homes in better neighbourhoods where the streets were kept cleaner than in the slums and where the refuse was removed more often, household cleanliness and non-toxic air were at least possible goals. For the rest, a measure of public cleanliness had to come first. Edwin Chadwick's report recommended uniformity of action throughout Britain to improve public drainage and sewers, to remove waste from the streets, to provide good water supplies. This would, he asserted, help to eradicate contagious disease, increase life expectancy amongst the working classes by thirteen years at least, and – of course – improve their moral condition, for 'sound morality and refinement in manners and health are not long found co-existant with filthy habits'.

The depressing effect of damp on household standards is a common theme in Chadwick's report; many a cautionary tale is told. Like that of the young woman who was neat and clean and the acme of respectability until she married and went to live with her husband in a wretched worker's cottage. She became dirty and slatternly, worn down by the persistent, pervasive damp of the place. The damp rose through the floor and when it rained the roof leaked everywhere: 'large drops fell upon her as she lay in bed . . . in short, she had found it impossible to keep things in order, so had gradually ceased to make any exertions'. Removed to another cottage, this worthy female was saved from filth and damp and resumed her former good habits.

The idyllic English cottage is given a poor bill of health in Chadwick's report. Most workers' cottages are characterised as 'damp, low, cold, smoky, and comfortless', with pigsties and dunghills perilously close the the living quarters. The occupants are not blamed by the medical officers making the reports, although these gentlemen do allow themselves an occasional sideswipe at the workers' moral character, which is assumed to correspond to the degraded state of their homes, and many reproving comments are made about intemperance and vice, both of which apparently thrived under damp, thatched roofs in the country. But this aside, many of the men making their reports concur with the sentiments of one Mr John Fox who wrote about labourers in Dorset that 'if their wages were sufficient to enable them to rent a·decent cottage, I have no doubt they would soon regain their lost spirit of cleanliness'.

Damp was a great disincentive to cleanliness and judging from Chadwick's report, damp reigned supreme in most British dwellings: in cellars, in cottages, in large old houses, in tenanted blocks of flats. It still does, in my experience. Having lived in many different kinds of homes both in Britain and in North America, the damp I encountered so repeatedly in Britain outclasses anything I have met elsewhere. In my early years in Britain I lived with wallpaper bagging moistly on the walls of rented houses; I witnessed lines of damp moving visibly up newly painted walls; I became accustomed to overpowering smells of mildew, clothes never fully dry, walls clammy to the touch, towels that developed mildew between baths. The few patches of mildew and damp I have done battle with in various closets, bathrooms and basements in Canada are a mere nothing compared with the perils of living in older housing in Britain. Chadwick's report is entirely correct in pointing out that it is hard to feel either clean or healthy in a damp place. 'The greater facilities and inducements to cleanliness in a dry house would, in the course of time, form a more cleanly people, and superior healthiness would follow.'

After many long years of thankless struggle, Chadwick did win the day. Largely because of the shocking material in his report, the first Public Health Act was passed in Parliament in 1848. From that point onwards public sanitary reform remained firmly upon the legislative table.

In America the burgeoning new cities all faced overwhelming sanitary problems in the nineteenth century, none more so than New York, that mecca for immigrants. Descriptions abound of the filth in the streets, the disease, the overcrowding; of how epidemics of cholera, yellow fever and typhoid followed one upon the other. In New York in 1864, the Citizens' Association decided to take action. Their Council of Hygiene and Public Health undertook an ambitious investigation into the sanitary conditions of the city, employing the services of thirty-one physicians who inspected different areas of the city.

The picture that emerges of life in New York City is smelly, nasty and dirty: 'our Sanitary Inspectors have, throughout the entire period of their labors, reported the prevalence of universal filthiness, the only exceptions being a few streets and places that are daily cleaned by private enterprises.' A few favoured areas of the city were acceptably clean and graced with elegant residences with lawns and gardens. 'Along the banks of the Hudson are the stately mansions of the rich, with the usual complement of domestic servants, gardeners, hostlers, coachmen, stable-boys etc.' Within close range of such houses, however, lay 'the most loathsome and filthy lane . . . rank with filth and stench . . . unsewered, unguttered, reeking with filth'. In such undeveloped streets of the growing New York, shanty-dwellers lived in intense squalor, but recent arrivals to the city who found their way into the overcrowded brick tenements were not much better off.

The horror of these 'tenant houses' is the most consistent theme in the report, which estimates that nearly half a million people in the city inhabited these densely packed buildings. Variously described as 'fever nests', 'hives of sickness and vice' and 'poisoned abodes of physical decay' by the medical gentlemen carrying out the sanitary inspections, these tenements not only had little air or light – many rooms were without windows – but they rarely had a good water supply and often featured communal privies in their narrow, well-like courtyards.

The filth of these dark, dank 'yards' rivals similar descriptions from the slums of London and Liverpool. Slops would be thrown from the windows; the ground would be piled deep with filth; the privies would be badly drained or overflowing. According to one inspector:

> The water closets are located between the front and rear houses, many of them covered and surrounded with filth, so as not to be approachable, others so much out of repair as to endanger the life of those frequenting them. Some of them are merely trenches sunken one or two feet in the ground, the fluids of which are in some instances allowed to run into the courts, stones and boards being sometimes provided to keep the feet out of the filth. One-half of the tenant-houses have no sewers connected with them; consequently the stench from all of the water-closets, during the summer, is absolutely unbearable and perilous.

The 'special nuisances' of New York City included manure

yards, fat melting and bone boiling and hide curing establish-ments, stables and, worst of all, slaughterhouses. There were 173 in New York City at the time. The smell, the animal waste, the noise, the heaps of offal all combined to debase already blighted localities even further. In one district after another of the city, the medical officers write with lively horror of the 'gross filthiness of the streets, courts, and alleys, the putrefying masses of animal and vegetable matter, together with dead animals, obstructed sewerage and drainage, and poisonous exhalations from manufactories of various kinds, combine to pollute the atmosphere of the entire city'.

Public health measures in England were well known to the writers of this American report. They cite the recommendations of Miss Nightingale concerning sanitation and ventilation in homes of the 'industrial classes' of London, and the success story of the district of St Giles is held up as an example. There, in one year, the mortality rate was reduced by 50 per cent, 'by means of cleansing and ventilation'.

The report concludes that public cleanliness should be enforced in New York. The Citizens' Association called for a 'sanitary government', an 'enlightened Board of Health' and also recommended the 'employment of sanitary missionaries and lecturers' to work among the poor. The report also called for the removal of slaughterhouses from densely populated areas and for improved sanitation in areas with stables, where the 'daily employment of coal tar or the chlorine compounds, and proper absorbents' is recommended. Within a year of the report being presented to the state legislature, a Metropolitan Board of Health was created and given the power to enforce sanitary measures.

The faster cities grew in North America, the worse their prob-lems, and in the late nineteenth century cities were growing wildly and rapidly. In the 1860s in Canada, the new city of Ottawa was emerging messily from a stretch of mud and wilderness. Sandra Gwyn's vivid portrait of the place in *The Private Capital* (1984) tells of unrelenting filth: 'These were dirty, demanding times . . . The roads were full of mud and manure; the wooden sidewalks covered with clots of spittle, tobacco juice and worse.' Even the most agreeable houses were plagued by 'the putrid, overpowering stench of stagnant water and human faeces'. Sewers and running water did not come to Ottawa until 1874, and until then the inadequate wooden drains stank to high heaven during the hot summer months.

'Stench intolerable, add to which the combined odours of chlorine and lime, carbolic acid and other diabolical disinfectants that I have been using freely.' Edmund Meredith's domestic plight is recorded plaintively in his journal. A civil servant living in Ottawa in the 1860s and 1870s, Meredith chronicles the private miseries of living in such a raw, new place. His dismay at discovering the clogged drains under his new house is pitiable: 'Drains, Drains, Nothing but Drains', he says in a journal entry of June 1872. 'Garden torn up, cellar floor. Drain outside found to be choked up, pipes are of common red clay, not glazed, joints not cemented.'

Water was expensive. The Merediths paid 15 cents a gallon in the summer and 25 cents a gallon in the winter for their water, which came from delivery carts that went from door to door. Keeping themselves and their clothes clean must have been not only extremely hard work, but very costly. Keeping the new house clean, built in 'a treeless wasteland of mud', without even a wooden sidewalk nearby, would have been a nightmare.

Accounts like this make urban Britain, with all its attendant problems, appear exceptionally well-serviced. But small cities like Ottawa knew nothing of the massive problems of older and bigger industrial cities, nor did they need to convince a large existing population about the grave necessity of keeping clean. This need to educate and inform a large population led to extraordinary efforts on the part not only of public officials, but also – and perhaps chiefly in some settings – on the part of volunteers.

In Britain, countless voluntary agencies sprang up in the nineteenth century whose aim was to relieve the poor and to help the needy in the ever more crowded and polluted urban centres. Middle-class women, freed from their own domestic chores by their ability to hire servants, became front-line workers, taking direct and public action in their own cities and towns, doggedly going from house to house to try to improve the lot of the poorest of the poor. They gave advice, they fed, they clothed, they sewed, they washed, and – of course – they cleaned, and exhorted others to clean. Along the way they distributed innumerable Bibles and quoted a great deal of Scripture, for a strong religious zeal lay behind many, perhaps most, of these philanthropic agencies.

Radiating self-assured virtues, certain that God was on their side, these women were indefatigable, visiting all the poor in district after district of major cities. Time and again they found themselves in desperate, filthy, disease-ridden hovels, doing what they could to feed, clothe, nurse and clean up. As the historian Frank Prochaska puts it: 'these foot-soldiers of the charitable army went from door to door to combat the evils of poverty, disease, and irreligion . . . they sought to reform family life through a moral and physical cleansing of the nation's homes'.

This connection between moral cleansing and physical cleansing is much repeated in the writings of social reformers. Dr Southwood Smith declares that:

A clean, fresh and well-ordered house exercises over its inmates a moral, no less than a physical influence and has a direct tendency to make the members of the family sober, peaceable and considerate of the feelings and happiness of each other; whereas a filthy, squalid, unwholesome dwelling, in which none of the decencies common to society are or can be observed, tends directly to make every dweller regardless of the feelings and happiness of each other, selfish and sensual.

In similar vein, the authors of the 1865 report on the sanitary condition of New York City frequently equate the physical and moral purity of the city's dwellers. Many of the inspectors who contribute to the report stress that the prevalent disregard for 'personal and domiciliary cleanliness' reflects lax moral habits. The dark, filthy courtyards of the city's brick tenements were condemned as 'pernicious at once to the health and morals of such localities; they inevitably become haunts of social debasement and vice, as well as of fevers and every bodily disease'. The report quotes a journalist who writes with outrage about these tenements where 'poverty, disease and crime find an abode . . . Unholy passions rule in the domestic circle. Every thing, within and without, tends to physical and moral degradation.'

Such emphasis on the moral virtues of cleanliness was only to be expected; a sign of the times. The *Encyclopedia of Domestic Economy* of 1844 strikes a particularly self-righteous pose. In extolling the superiority inherent in cleanliness, the authors do not draw back from the logical conclusion of their argument; if cleanliness is a conscious virtue – it is described as the 'parent of virtues' – then dirt is a deliberate vice:

> As a habit, [cleanliness] has moral as well as physical advantages . . . it is an emblem, if not a characteristic, of purity of thought and propriety of conduct. It seems as if it could not be associated with vicious pursuits; so rarely, in the habitually profligate character, are the active and wholesome habits of cleanliness perceptible. The squalid wretchedness, which sometimes engages the pity of the philanthropist, is oftener found, on investigation, to be the effect of vicious idleness rather than of unmerited misfortune; while cleanliness, if it cannot totally indemnify us from the evils of poverty and disease, can keep them far removed from utter wretchedness and misery.

This is unforgiving stuff. Many joined the moral chorus of praise and blame. 'Filth is more frequently evidence of depravity than of destitution,' reports a medical officer in the 1840s. The Reverend Francis Kilvert records his surprise when he sees the flecklessly clean home of a couple who, although now married, had once lived in sin; he had fully expected the place to be dirty. Another reverend gentleman intones that 'All who know the lower classes will testify that the last want felt by the dirty is cleanliness'.

Mercifully, most reformers knew that cleanliness requires not only an effort of will and correct morals, but certain basic commodities like water and decent drains. Time and effort and a little money were also essential, for soap or for a spare set of clothes to allow the other to be washed. Having a place to live in which one can reasonably take some pride would also be a boon. With none of these advantages, why should people even try to keep themselves or their surroundings clean? With none of these advantages they are virtually defeated before they even start.

Herculean efforts by town and city planners, by health officials, by charitable groups all combined to create much cleaner cities by the late nineteenth century. Better drains, better water supplies and cleaner streets meant that the terrible urban outbreaks of typhoid and cholera were greatly reduced by the 1890s. Much of the public cleansing that led to this enormous improvement grew out of the efforts of people whose understanding of the spread of disease was uncertain, but whose belief in cleanliness was none the less absolute.

The germ theory of disease was not widely accepted even by the medical community until the late nineteenth century. By the time the germ theory began to filter through to the non-scientific community, the long-fought-for improvements in public sanitation were largely in place. At this point, health reformers and sanitarians began, with great energy, to focus their energies on those new public and private enemies, *germs*. Once they began to spread the word about these pernicious microscopic creatures, housecleaning would never be the same again.

7

GERMS

THE RADICAL EFFECT OF THE GERM THEORY

Song of the Microbe

I'm in the air,
I'm everywhere,
I'm after all of you;
You can't escape
My little shape
If I choose to pursue.
I'm in your food,
E'en bad or good,
I'm with you day and night;
I'm in your meat,
And all you eat,
Though I am out of sight.

I'm on the brink,
I'm in the drink,
I'm in the bucket old;
O, haughty Miss
I'm in the kiss,
I'm in the soda cold.
I'm here and there,
I'm everywhere,

My grip I never lose
My little shape
You can't escape,
If I choose to pursue.

(*refrain*) Just a little microbe,
Just a tiny mite;
Merely playing possum,
Always out of sight.
Lying low and waiting,
Perhaps unknown to fame;
Just a little microbe,
I get there just the same.

By the time this ditty was printed in the *American Kitchen Magazine* in September 1898, the unlikely notion that invisible micro-organisms were responsible for disease had captured the public imagination. This idea was bizarre, astonishing, and more than a little frightening. Once it entered the public arena it spread quickly. Educators, health officials, home economists and advertisers all began to repeat the same message; germs, the purveyors of everything evil, lived and thrived in dirt and they must be killed. Scrupulous cleanliness was the answer, more scrupulous than ever before.

Once germs became an accepted part of everyday life and understanding, crude though that understanding was and often still is, the pursuit of cleanliness changed for ever. A new and terrifying enemy had been revealed and our understanding of the very nature of dirt was radically altered. As Mary Douglas says of the germ theory of disease in *Purity and Danger*: 'So much has it transformed our lives that it is difficult to think of dirt except in the context of pathogenicity.'

In *Objects of Desire*, Adrian Forty points out how the vigorous new concern about germs took the health reformers out of the public domain and into the private home in a way that was entirely new. Germs were known to be carried by flies, on dirty hands and clothes, in unclean food and, it was widely believed, in dust. None of this fell within the remit of municipal cleansing projects, so if these germs were to be conquered domestic habits had to be improved and every individual must be educated about hygiene and cleanliness. The word must be spread into every home, to every man, woman and child; here, on the home-front, lay the new battleground. 'Kill The Germ' became the battlecry. Household advice manuals and advertisements encouraged homemakers to think that they could indeed kill each and every hostile germ in their homes, with concentrated effort, with the right products and with sufficient know-how; not only was this possible, it was their bounden duty.

The germ theory of disease took a long time, however, to work its way into the public consciousness. The revolutionary work with disease micro-organisms carried out by Louis Pasteur and others became known in the early 1860s, but even the medical establishment did not fully accept or act on these discoveries until nearly two decades later. Therefore a vast amount of public health work, including major sanitary improvements and the heroic battles against epidemic disease of the nineteenth century was carried out with a notable degree of success by people who had absolutely no truck with the germ theory. The miasma theory of disease held sway.

Florence Nightingale was of the old school. No one knew better the importance of sanitation in hospitals or fought more strongly for improved cleanliness in the care of the sick. Miss Nightingale virtually invented the modern science of nursing in her work during the Crimean War. She knew that cleaning saved lives, she knew that accumulations of filth were dangerous; she knew that porous surfaces somehow held disease; she knew all this because she had seen and experienced it in hospitals. But germs were not in her vocabulary. She lived and worked at the same time Louis Pasteur's theories were being debated by the medical community, she lived through the era when antiseptic techniques in surgery were becoming the norm, and before she died in 1910 the germ theory was widely accepted, though she graced it with little attention.

Many eminent medical people of the latter part of the nine-teenth century, doctors and surgeons with far more qualifications than Florence Nightingale, strenuously resisted the germ theory of disease, even though they knew that cleanliness – and in some cases antiseptic practices – were extremely important. Arthur Newsholme, who studied medicine in the mid-1870s at St Thomas's Hospital in London, describes the indifferent understanding his superiors had of germs and contagion. Instruments were sterilised in alcohol during surgery, to be sure, but Newsholme witnessed one surgeon drop a forceps on the floor and use it again; he saw sponges that had been used to swab a patient rinsed out in a sink and used again; he even saw one surgeon taking snuff while he performed surgery. Some surgeons operated in old frock coats, never properly cleaned and certainly not removed between operations, and Newsholme recalls seeing needles threaded with dangling silk threads attached to one such well worn and grubby coat, all ready to be used for suturing. The medical gentlemen who practised in such a fashion were far from worried about micro-organisms. Yet when the change came it came fairly quickly, and by the mid-1880s after yet more disease bacteria had been identified and isolated, the germ theory of disease was broadly accepted in the medical community.

On the sidelines, interested lay observers had long been commenting on the germ theory. Amongst the household experts, one of the earliest to pass comment was Catharine Beecher, characteristically ahead of her time. In 1869, in *The American Woman's Home,* she mentions 'microscopic plants' found in the blood and body fluids of typhoid sufferers and smallpox victims, adding in a tone of curious wonderment that the typhoid plants 'resemble in form some kinds of seaweed'.

Over a decade later, the ever-enthusiastic Harriette Plunkett was volubly interested in germs. In 1885, in her book *Women, Plumbers and Doctors,* she writes:

Five years ago it would have been presumptuous to declare unqualifiedly that typhoid fever, diphtheria, cholera and all the diseases that become epidemic, are produced each by its own specific *contagium,* which consists in an infinitesimal *seed* capable of retaining its vitality for an indefinite period.

She goes on to say that now 'the conviction is spreading and gaining daily in strength, that reproductive parasitic life is at the root of epidemic disease'. Mrs Plunkett pours scorn on disbelievers, like 'the man who says he "is sick to death of all this germ nonsense"'.

Mrs Plunkett was writing at a time when the sanitation and hygiene of every home were becoming the dominant themes in household advice books. Not all advisers are as forthright as she about the germ theory; most allude in generally laudatory terms to the importance of scientific knowledge, and insist that every woman in charge of a house must inform herself about the spread of disease and the importance of hygiene. An excellent example of this vague type of advice is the book *Home Sanitation: A Manual for Housekeepers* which appeared in 1887. It declares:

> The day is past when sickness was held to be a direct interference of Providence, as retributive punishment. Pestilence, fevers, and weakness are, indeed, penalties for sin, but it is for the sin of ignorance. In this age of scientific enlightenment and invention and wide-spread information, ignorance of the primary conditions of health and vigor is unpardonable. A knowledge of sanitary principles should be regarded as an essential part of every woman's education, and obedience to sanitary laws should be ranked, as it was in the Mosaic Code, as a religious duty.

While some understanding of germs certainly lies behind the advice given in *Home Sanitation* – it speaks of 'the general acceptance of the germ theory' – this book and many others of the same ilk tend to speak of sanitation and hygiene in terms that are far more emotional than scientific. A strange combination of moral fervour, common sense and downright threats is used to drive home advice about how to safeguard a home against germs and infection. Some decidedly odd ideas come into play also: *Home Sanitation* recommends, for instance, that furniture be varnished or oiled to prevent 'the absorption of poisoned gases'. The language is consistently flowery; to 'propitiate the goddess of health' all 'unsanitary' furnishings and fabrics, including carpets, draperies and cornices, should be banished in favour of easy-to-clean hard surfaces.

Women are not asked in *Home Sanitation* to try to understand theories of micro-organisms but they are expected to understand fully that water should be pure, drains and earth closets and water closets and privies be regularly disinfected, garbage be carefully disposed of, cellars be dry and regularly whitewashed. Fiercely and repeatedly readers are told that the stakes are high: 'One of the most dangerous qualities of the unsanitary house is that it does not always and at once produce a definite and virulent disease, such as typhoid fever or diphtheria, though such is often its result; but, without doubt, it slowly and insidiously causes ill-health and general languor.'

Outspoken enthusiasts of the germ theory like Mrs Harriette Plunkett expected more of women than a general apprehension of germs and their ways. In an article in the *American Kitchen Magazine* in February 1899, entitled 'How can any woman become a Sanitarian?', Plunkett is more committed than ever to encouraging women to take an intelligent interest in the whys and wherefores of sanitary practices. She writes thrillingly of new discoveries:

> The whole science of bacteriology has been developed within these last wonderful twenty years, and the sanitarian must study that; and its almost miraculous truths have been set forth, by gifted writers in plain but fascinating language . . . a woman must read and study and observe, she must mark and inwardly digest, and then she must rise up in all her womanly might, and translate her knowledge into action, – absolute, aggressive, ceaseless action, against the kingdoms of dust and filth and dampness and bacteria – then indeed her children will have true occasion to rise up and call her blessed.

Mrs Plunkett also expresses the hope that women's clubs will take up the study of sanitation, for, she says witheringly, 'while not decrying the aesthetic and philosophical, one cannot but feel that the presence of typhoid germs in the well is of more consequence than theosophy or palmistry, or the recovered verses of Bacchylides, or even of hypnotism, or the position of women in ancient Greece and Rome'.

The 'absolute, aggressive, ceaseless action, against the kingdoms of dust and filth and dampness and bacteria' recommended by Mrs Plunkett, or the 'eternal vigilance' advised by *Home Sanitation*, succeeded, along with much other advice, in frightening women into a new level of anxiety about household cleanliness. Because germs were understood to thrive in dirt, the equation was simple. Dirt, visible and invisible, must be banished if disease germs were to be banished. No alternative and no escape existed for a right-thinking housewife once she realised what she was up against, for epidemics of cholera and typhoid were still a grave danger, diphtheria and tuberculosis and scarlet fever were the bogeymen of every mother. If germs were the cause of all this misery, they must be eliminated in the home in mortal domestic combat; their breeding grounds must be stamped out, and the germs themselves must be killed and killed and killed again.

Here was a real job for women. The president of the British Medical Association is quoted by Mrs Plunkett saying that 'it is the woman on whom full sanitary light requires to fall', pointing out that the housewife, 'the presiding genius of the home', was responsible for stopping the spread of disease in the home. The American Medical Association, a few years later, announced in an editorial in the association journal that women must be trained to 'establish a sanitary regime in every room in the home as well as in the kitchen and dining room.' Domestic scientists concurred enthusiastically, appealing fervently and repeatedly for women to learn about household germs and disease microbiology.

To be on the safe side, however, much domestic advice from the late nineteenth century manages to combine both new and old beliefs about the spread of disease, offering solutions that cover both the germ theory of disease and the lingering popularity of the 'miasma' theory. Mrs S.A. Barnett's book of domestic economy, *The Making of the Home* (undated), is concerned both about bad air and about disease microbes. Mrs Barnett expresses a particularly lively concern for airborne germs emerging from an infected household:

> If the fever-germs are not killed by a disinfectant, they will go on growing and breeding in the drain, and one fine day rise up above the ground through the little openings in the road, and entering into some passer-by with the air which is breathed, they will bring trouble, weakness, and pain into another happy family.

Mrs Barnett's solution is simple: get rid of both the germs and the bad air in one fell swoop. To do this the housewife must disinfect, and disinfect with a passion, especially if there is illness in the house; she must kill germs, kill odours, keep the drains free of infected matter, and keep the air fresh and clean. In a household where there is fever, Mrs Barnett recommends using 'green copperas' (sulphate of iron), a pound and a half to a gallon of water – 'a tea-cupful of this should be added to all that comes from the patient'; slops from the sickroom should be disposed of down the drain only when the disinfecting solution has had time to work. In addition, every single thing in the sickroom must be disinfected repeatedly. Mrs Barnett recommends keeping two tubs of water in the sickroom, adding disinfectant, and into these plunging all crockery and cutlery and sheets and nightshirts.

Nursing patients at home when they suffered highly infectious diseases always meant ceaseless work for the woman of the household. Domestic advice manuals of the nineteenth and early twentieth centuries almost invariably include long chapters on the care and nursing of the sick. A great deal of this advice deals with cleanliness, with laundry, and with means of disinfection. The tone of such advice is fearsome. 'It is impossible to reprobate too strongly the conduct of those who wish and endeavour to shirk the expense and trouble of proper disinfection,' says *Spon's Household Manual* (1887).

Proper disinfection, both during and after an illness, meant a staggering amount of work, according to *Spon's*. Linen was to be disinfected before leaving the sickroom; handkerchiefs burned; the sickroom emptied of all fittings and furnishings and carpets and clothing and draperies; the bare floors sprinkled regularly with disinfectants; the slops from the patient soaked with strong disinfectant. Like Mrs Barnett, *Spon's* emphasises at one and the same time the importance of ventilation and clean air and the war against 'the germs of disease'. Windows were to be left open in the sickroom, top and bottom; attendants must be sure to stand between the patient and the window rather than between the patient and the fire; anyone in the room must breathe through a sponge soaked in carbolic acid, not swallow their saliva while in the room, and 'expectorate and blow the nose immediately on leaving the sickroom' as well as rinsing out the mouth, throat, eyes and nostrils.

In *The Making of the Home*, Mrs Barnett devotes a special chapter to scarlet fever. She recommends that the patient be isolated in a room with carpets and all hangings removed, and that outside the door a wet sheet soaked in disinfectant must be hung (she recommends carbolic acid or permanganate of potash). 'The object of a disinfectant is to render harmless the germs of scarlet fever which, as I have told you, come from the skin or exhalations of the patient, and float about in the air of the room.' Behind the wet curtain in the sickroom, the most conscientious disinfecting practices must be maintained; of the patient's clothing, dishes, and everything with which he had contact. When the fever had abated, a local 'disinfecting officer' must be called, and he would arrive bringing a 'disinfecting instrument' with him – presumably some sort of brazier – in which half a pound of sulphur would be burnt in the carefully sealed off sickroom. All bedding and clothing and toys and books used during the illness would be spread out in the sickroom, chimneys and windows would be blocked, and the sulphurous fumes would then do their worst.

Such advice and such practices are not very distant in time and in spirit. My mother recognised them instantly. When her elder brother was ill with scarlet fever in the mid-1920s, the scene described by Mrs Barnett was enacted almost to the letter.

My mother recalls her childish fascination for the disinfectant sheet soaked in carbolic solution that hung over the door to her brother's room. A public health notice warning of the infection was mounted forebodingly in front of their house, no visitors were allowed, and great was the fear in the household. No one but my grandmother went near the sufferer during his illness. When he recovered my grandmother went, coughing, from room to room carrying a scuttle full of hot coals sprinkled with sulphur, fumigating the entire house to prevent her other children from inhaling the deadly germs. None of them caught the disease.

No antibiotics existed then. This one simple fact explains much about earlier disinfecting practices, about the high anxiety and great effort associated with trying to kill disease germs. There was no magic bullet available to combat dangerous disease; it was impossible to be too vigilant or too wary of germs. Disease germs were insidious and frightening, their number incalculable, their ways evil, their influence and their ways invariably malignant: 'take heed and avoid them . . . they love darkness and hate sunshine', declare the authors of the Canadian school text from 1911 entitled *How To Be Healthy*, going on to describe how a communal drinking cup 'was taken from a school to a doctor, who found a great many different kinds of germs, and over the whole cup he estimated that there were about twenty millions of microbes'.

The mixed and muddled welter of propaganda about germs and cleanliness that began in the late 1880s carried on unchecked for several decades, generated by a host of well-meaning reformers. These included home economists, public health officials, teachers, social workers, health visitors and volunteers; most of their efforts were aimed at the working classes, the immigrants, the ignorant poor of society. Schools started to teach personal hygiene, notices prohibiting spitting went up in public places, drinking fountains with continuous streams of water rather than cups were put in public places, home visitors talked to mothers about clean milk and child care, lessons in 'housecraft' were given to slum dwellers. In America there were repeated and vigorous campaigns to eliminate spitting in public, to kill flies, to encourage hand-washing amongst children. Women's Institutes, Boy Scouts, churches, schools, insurance companies, government agencies all became involved in the countless zealous campaigns to raise standards of cleanliness in the home.

'The very health and body of the family depends to a large degree upon the . . . intelligent practice of sanitation and hygiene, the comprehension of bacteriology,' wrote Mary Pattison in 1915. In domestic advice literature, in school texts, in home economics books and in advertising, the battle lines were drawn and were clear; no middle ground was admitted. All germs were potentially harmful, all dirt was potentially dangerous. The lesson was stark. 'Where there is dirt there are pathogenic germs, where there are pathogenic germs, there is disease.' An elderly lady recalls those words spoken at her first lecture when she was a nursing student in the early 1930s. No allowance was made that some dirt – even some germs – might be fairly harmless.

Advertisers of cleaning products were quick to realise that a highly vulnerable market was now open to them. In their able hands, 'information' about germs and how to kill them was quickly disseminated to concerned housewives. Never mind that the advertisements were often misleading; here was a means of spreading the word about germs that had, and arguably still has, no equal. I myself have heard more and seen more 'information' about household germs in advertisements than I ever picked up in school or from health education classes. The advertising that mentions germs is powerful and insidious stuff and easily remembered. Because some grains of truth do lie within such a selling strategy, it has proved both lasting and potent.

At the dawn of the twentieth century advertisers had a clear field and could make staggering claims for their products with few holds barred. Clearly, simply and bluntly, various products announced their battle strategies. Disinfectant solutions like Lysol, Sanitas, and Platt's Chlorides led the way, hinting at the extravagant powers of their products to deal with germs. 'DIPHTHERIA' declares an 1898 advertisement for Platt's Chlorides, the one word written in large black letters. The small-print text beneath goes on to explain how this disease thrives in the winter in badly ventilated rooms, and that regular disinfection of drains and household surfaces with Platt's Chlorides will 'insure pure air in the home'. Without actually claiming that this product can prevent diphtheria, the advertisement gives the impression of just that. Another Platt's Chlorides advertisement is dominated by the word CONSUMPTION, and says that 'Rooms occupied by consumptives can be kept free from odor and contagious dust by frequently sprinkling the floors (particularly before sweeping) with Platt's Chlorides'.

The deeply held and widespread belief that dust contained disease germs inspired countless advertisements. Sales of vacuum cleaners capitalised on this for decades, egged on by advisers like Christine Frederick who was adamant that with these new machines a superior level of 'sanitary' cleanliness was possible. In eulogising the hygienic properties of vacuum cleaners she declared:

> This electrical appliance, whatever the specific model, extracts dust, holds it, absorbs it, actually removes it . . . vacuum cleaning method is based on a . . . much higher standard of room and home cleanliness. It is based in fact on a very superior principle of hygiene: freedom from dust and germs, and ultimate disease . . . What housewife could refuse to accept such an offer, and even skimp and save if need be, to purchase the device that would bring more health into her home?

All vacuum cleaner advertisements sang the same tune. Hoover warned of the 'continual accumulation of germ-breeding dirt in the depths of one's rugs', claiming that it could 'minimise the danger of sickness' and produce an 'ever-clean home'. The Croydon Electric Vacuum Cleaner 'revives and preserves the colour and beauty of carpets, curtains, and upholstery . . . ensures a bright, clean, and thoroughly sanitary home.' The Eureka Vacuum Cleaner ads advised women to 'Welcome the Eureka Man' to their door; 'he has been schooled thoroughly in modern cleaning methods' and 'he brings new standards of home sanitation'.

Soap advertisers were equally canny. Claims made for various soaps often implied that their product was part of this modern warfare against germs. The Lifebuoy Soap label declared the soap worked 'for preservation of health and prevention of sickness', while Ivory Soap declared itself to be the very 'Spirit of Cleanliness'. Words like 'hygienic', 'healthful' and 'pure' appeared regularly on soap labels and in soap advertisements, as well as 'sanitise', 'disinfect' and 'antiseptic'. Imprecise and inexact as it was, and indeed still is, the use of such words in advertising led buyers to believe that in using the product they were killing germs and promoting health.

As the advertising age gained pace and confidence in the late nineteenth and early twentieth centuries, more and more products became available promising to banish disease and germs. Killing germs became an obligatory blood sport in every household, and advertisements became ever bolder:

> Ordinary washing of cooking utensils passes over whole hidden nests of little wigglers – commonly called germs. Gold Dust is a sanitary washing powder that not only removes the visible dirt and grease but digs deep after every trace of germ life – sterilizes pots, pans, pails and kettles – leaving them clean, wholesome, safe.

In truth, the chances of a washing powder sterilising anything are slight, quite apart from the obvious question of why anyone would want to sterilise all their pots and pans in the first place.

Advertising for every imaginable product capitalised on the growing awareness of germs. In the October 1913 edition of the *Ladies' Home Journal* roasting pans were advertised as sanitary, lightshades as hygienic. Mops and wallcoverings were not left behind: a 'modern wall covering' called Sanitas deplores old-fashioned dusty walls, claiming it can provide 'the healthful uplift of pure air' as well as 'the spiritual uplift of beauty' to your bedroom walls; while a 'Sani-genic Polish Mop' advertisement promises to get 'into the corners, under radiators, beds, over doors and mouldings where dirt and germs lurk'.

Scare tactics were common. 'Do you live in a haunted house?'

enquires a Lysol ad from 1918. 'Is your house germ-haunted? It is, and so is every home that is not regularly disinfected.' The ad goes on to discuss at length how Panama had been changed from a 'pest-hole to a health resort' by disinfection, yet 'In our cities [disinfection] is optional, hence neglected by those who refuse to believe in germs'. Readers are encouraged to do their bit to fight epidemics and disease by disinfecting their homes regularly with Lysol which 'annihilates all germ-life at the instant of application'. A paragraph entitled 'How to Banish the Ghost' gives instructions: 'Get a bottle today, mix a little of it with water, and use the solution regularly in garbage cans, toilets, sinks, and drains. Use it in scrubbing-water, in dark, sunless corners, and in summer, wherever flies gather.'

As the twentieth century has progressed, advertising has become an ever more refined and sophisticated business. Yet when it deals with any product that claims to kill germs, advertising often remains crude and obvious. Bottles of magic germ-killing potions still stand on gleaming countertops and shining floors, while children – saved from the perils of germs – beam toothily at their mothers who are smiling in relief, believing that all germs on every kitchen and bathroom surface have been zapped. This simplistic approach to killing germs not only encourages us to believe that we have purified our kitchens, our toilets and our entire homes, it depicts housecleaning as a highly moral endeavour. If we do our work properly, we defend our families from those evil little germs; we kill that which is bad, allowing that which is good and pure to triumph. Such messages have been persistent and insidious for several generations; their effect has been daunting.

The widespread acceptance of the germ theory, coming as it did during a period when women were beginning to re-evaluate their social role in countless different ways, did nothing to liberate women from the home. It added a grave burden of semi-scientific knowledge which only increased the work and the responsibility of running a home. At the same time, servants were beginning to abandon ship, technology was changing rapidly, and homes were beginning to be run as one-woman operations. Work enough was the result of such changing conditions, but combined with the knowledge that unpleasant germs could lurk menacingly within a household, ever more came to be expected of women and imposed upon women in charge of their own homes. Their mission – if they decided to accept it – was to purge, disinfect, sanitise their surroundings; to be on guard, to defend and to attack. Germ-bashing propaganda was, and continues to be, highly successful; it was, and it continues to be, instrumental in keeping at least some women off the streets.

8

MOVERS AND SHAKERS

THE DEVELOPMENT OF HOME ECONOMICS
AND HOUSEHOLD ADVICE

Doughty, confident and determined, a number of reforming women appeared on the domestic scene in the late nineteenth century in America. These were the movers and shakers of the new domestic science movement; their mission was to acclaim housework as an honoured science and to establish it as a serious study in schools. Their writings exhort women to become professional in matters domestic; to inform themselves not only about cooking and cleaning and laundering, but about drainage, plumbing, ventilation, sanitation, household engineering, the spread of infection, the contamination of milk, the efficiency of kitchen design, the inner workings of domestic appliances. The influence of these women was enormous; their style fervently expressive.

   In women's magazines, in books, in public lecture halls a clarion call went out advocating new methods and new attitudes towards household affairs. The writings of the domestic crusaders are highly polemical; they did not see themselves merely as dispensers of household advice, they certainly did not write with the humble aim of passing out instructions about the correct way to dust. They saw themselves in all earnestness as leaders of a movement, 'high priestesses of the new religion of right living', as household scientists and engineers and sanitarians. They brought 'science' to the housekeeper's attention; they began to preach a 'gospel of cleanliness' that included an entirely new level of information about germs, about contagion and infection. They aimed to educate the homemaker, elevate her calling, make her see that 'Science is her handmaiden; invention a servant following her'.

This kind of high-flown talk was common by the late 1890s. It appears in books, pamphlets and magazines. An article entitled 'Foes in our own household' appeared in 1898 in the *American Kitchen Magazine*. It declares: 'Women have lacked respect for nature and her laws. They have feared the thunder and ignored the microbe . . . They have allowed the sink drain to feed the well and the dark, damp cellar to furnish air to the house . . . They need the influence of the scientific spirit.' All of the writings in this vein stoutly maintain that the scientific spirit is a liberating force for women:

> Progressive women have perceived with a growing sense of freedom, how that which has seemed such endless drudgery can, by a clear understanding of underlying principles and the application of scientific methods, be changed into a beautiful harmony of law and order. . . . Why has woman, so eager for light in other directions, been content to remain so long in such medieval darkness as regards her domestic affairs? Too many women regard housekeeping as a sort of Moloch upon whose altar an unkind fate has decreed that they must, however unwillingly, sacrifice their time and strength, to say nothing of temper and nerves.

Most of the domestic reformers of the late nineteenth and early twentieth centuries were keen to spread the teaching of home economics into the schools. Nothing new with this; the teaching of domestic skills in the American classroom dates back many years before the time of these domestic crusaders. Five decades earlier Catharine Beecher was working to establish 'domestic economy' as a science in the classroom. However, the idea did not really take root until the 1890s when the teaching of domestic science spread steadily, although not quickly, into schools. By 1895 some ten agricultural colleges in America offered courses in domestic science; by 1905 there were thirty-six, and at the same time, cookery schools were thriving. Courses were offered in food chemistry, sanitation, heating and ventilation, lighting, waste disposal, methods of housework and laundering. Domestic science was presented as a prodigiously worthy subject, one which embraced serious disciplines like bacteriology and chemistry, and one which should be undertaken as an almost pious duty by all young women.

The early home economists, or domestic scientists, shared one impressive characteristic; they believed in and they spread the word about germs. The germ theory was not widely accepted even in medical circles in the United States until the early 1880s, but by the 1890s it had filtered through into the popular imagination. Domestic scientists played an important role in educating women about germs, probably their single most important contribution to health and cleanliness of the home. In their critical study of domestic advice, *For Her Own Good: 150 Years of Experts' Advice to Women*, Barbara Ehrenreich and Deirdre English have this to say:

> For the Domestic Science experts, the Germ Theory of Disease pointed the way to their first victory: the transformation of cleaning from a matter of dilettantish dusting to a sanitary crusade against 'dangerous enemies within.' Here at last was a challenge suitable to the energy and abilities of educated women.

In domestic science classes and lectures, in articles and books, the domestic scientists explained in layman's terms just how easily milk could be contaminated with disease germs; they condemned flies as carriers of microscopic organisms of infection; they emphasised the importance of clean water. They addressed themselves exclusively to women, interpreting and passing on scientific information, firmly believing they were the prophets of domestic revelation. A brave new world was just around the corner; the twentieth century would soon dawn and, with the help of science and technology, the work of women within the home would never be the same again.

The early domestic scientists were intensely serious; none of these worthy women appears gifted with even the slightest sense of humour or irony. Their sense of self-worth is awesome. 'During the years of my teaching of domestic science,' writes one teacher in 1899, 'a sense of the true meaning and dignity of our calling has impressed itself upon me as its ethical value has unfolded. There is perhaps no branch of pedagogic work which is on the surface so discouraging as ours.' She continues that a good teacher will know how to teach 'not only the industrious cleanliness of the unlettered drudge, but to train the new generation to a new and broader view of the home and its intention and requirements'.

According to Mrs Harriette Plunkett, a woman's first duty in her home lies in understanding its plumbing. Her book on the subject is unnervingly thorough: *Women Plumbers and Doctors, or, Household Sanitation*, published in 1885. Mrs Plunkett describes at great length the complex responsibilities of learning about pipes and cesspools and wells and drainage. These preoccupations also appear in the many articles Mrs Plunkett wrote about home sanitation: 'The immediate household environment of many a woman in this country is a wet cellar, and perhaps a wet, undrained house-site.' She describes the millions of disease germs emanating from the damp, decaying vegetables that are surely mouldering away in such a cellar. 'The home environment', she continues, 'may be further aggravated by a well so situated as inevitably to become polluted by animal wastes, both from the barn yard and the inadequate and badly made and located cess-pool or privy. There are thousands of them at this hour killing by the direct communication of disease-germs and undermining health, by the indirect method of introducing small doses daily of organic poison.'

Of all the domestic science crusaders, Ellen Richards is probably the best known. A pioneer of the home economics movement in America, sometimes called the 'mother' of home economics, she worked as a sanitary chemist at the Massachusetts Institute of Technology, where she was the first female faculty member. She became a firm believer in the application of science to the problems of running a household. Convinced of the need for education for home life, she was the main organiser of the 1898 Lake Placid Conference on home economics in New York State. This gathering brought together a group of people who represented many different areas of study: chemistry, biology, physics, bacteriology, sanitary science, hygiene, even psychology and sociology. Anyone who had anything to contribute to what Mrs Richards called the 'home life education movement' was at Lake Placid. From this conference and from subsequent annual conferences, home economists went forth insisting that their discipline be better known, better taught and better respected.

Nine years after the first conference, the 1907 Lake Placid conference deplored the still pervasive belief that home economics education was not necessary outside the home. The movement soldiered on in the face of many questions and doubts about what home economics really *was*, and whether it should be essentially academic or practical in nature. An increasingly broad range of subjects came under its umbrella; architecture, home decoration, child care, economics, aesthetics, mathematics, physiology, history and anthropology. The arguments about the real nature of home economics and its real aim became ever more tangled; arguments which have continued unabated thoughout the twentieth century.

Back in the 1890s, however, Ellen Richards was a woman of straightforward and unusual vision. She was adamant that women must understand at least some science in order to run a home responsibly, and firm that the monotony of housekeeping could be alleviated by 'the zest for intelligent experiment'. Given that a small dust particle teems with microscopic organisms, she insisted that cleanliness was 'a sanitary necessity of the Twentieth Century', and to achieve cleanliness women must fully understand the nature of dirt and disease. In 1899 she wrote:

Women are thinking. Not all women, but in every town some women. This is a great gain. In every one of the two score audiences which it has been my fortune to address the past winter I found a few earnest souls who are ready to accept what the science of the twentieth century will undoubtedly offer to them . . . The young women of today can hardly escape from a little knowledge, however superficial, of the general trend of progress in social, sanitary and economic science – the sciences which will most certainly profoundly affect home life in the next century.

Ellen Richards was a prolific public lecturer, giving talks on subjects such as 'Bacteriology in relation to daily living' and 'Public hygiene as related to the housekeeper'. Calling for a 'revolution in ideas' amongst women, she had little patience with unprogressive attitudes of women towards housework:

Why is the daily care of the house considered drudgery by so many women? Because they are ignorant that 'safety' today means good food, good air, cleanliness; that far more important today to the ideal of home is it to have good plumbing, good ventilation and such good as will make the inmates of the house healthy, happy, contented individuals – than to have the mistress make her own or her children's clothes or to clean her silver.

Unquestionably high-minded and original, Ellen Richards was a woman of enormous energy and far-reaching ideals. She truly believed that scientific information and better education would be the keys that would set women free from the drudgery of housework. Yet driven though she was by this higher vision of housekeeping, she had little sympathy for the muddled ordinariness of most women's lives. A well-off, happily married, childless woman, she was one of many domestic science theorists whose ideas often seem strangely disconnected from the practicalities they claim to address.

The Cost of Cleanness is one of Ellen Richards's books, and she reverts to its theme over and over again – that keeping a home clean is expensive: 'when the sanitary engineer and the home economics teacher preach the Gospel of Cleanliness to the distraight [sic] housewife, it behooves them to know just what they are demanding of her in the cost of time, money and strength.' To keep a house in a 'really sanitary' condition requires half what a family pays for rent, or approximately 12.5 per cent of their overall income, according to Richards. Not surprisingly in reaching such a figure, her standards of cleanliness were high. She unflinchingly outlines the amount of work in cleaning an ordinary home, an amount of hard labour that sounds absolutely ghastly.

> To remove dust and tracked-in dirt in an ordinary eight room house costs eighteen hours a week, fifty weeks in a year, or nine hundred hours. If there is a furnace and frequent open fires, four special cleanings of twenty hours each, in the year, or eighty hours, are sufficient. The washing of windows takes ten hours a month, of blinds and porches eight hours more, or seventy-eight hours a year. The washing of walls and paint needs fifteen hours twice a year; and with a library, fifteen hours four times a year, or ninety hours. The laundering and cleansing of textiles, curtains and draperies etc., uses eight hours a month or ninety hours, making a total of 1244 hours, or the time of a maid at 56 hours a week for 22 weeks in the year.

Ellen Richards was a member of the Sanitary Science Club, a club that in 1887 produced *Home Sanitation: A Manual For Housekeepers*. This book sets out for women where their duty lies, stressing that in the pursuit of sanitation in the home, they must become actively and *publicly* engaged, following the discussions of 'sanitary congresses, boards of health, and other authorities'. These public duties come in addition to the private obligations of women: 'Our social order gives to most women, during a greater portion of their lives, the responsibility of creating and preserving the conditions of home life. Upon these conditions depends, in large measure, the health of the household, especially that of young children.'

Responsibility for young children is a theme repeated over and over again in the writings not only of the domestic crusaders but of all writers who have ever dispensed household advice. A time-honoured way of making women pay attention is to tell us we are not doing our duty towards our children, that we are endangering their health through our disregard of cleanliness: like it or not, willingly or unwillingly, we feel compelled to listen. In the late nineteenth and early twentieth centuries, the domestic scientists were extremely concerned about contaminated milk being given to young children. The point is hammered home repeatedly that milk should be clean, that it should be officially inspected, that mothers should be extremely cautious about the milk they give their children and in how they clean babies' bottles. Dispensing this kind of advice, however heavy-handed it may now seem, undoubtedly saved the lives of countless infants.

Encouraging a scientific, germ-conscious method of house-keeping went hand in hand with a new attitude towards 'efficiency' in the household. In 1899 Ellen Richards wrote: 'How long should it take to clean a chamber or to do the chamber work of the family of three or five? It would not be difficult to settle this if women were amenable to reason, or if they had any training in mechanics, so that they could tell whether the person were wasting time and strength in passing to and fro ten times where once would serve.' Such comments foreshadow the time and motion efficiency studies that later came to dominate the writings of several of Ellen Richards's successors, most notably Christine Frederick.

Christine Frederick was a zealot on the subject of household efficiency, strongly influenced by the work of the newly emerging breed of industrial efficiency engineers. Her husband was a businessman and market researcher who worked closely with efficiency experts as they analysed the industrial workplace and the expenditure of time and motion amongst workers. Mrs Frederick was able to observe the new methods of improving industrial production, and she then translated these methods into improving the work habits in her own home. With boundless energy she set about organising domestic work into a coherent schedule; organising tools and equipment and work surfaces, reducing stooping and lifting, and eliminating extra steps. The challenge excited her: 'Household problems, large and small, became invested with entirely new interests and new possibilities. Instead of being something upon which to slave, they became objects of keen mental interest – quite the same . . . as the tasks of the business and industrial world which men tackle with zest and results.'

Christine Frederick carried out exhaustive studies both in her own kitchen and in those of other women. She timed various tasks, took photographs, assessed the amount of energy and muscular movement required for different jobs, came up with detailed analyses of even the smallest chore, and finally arrived at her suggestions for saving time and improving efficiency in the home.

The introduction to her book *The New Housekeeping* (1913) was written by Frank Gilbreth, one of the better-known efficiency engineers of his time. He is effusive:

> Nothing is more worth while than bringing efficiency into the home. When housekeeping becomes a science, as well as an art, when it is based on measurement – then it becomes worthy of the best brains and highest endeavour. Mrs Frederick has rendered a real service to this country, in that she has eliminated from housework that monotony that comes from doing uninteresting and repetitive work without an incentive, and in that she has seen the necessity for making the home a laboratory, – a training school for the women and children in it, and perhaps an example to the men.

The New Housekeeping is based on four articles that appeared in the *Ladies' Home Journal* in 1912. The editors of this worthy journal provide a description of how a bricklayer's performance at his job improved radically by following the suggestions of an efficiency engineer, and they herald Mrs Frederick's contribution to domestic work like this: 'It is housework's turn now to get revolutionized, and these articles tell in detail just how it is being done.'

Mrs Frederick begins by plunging into a welter of detail: 'Usually after our dinner I wash forty-eight pieces of china, twenty-two pieces of silver and ten utensils and pots, or eighty pieces in all; and for years I never realized that I actually made eighty wrong motions in the washing alone.' Imagine doing all that counting. But she excelled at such tasks: she measured, she counted, she timed; then she did it all again, then she tried a new method and went through it once more, and then yet again; astonishingly she never seems to have tired of it all.

By changing the height of her dishpan, moving her drainboard, altering the method of scraping her dishes, Christine Frederick claims she reduced the time for washing dishes by one third. She also describes how she improved her methods of dusting and sweeping and cleaning windows by doing one task at a time, never trying to accomplish everything at once. Jumping from one kind of work to another is grossly inefficient, she claims, requiring 'nervous adjustment' and fatigue. '*Every time there is a change of shift* (from sweeping to scrubbing or from any one step to another), *there is waste motion and effort.*'

A firm believer in making lists, taking inventories, keeping to schedules, Frederick was hideously organised. She transposed most of her household activities into a card-file, recording the location of every pair of mittens and the cost of every brush. She even labelled each hook and space on the shelf in her cleaning closet to ensure that tools and cleaning products were neatly stored in their proper place. 'If [the labels] are pasted on and shellacked, they will stay in place for years,' she assures us. She maintains that cleaning instructions should be written down and followed to the letter on the appointed day for that job.

In 1915, in her later book, *Household Engineering*, Frederick declares that 'The reason why our meals are so often better cooked than our rooms are cleaned, is almost solely because there have been no written directions or "practice" for the latter, while there was for the former.' She recommends having a set of written instructions for cleaning each room, which should be 'pasted or tacked in an inconspicuous part of the room'. These instructions, like a recipe, include tools, method and recommended length of time for the job. Far more madness than method is at work in setting up such tyrannical little systems, but Mrs Frederick defends her position to the hilt: 'I notice that the women who say that they hate "system" and methods, and that all this seems too mechanical and formal for them to follow, are the very women who are forever talking about "home drudgery".'

For the less well organised amongst us, Mrs Frederick shows not one iota of sympathy. She bulldozes ahead, outlining her ever more efficient and scientific and sanitary ways of running a home. In everything she writes she is thorough and didactic and ringingly earnest:

> I would feel very badly about it if my earnest plea for a more efficient attitude of mind should result in nothing else but increased slavish devotion to work. . . . Efficiency would be a sorry thing if it simply meant a prisonlike, compulsory routine of duties. *But it doesn't, please believe me.* Its very purpose is more liberty, more leisure, a shrewder sense of values, and the elimination of wasted energy.

Such special pleading is entirely unconvincing. Those who would either wish to follow or succeed in following Mrs Frederick's instructions for cleaning and housekeeping are small in number, and possibly quite demented.

Yet despite her impossible demands, Christine Frederick is an engaging writer. While she must have been a most tiresome woman, opinionated, unsquashable, and horridly capable, her boundless confidence in her own methods and opinions, and her busy attention to small details, inspire a dazed kind of admiration. Energetic advice pours from her, always backed by extensive and close observation of women at work. 'Expand the chest', she commands, 'while using the arms with broom, mop, etc. Never prostrate and shake the body as in usual floor scrubbing, but choose some tool that will permit standing work. . . . Train the hands to quick, deft action. . . . In this way the highest results and exercise will replace drudgery.'

While cleaning, we are told to dress for success, 'because right, neat clothing affects one's self respect . . . a worker does neater, more careful work if she is neatly attired. . . . It is possible to do even mopping and cleaning without becoming a "sight". Recommended cleaning garments of 1915 were 'a plain, short, gored skirt and a jumper waist like a middy blouse . . . It should have elbow sleeves and low collar and can be made in seersucker, chambray or similar materials . . . A cap is also a needful accessory, keeping the hair from coming loose about the face, as well as serving as a dust protector.' Do bear all this in mind the next time you find yourself with your hair falling in your eyes, in dirty jeans, prostrate on your hands and knees cleaning behind the toilet.

Christine Frederick disdainfully dismisses all cleaning practices of the past as 'scattering'. The only result of old methods of cleaning, she says, was to scatter dust and dirt from one place to another: the corn broom scattered dust from the carpet into the air; the feather duster in turn scattered the dust from the pictures and ornaments back to the floor. But salvation from these methods was in sight, for the 'new sanitary ideal today has for its watchword "absorption"'. This means the use of a dustless (that is, a treated) duster, and the modern vacuum cleaner.

'No one invention is so responsible for new cleaning methods as is the so-called vacuum cleaner,' she declares. Several pages are then devoted to discussing the different types of vacuum cleaners on the market, some of them hand-operated by bellows, some electrically operated, and she even mentions 'permanent vacuum systems' operated by electric motors in the basement which required the installation of pipes throughout the house, to which suction hoses could be attached. Interestingly, Christine Frederick's time studies indicate that little if any time was saved by using these early vacuum cleaners, for they were slow and cumbersome to operate, but the vacuum cleaner 'necessitates less *frequent* cleaning, which is the great advantage'.

The comfort and efficiency of our modern homes owes much to Christine Frederick and to others like her. As one of a handful of women engaged upon genuine domestic research, looking for real improvements in the 'work-space' that was the home, Mrs Frederick established her 'Applecroft Efficiency Experiment

Hannah Cullwick, photographed in 1872. Then 39 years old, she had entered full-time domestic service at the age of eight in 1841

———

Florence Nightingale in 1891. Her stern admonitions about cleanliness are widely quoted in nineteenth-century household manuals. She strongly disapproved of 'flapping' as a method of dusting

———

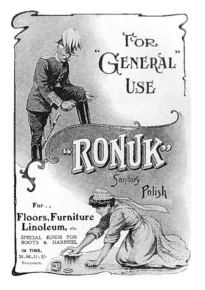

Like many other cleaning products in the early twentieth century, Ronuk Polish claimed to be 'sanitary', both responding to and feeding the ever-increasing anxiety about hygiene.
(From the Illustrated London News *of 1906.)*

———

The Morning Gossip *by George Cruikshank
(1792-1878). Housemaids gather in a London
street. For some, sweeping the front steps might
be the only fresh air they get all day*

Taking up the cudgels against the demon dirt.
According to the magazine The Delineator *of*
April 1915, these weapons were:

1 *Radiator brush*
2 *A new window-cleaning device, with*
wool-padded edge
3 *Mitten duster for polishing*
4 *Lamb's wool wall brush*
5 *Handy box of assorted tacks, etc*
6 *Carpet sweeper, vacuum type*
7 *Wire upholstery beater*
8 *Painter's brush for dusting crevices*
9 *A convenient broom holder consisting of a*
metal spring to be attached to the wall
10 *Putty-knife for repair work*
11 *Folding chair and 'steps' in one*

———

The 'Dust Pan Parade' of maids-in-training as they receive their morning's instruction before a class at Lapsewood Domestic Training Centre in London in 1938. This government-run centre opened in 1932, offering girls three months of domestic training and assuring them a job at the end. Anxiety about the 'servant-girl problem' led to many training initiatives to attract girls into domestic service

'You can never tell when they are lurking about the house.' (From Better Homes and Gardens, *1929.) Fear of germs was heavily emphasised in advertising from the 1890s onwards as ever more disinfectant products came onto the market*

Gillett's Lye struggles to enhance the image of toilet cleaning. Throughout the twentieth century advertisers have routinely promised to make cleaning effortless and genteel, magically removing the 'work' from housework

Advertisers' pressure on mothers to maintain germ-free, socially acceptable households has been relentless and blatant. This advertisement for Harpic is typical of many

(Previous page and above)
Advertisers successfully sold the idea of
well-groomed women tending their equally
well-groomed houses, their cleaning made easy
by machines in a never-never land where
housework involves no mess, no fuss, no bother
– and not a hair is out of place

Kitchen' at her home in Long Island. Here she tested and assessed a wide variety of domestic appliances and tools and carried out endless efficiency studies. She investigated every form of domestic activity: cooking, laundry, shopping, cleaning, and she never failed to come up with suggestions to save time and effort. Few of her ideas outlived her, but she is at least partly responsible for some of the domestic arrangements we now take for granted, like the height of countertops, design of kitchen workspace, proximity of sinks and stoves and refrigerators, placing of windows and cupboards in the kitchen.

Like so many other domestic scientists, Christine Frederick was profoundly conservative. Despite her repeated desire to liberate women from household drudgery, she never wanted them to participate in activities beyond the household. The proper study of home economics was, to her, one way to keep women usefully and happily at home. In *The New Housekeeping* she wrote that 'if you are wise, you will wish your daughter to know *more* than you know – old time methods and ideas are changing, and the school will teach your daughter new methods, tell her of new equipment, and inform her of the new housekeeping which means less drudgery and effort than you have put into your work all your life . . . It is a fine antidote against the unnatural craving for "careers" and the reluctance to give attention to and take pride in those things which a woman's part in life makes it imperative for her to know, sooner or later.'

Such direct references to women working outside the home are unusual in domestic science writings; an attitude of firm disapproval is usually *assumed* rather that stated. That home *should* be the primary object of a woman's life is abundantly clear, whether in advice literature from the 1880s or the 1920s. Huge changes for women occurred during those years, but home economists continue to sing the same tune: that the proper pursuit of housewifely skills is more than enough for a woman, that she should study domestic science and learn to do her job properly.

As the home economics movement matured and moved into the twentieth century, this implicit disapproval of women working outside the home became increasingly evident. To be a 'working woman' with keen outside interests was the antithesis of the heavily promoted image of the homemaker. She should be a ladylike, enthusiastic and fully occupied woman making an intelligent and challenging and 'scientific' career for herself within the four walls of her home. As the authors of *The House and Home* effused in 1896:

> Science and invention have revolutionized housekeeping. They have made it possible for a woman to fill the office of a housekeeper and yet have leisure to enjoy the graces of life . . . [they] have freed her from labor that women of preceding generations were compelled to do with their own hands . . . Whether woman will abuse the freedom, and in the first flush of liberty that should mean leisure enchain herself to outside responsibilities, until home becomes the secondary, not the primary object of her life, future years will determine.

Although this kind of message dominates the early decades of the home economics movement, a few outstanding and outspoken women wrote about domestic matters in entirely different terms. They maintained a woman had the right – and indeed the duty – to engage herself fully outside the home. Charlotte Perkins Gilman was the most remarkable of these writers.

A socialist and feminist – 'the most original feminist the United States has ever produced', according to Dolores Hayden in *The Grand Domestic Revolution* (1982) – Charlotte Perkins Gilman fiercely believed that women should rethink their willingness to act as 'feeders and cleaners' of their families. She hoped for radical change on the domestic horizon; change that would free women to take charge of their own lives. Writing at the beginning of the twentieth century, she was fired by the possibilities that lay ahead: 'The girls today, in any grade of society, are pushing out to do things instead of being content to merely eat things, wear things, and dust things. The honourable instinct of self-support is taking the place of the puerile acceptance of gifts.'

Gilman had no time or patience for women who continued to

tie themselves to a self-sacrificial domestic wheel. Her annoyance is particularly sharp on the subject of housecleaning:

> It is amusing heretofore to see how this least desirable of labors has been so innocently held to be woman's natural duty. It is woman, the dainty, the beautiful, the beloved wife and revered mother, who has by common consent been expected to do the chamber-work and scullery work of the world. All that is basest and foulest she in the last instance must handle and remove. Grease, ashes, dust, foul linen and sooty ironware – among these her days must pass.

Women are often their own worst enemy, in Gilman's view:

> The economically dependent woman, spending the accumulating energies of the race in her small cage, has thrown out a tangled mass of expression . . . she has crowded her limited habitat with unlimited things, – things useful and unuseful, ornamental and unornamental, comfortable and uncomfortable; and the labor of her life is to wait upon these things, and keep them clean.

According to Gilman, the obvious solution lay in the idea of cooperative housekeeping. If only people would live in purpose-built accommodation featuring central kitchens and dining areas and central laundry and cleaning services, then all cooking and cleaning could be done for them and they would be free to pursue other interests. She is convinced that many women would leap at the idea of being so freed from domestic concerns. She speaks of the 'hundreds of thousands of women in New York City alone who are wage-earners, and who also have families', not only poor and unskilled women, but 'business women, professional women, scientific, artistic, literary women . . . These women want homes, but they do not want the clumsy tangle of rudimentary industries that are supposed to accompany the home.'

Charlotte Perkins Gilman was not alone in speaking with such expressive disdain of this 'clumsy tangle of rudimentary industries' – particularly cleaning and cooking – that characterise a home, nor was she alone in her radical suggestions for changing how the work of the home could be done. She was one of a significant and influential few, now known as domestic or material feminists, who favoured socialising housework and who also demanded pay for housework. The material feminists argued for more efficient living conditions, not to enable a woman to take ever better care of her possessions and her family, but to enable her to occupy herself more fully in social or professional or economically independent action outside the home. The movement lasted from the late 1860s until the early 1930s, experimenting with and establishing a number of cooperative housekeeping ventures.

Calls for basic social change underlay everything the material feminists said; a rejection of the inefficient single-family household, a radical rethinking of the economic dependence of women, a call for women to turn from their traditional power base within the home to fix their sights on broader issues. But the material feminists were asking too much, and they were asking it at a time when the new cult of domestic consumerism was growing rapidly. The icon of the single-family dwelling, filled with gadgets and devices and governed by a non-working housewife, grew more powerful all the time. In the face of such a potent and heavily marketed icon, the challenges of the cooperative housekeeping movement and of the material feminists never stood a chance. Charlotte Perkins Gilman's cool. and intelligent criticism of private homes as 'bloated buildings, filled with a thousand superfluities' was true at the turn of the twentieth century and its truth became even more evident and biting as the century progressed. Others in the material feminist movement raised similarly prophetic voices, but their voices were all drowned in the tidal wave of consumer culture.

Domestic scientists paid ever increasing lip service to the notion of freeing the housewife from drudgery. At the same time they were so hell-bent on establishing a new 'profession', a new 'science' of housework, that their rhetoric became an appalling jumble of exaggeration and outright lies. Every activity in the household, from scalding the drains to scrubbing the floor, came to be described as a 'science'; every bit of domestic lore about killing germs or airing rooms was hailed as a professional achievement. No one ever says that such work is inevitably ordinary, repetitive and dull. In 1915, in *Principles of Domestic Engineering*, Mary Pattison, who carried out work similar to that of Christine Frederick, wrote that 'even if one's work is never done, it may with proper appreciation and encouragement become one's play, one's profit, and one's choice, and as to drudgery, that conception merely exists from ignorance as to point of view, and is not a necessary reality.'

Such a Pollyanna-like attitude is clearly impossible to maintain. Everyone knows now, everyone knew then that the work of cleaning and maintaining a home is time-consuming, grubby and often graceless. The drudgery of former times is hailed with dismay, yet the detailed descriptions of daily housework at the dawn of the twentieth century reveal exacting standards that would be extraordinarily difficult to meet. Even with occasional help the woman of the house would find the amount of work vastly time-consuming if she were to follow faithfully the advice of domestic scientists. Women were unlikely to have much extra time if they were so busy being ever-more-excellent and 'professional' housewives. As the new century advanced, the vision of early domestic scientists like Ellen Richards, with their idealistic beliefs about educating women to a more intelligent understanding of their households, gave way to a persistent badgering of women to raise household standards and to improve efficiency.

Barbara Ehrenreich has written that 'Housework-as-we-know-it . . . was invented . . . around the turn of the century for the precise purpose of giving middle-class women something to do', in other words to keep them off the streets, out of the suffragist movement, out of the workplace. Ehrenreich is not amused by this, nor by its instigators: 'Enter the domestic-science experts, a group of ladies who, if ever there is a feminist hell, will be tortured eternally with feather dusters. These were women who made careers out of telling other women they couldn't have careers, because housework was a big enough job in itself. And they were right, since their standard for a well-kept home was one that revealed no evidence of human occupation.'

So Ehrenreich dismisses the whole lot of them, all of the domestic science experts, as creators and preservers of the domestic standards that developed into such a trap for women. She is right. Worthy though these women's motives may have been, worthy though their aims, the early domestic scientists set the stage on which the twentieth-century housewife would enter. The role she was required to play, and the standards she was expected to achieve, were impossible, stultifying and imprisoning. In the end, the women who crusaded for a scientific and efficient approach to housework only succeeded in creating a more complex domestic trap for women.

9

IMPROVEMENT AND IRONY

HOME APPLIANCES AND HIGHER STANDARDS

As public and private cleaning practices evolved, the practical problems of keeping clean eased in countless ways. In the early decades of the twentieth century *things* of every description became easier to clean; clutter became unfashionable and therefore dirt became easier to spot. House design altered beyond recognition, as did fashion in decoration, fabrics and household surfaces. The dominant reds and browns and dark greens of the Victorian age gave way to white paints and finishes, and the curlicues and fringes and frills and furbelows beloved of late nineteenth-century drawing rooms fell out of favour with a thud. Architectural aesthetics changed completely, allowing the architect Le Corbusier, in the 1920s, to advise his clients to aspire to a light, uncluttered, uncarpeted and hygienic environment with bare walls and built in furniture.

Although many domestic advances have proven to be of questionable value, without any doubt we owe much to a number of domestic campaigners and manufacturers who set out to improve basic household facilities. The tireless search for specific household improvements is, at its best, impressive, for it completely transformed the home by introducing the many shining conveniences we now take for granted.

Take household surfaces. As knowledge spread about sanitation, genuine concern about the cleanliness of household surfaces appeared, a concern forcefully voiced back in the mid-nineteenth century by none other than Florence Nightingale. Her intolerance of absorbent surfaces was absolute. Anything in a room that could attract, hold, or distribute 'organic matter' was not to be countenanced. She despised carpets and draperies; she scorned wallpaper and even plaster; although 'the plaster can be redeemed by frequent lime-washing', she recommended that walls be painted with oil paint; in hospital wards she wanted walls of 'pure white non-absorbent cement or glass, or glazed tiles'. For sinks in the scullery and in the bathroom Miss Nightingale approved of the new porcelain, with hot and cold water laid on. She abhorred stone sinks, for 'That great surface of stone, which is always left wet, is always exhaling into the air'. For 'eating, drinking, and washing vessels' she preferred glassware or earthenware rather than tin or any other metal: 'Some kinds of tin vessels cannot by any amount of cleaning be freed from an unclean smell.' For floors she favoured oak:

> The reason for using oak wood is, that it is capable of absorbing but a very small quantity of water. And it is very desirable to diminish even that capability, by saturating it with beeswax and turpentine ... Practically, with care, a well-laid oak floor, with a good bees-waxed surface, can always be kept clean by rubbing; but *the means of producing a really good impervious polished surface with little labour, have yet to be discovered.* (my italics)

Just imagine keeping a home clean without 'a really good impervious polished surface'. Christine Frederick was still pondering this problem in 1915, in *Household Engineering*.

> What material, then, is best for the kitchen floor which receives a heavy daily quota of dirt, grease and water? All wood no matter how treated is absorbent of grease, and collects dirt particles ... There are three groups of sanitary floor coverings with definite points of merit and fault, i.e. linoleum, 'composition flooring' and tile.

Going on to discuss these floorings, Frederick comes out strongly in favour of that ever-improving invention, linoleum.

In *Housewifery*, first published in 1919, the redoubtable Mrs Lydia Ray Balderston is still hard at it, seeking out the perfect household surfaces. She has much to say about wooden sinks and drainboards, none of it good. No modern house should tolerate them, we are told, although they were still to be found in some homes: 'It soaks up water, becomes slimy, slowly softens, rots, and splinters. It is almost impossible to keep it sweet smelling and free from grease.' Her first choice for both sinks and washtubs is enamel or porcelain, followed by galvanised iron, slate and soapstone. She also speaks favourably of the new 'monel metal', an alloy of nickel and copper.

Most domestic writers engaged earnestly in this discussion of household surfaces, recommending linoleum, porcelain or enamelled sinks, oil-based paints, zinc-topped tables. Christine Frederick is typical of many in her adamant dislike of wood: 'Wooden surfaces of all kinds must yield to the pressure for more perfect sanitation. The exposed wooden kitchen table top or drainboard absorbs water, stains, and grease. This means wasted effort in continual scrubbing and scouring.' Manufacturers of floor and wall coverings, kitchen furnishings, and non-absorbent surfaces thrived, turning out highly successful products for the new and modern kitchen.

The new easier-to-clean surfaces came as a real liberation to homemakers. Having always lived in houses graced with formica, arborite, stainless steel and porcelain and countless other easy-care surfaces, I was utterly horrified the one and only time I had to clean a wooden drainboard. Slimy and discoloured, it lay festering in the corner of an elderly friend's home beside her equally elderly kitchen sink. For all the boiling water and bleach I threw at it, the drainboard remained a thing of darkness during my stay. No doubt had she scrubbed it daily with washing soda, as the books recommend, it would have been in better condition, but she was never one for that kind of housecleaning.

In reading the children's story *Bedknobs and Broomsticks* when very young, I remember being puzzled by the mysterious Miss

Price. Not because she was a witch, nor because of her magical powers, but because of her fierce attachment to her new and dearly beloved stainless steel sink: '. . . she ran a loving hand across the gleaming surface of the sink. "But this is rather jolly, don't you think? Forty-three pounds seven shillings and tenpence, excluding the plumbing. But worth it in the end, wouldn't you say?"' The book is so full of magic, with time travel on a charmed brass bed, with awestruck children coming to know strange characters from the past, that Miss Price's devotion to her stainless steel sink struck me as incongruously mundane. When, at the end of the book, she decides to travel back to the seventeenth century for what looks to be a permanent stay, she insists that all her new plumbing go with her.

Bedknobs and Broomsticks was first published in the late 1940s, when stainless steel sinks were still something of a luxury in Britain. Reading the book, as I first did, in a home in which stainless steel sinks were the norm, I completely failed to see the importance of such an acquisition, or how it could merit so much attention. But Miss Price had probably lived for years with a wooden drainboard, or an old stone sink. Given this, her passion for her new sink seems entirely natural.

In conjunction with such important changes in materials, as well as in style and design, the availability of two basic domestic services enabled the transformation of private standards of cleanliness: hot and cold running water in the home, and the miracle of electricity. Without a ready supply of water, including hot water, sustaining high standards of cleanliness is very difficult; without a reliable and cheap source of household power, labour-saving appliances cannot enter the picture.

Little imagination is required to see how water and electricity in the home changed domestic life. Having frequently visited remote places in Canada where there is neither electricity nor running water, I know the feeling of returning to the blessed white gleam of my washing machine after weeks of doing laundry by hand; I know the relief of vacuuming a floor after sweeping muddy wooden boards day after day in the half light of winter; I know the simple bliss of turning on a tap and having hot water gush out after hauling icy buckets from a stream and heating them on a wood stove. As optional extras in my life I have enjoyed such experiences, as mandatory chores from which there is no escape I would enjoy them not one whit.

Electricity not only cast a new light on household dirt – dingy corners and dust showed up as never before – it also provided the power needed to chase this dirt energetically. Household appliances had been available in different guises for some time, most importantly vacuum cleaners and washing machines, but they never really caught on until homes were electrified; other means of powering them had been too cumbersome and too difficult. The foot-operated bellows that wheezily cranked up early vacuum cleaners was, not surprisingly, never a great hit.

High expectations greeted domestic electricity; it would, claimed a manual of 1914, turn 'a neurotic wife, worn out with the worries of housekeeping and domestic troubles' into 'a loving woman, bubbling over with mirth and joy'. 'Spring Clean With Electricity' declares an advertisement of the Electrical Development Association, showing a woman happily leaving her house, without a care in the world, 'no longer tied down by house-work'. Another bulletin of the same association poses this thrilling question: 'What is the stroke of magic which for the last few years has been transforming household tasks, formerly so burdensome, into a part of the daily routine cheerfully undertaken by mistress or maid? . . . Electricity provides the modern housewife with a perfect servant – clean, silent, economical.'

Such power in the home was miraculous. At the flick of a switch, electricity would remove dust, wash clothes, liberate the housekeeper, promising freedom from what Mary Pattison called, in *Principles of Domestic Engineering*, 'the primitive tripod in equipment, upon which housework has rested for so long . . . the broom, the coal stove and the washboard'. Like other home economists of her time, Pattison was in raptures about new technologies; advocating the vacuum cleaner she claims that she 'cleaned the seven rugs of the front hall, not long ago, while gloved and dressed for a reception'.

Advertisements for electrical appliances consistently promise less work and more free time for the overburdened woman who does her own housekeeping. 'Electrical Hands that Wash Clothes' declares one washing machine advertisement, rather improbably. In an article entitled 'The Business of Housekeeping' in *Good Housekeeping* (March 1922), a young woman eulogises about how her 'entire source of physical help lies in that great boon to modern housekeepers, electricity'. She describes how, by using her electric washing machine, electric iron and electric vacuum cleaner, she now does all her own housekeeping and looks after two small children. She also manages to arrange fresh flowers, and dust and prepare dinner, all of this in the mornings when her children obligingly sleep between nine and twelve – one does wonder in passing what drug she gave them. Such an air of great expectation is consistent in early advertisements and articles about electricity; its promise was unlimited.

By 1928 about two-thirds of American homes were wired for electricity. In Britain the spread of electricity was slower, particularly in working-class areas. Elizabeth Roberts' research into working-class neighbourhoods in Barrow-in-Furness and Lancaster and Preston indicates that electricity did not come into most homes there until the 1940s, although it was in place as much as a generation earlier in better-off British homes. And whereas washing machines were becoming commonplace in American homes by the 1940s, they were not widely installed in working-class British homes until the early 1970s. Vacuum cleaners, too, were normal features of the middle-class household scene in America by the 1940s; in Britain they were not in widespread use until the early 1960s.

As householders bought more and more electrical appliances, the advertisers kept up the promises: less work, more free time, virtually no effort. 'Swing through spring cleaning', happily announces an advertisement in *Good Housekeeping*, 'You set it and forget it', declares another for Bendix automatic washers. And from the earliest days, women have been promised more personal beauty as they benefit from their modern appliances. 'Which shall it be?' asked Hoover in 1927, showing a publicity photo of two women, a dishevelled one with a broom and a sleekly groomed one with a Hoover: 'The overworked woman in unsightly attire, or the attractive woman in neat attire who keeps her self-respect because she uses an electrical cleaning service?' Over the years, women with improbable hairstyles, wearing good dresses and high heels, have been routinely photographed smiling alongside their various appliances; their ease, their beauty, and their grooming somehow reflect the effortless efficiency of the gleaming piece of equipment at their sides.

Once accepted as part of the scene, major domestic appliances like vacuum cleaners, washing machines and dishwashers became helpmates that many could not now imagine living without. It is difficult to credit the resistance to them amongst consumers in the past, but such resistance was notable. My own grandmothers were both born in the 1890s; each of them was fortunate in having electric power and indoor plumbing and hot and cold water in the small Canadian towns in which they lived from the 1920s onward. Either one of them could have purchased labour-saving devices like vacuums and washing machines, yet neither rushed out to buy these devices. My maternal grandmother had neither vacuum nor washing machine when she died in 1953; in the 1930s she was still sprinkling damp tea leaves on the carpet prior to sweeping it, although later she owned a manual carpet sweeper. On the other side, the family had a vacuum cleaner available as early as the 1930s, but it resided in my grandfather's electrical repair shop and he rented it out as part of his business; my grandmother rarely if ever had the benefit of using it, nor did she own a washing machine until the 1940s. She was untroubled because these new machines were objects of suspicion to her. When my grandfather presented her with her first refrigerator, she was secretly appalled and refused to believe it was necessary for anything but butter and milk; these she allowed into the fridge, everything else she kept in her food safe on the back verandah.

In *Women and Families: An Oral History 1940–1970* (1995), Elizabeth Roberts points out that some women in her survey firmly believed that work done by hand was superior to that done by machine. She quotes a woman who obtained a new washing machine in 1962 when she had three young children;

shortly after, the same woman had six children, two of them in nappies at the same time, yet she states that she 'always washed the nappies by hand even when I had a washing machine. I would wash them with green soap. I never used to put any washing powder in. I gave them three or four rinses and I boiled them once a week.'

To this day, my mother behaves in just that way, believing that washing done by hand is somehow a superior offering of love and care. She, too, washed all her babies' nappies by hand, and when my own daughter was a baby my mother arrived to lend support. Whenever I wasn't looking, she could be found with her back turned ostentatiously on my brand new automatic washing machine, washing the nappies by hand in a bucket. As for delicate items or even clothes only lightly soiled, I was brought up believing they should always be washed by hand, an instruction I obediently followed for years. An American friend was astonished seeing me wash a sweater by hand. 'I have never, ever washed anything by hand in my life,' she announced. 'What's the delicate cycle *for*, for heaven's sake?'

Growing up in the 1950s and 60s in Canada, I came of age during the era of readily available domestic appliances. We had few of them but the more prosperous homes of my friends were graced with everything from electric can openers and knife sharpeners to automatic washing machines and dryers. We remained faithful to the old wringer-washer in the basement, and the clothes were rinsed by hand in the concrete tubs alongside. The work was slow and mesmerising. I liked loading the fat and shiny machine, pushing the lever to start the dignified sweep of the agitator, rotating the wringer with its shiny chrome tray from machine to rinse tub, pushing the clothes through the wringer, loading and reloading the machine. Several loads would pass through the same water, the dirtiest clothes last, leaving a scum of greyish soap curds on the surface of the water. The rinse water in the tubs would have to be changed a couple of times during the process, accompanied by much gurgling and swishing. Then I had to hang out the wash, either on the lines in the warm basement or outside if the weather permitted. Most of the time the laundry went outdoors, for drying clothes in the fresh air was, and still is, something my mother holds to with a passion. In the winter everything froze solid; sheets and towels were stiff like boards, dazzling white after a good hard freeze. According to my mother, subzero temperatures kill all germs stone dead; a belief shared by my aunt, much to the dismay of her eldest daughter.

After the birth of her first child, this cousin of mine had a lengthy visit from her mother. 'She made me – she *made* me – hang all of the diapers outside. Mum was determined to freeze all those germs to death – she was totally convinced that cold kills everything,' my cousin recalls. 'This was in Saskatchewan, in December!' My cousin's dominant memory of her first month post-partum is shivering at the clothes line, folding iron-hard nappies into a laundry basket and praying for her mother's visit to end.

How my aunt and my mother formed their firm opinions about the way laundry should be done is a bit of a mystery. Not through my grandmother; like many middle-class women in North America she never did the family laundry when her children were growing up in the 1920s and 1930s. She relied on a washer-woman who would arrive once a week on her bicycle to do the wash by hand. My grandmother would have soaked it overnight in a solution of soap and water. 'She used bars of Fels Naphtha,' my mother remembers. 'They were bright yellow. We would save it into a jar of water to make a glutinous solution for the clothes.'

Compared to her predecessors in the trade, this washer-woman, a Mrs Hutchinson, had it easy in doing my grand-mother's laundry. She had a plentiful supply of hot running water and a heated basement to work in. Having to do an entire week's laundry by hand in one morning sounds ghastly under any circumstances, but just consider what washday used to mean in earlier days.

Gruelling descriptions of laundry day abound in domestic literature. It was without a doubt the most hated and the hardest of household chores. Consider it from first principles: where did the water come from? the soap? the heat? If soap could not be bought or was considered too expensive it had to be made, and making it involved saving and rendering animal fat and boiling it up with a highly caustic solution of lye made from wood ash and water. The water for the laundry may have been from a pump nearby, or drawn from a well in the country or, for the fortunate ones, there may have been a water source in the kitchen or scullery or laundry room. The water was poured into and heated in large coppers on a stove, and then ladled into a washtub where the soiled clothes (which had been soaked overnight) were scrubbed with soap on a washboard before going into the refilled copper on the stove where they were boiled with washing soda and diverse other cleansing and bleaching concoctions. 'For a good half hour,' according to Mrs George Cupples in *The Home Friend* in 1882, for even longer according to others, the clothes being pushed down occasionally with a stick. After boiling, the wash was lifted out into clean water to be rinsed; at least two rinses appear to have been normal practice, certainly for whites which were rinsed and then 'blued' for extra whiteness, and then often starched before being wrung out either by hand or with a hand-operated wringer. On any one washday, all of the laundry was wrung at least three times before being hung out to dry. Think of the sheer physical labour!

Kate Mary Edwards, a mill-hand's wife from Huntingdonshire, recalls this labour in recounting how she did her family's washing in the 1870s and 1880s. 'You had to be as strong as a man to lift the great wooden wash tubs, allus left full o' suds, to keep 'em binged [soaked], even without the weight o' the wet clothes; and then you had to lift the great iron pot, full of water, on and off the pot hook over a hot turf fire, and drag the wet washing in a clothes basket to the line down the garden, and put it in and out again, perhaps four or five times if it were a wet day.'

Mrs George Cupples tries to cast a sunny eye upon the

proceedings: 'The washing day in mostly every house is looked upon as a sad bugbear, and yet . . . I say there is nothing more interesting in all the weekly routine of a house. Indeed, I will go further and say that an amount of actual pleasure can be got out of the whole business, first to last.' Emphatically, Mrs Cupples is not to be trusted here: she clearly never did this work herself.

Even the different substances used in the wash are difficult to imagine. Given that we now rely on scented scatterings of pure white powder for our washing machines, the contents of earlier laundry tubs seem simply disgusting. The use of gall was common; the gall bladders of oxen salted down and sometimes perfumed. Not just a little gall, either. Mrs Cupples recommends that if clothes are greasy, gall should be added 'in the proportion of half a pint to six quarts of water'. That's one part in twelve. According to Caroline Davidson in *A Woman's Work Is Never Done*, stale urine, which contains ammonia, was commonly used in the washing water until the mid-nineteenth century; also dung. And there was lye, used either alone or combined with soap, in solutions often so strongly alkaline that if the wet clothing were rubbed hard against the skin 'the latter is frayed, and sometimes rubbed off'. Commercially produced washing soda, that strong and caustic derivative of salt, took the place of lye as the century advanced. Other additives to the washtub included kerosene, and in the various rinses there were many bluings and starches to contend with.

The washer-women who knew the mysteries of this trade were large in number. They went from house to house, working long and hard hours over steaming tubs and cold washlines. In Britain, according to Caroline Davidson, the upper classes with their more plentiful supplies of linen and clothing washed less frequently than the lower classes, but as the nineteenth century progressed, washday generally became more frequent. 'Some families wash only once a month; but once a fortnight would be better,' say the authors of the 1844 *Encyclopedia of Domestic Economy*. Later in the century, laundry became an accepted weekly task in most homes, one to which at least a full day of labour was devoted. Yet though laundry became an ever-more important task, it remained, on the whole, mechanically unaided. There were many experiments with domestic washing machines from the late eighteenth century onwards, and while some of them were both patented and marketed, they never caught on until there were reliable sources of water and power. In the meantime laundry work relied on a seemingly endless – though grudging – supply of female labour.

Sprained wrists, swollen joints, skin rubbed right off, eternally chapped hands: such were the joys of doing a heavy wash in tubs and on washboards and of wringing by hand. Yet when the early electrically powered washing machines came to the rescue of women, again there was initial resistance. One of the older women I interviewed recalls her mother's disbelief and her reluctance to trust any machine to do the job as well as she could herself. 'She would say, "How can clothes get clean when you don't put your arms into the water and bring them up and check for dirt? The way I used to do it, everything was checked over and I made sure it was really clean – this new machine just can't do such a good job."'

When wringer washing machines were eventually displaced by automatic ones, reaction was comparable. My own mother did not own an automatic washing machine until the late 1970s when she was more or less forced into buying one simply because she could not find another wringer-washer. How she loved that old Beatty; its shining chrome, its green and yellow enamel, its friendly rubber rollers, its agitator that she always removed and polished. 'You can't really control these automatic machines,' she still declares, frowning with disapproval at the instructions on the inside of the lid.

My mother is perfectly right. To think we are in control of the labour-saving machines in our homes is an illusion. Once our resistance is overcome, there is no looking back. A complete dependency soon builds up and before we know what has happened, the machines control us. Marcia ponders this point in Robert Irwin's novel *The Limits of Vision*:

> I force the Hoover's head down so that it is made to eat the dirt that lies at my feet. It snuffles and snorts around my ankles. As long as I have the Hoover I know that I have nothing to fear from the dirt. Princess and the domesticated monster, we are figures from some mysterious book of emblems. A metal chain connects us. It is not clear to me who is in bondage to whom.

The greatest irony of the domestic scene in the twentieth century is that the term 'labour-saving device' has turned out to be an oxymoron. Although changing the nature of the work, such machines have not reduced the amount of work at all. When first faced with this notion, I could not believe it. Whatever else I assumed about housecleaning I had taken for granted that I cleaned more efficiently and probably in less time than my grandmothers and great-grandmothers. After all, I have always had the essential machines to help me, at the very least I have lived in homes equipped with a vacuum cleaner and a washing machine. Yet the verdict is widespread and unanimous, it is in many sources and for all to see, and it has been well understood and well documented for a long time: labour-saving devices have not substantially reduced the time and effort spent on housework. Indeed, during the years domestic appliances became widely accepted in the home, the hours devoted to housework appear to have increased.

Take the use of washing machines, for example. One study claims that 'the time devoted to laundry has actually increased over the past fifty years'. The machines make feasible having clean sheets once a week, or even twice if we so choose, to do laundry daily, to wear clothes only once, practices now common to many households but which would have been undreamed of in our great-grandmothers' times. Their washday practices were certainly brutally hard work, but such work was never a daily event. Equally, vacuum cleaners enable us to achieve dust-free carpets wall-to-wall, a task that, taken on seriously and regularly, is just as time-consuming as the sweeping of floors and beating of rugs was for earlier generations. As an article in the *Ladies' Home Journal* in 1930 commented, 'Because we housewives of today have the tools to reach it, we dig every day after the dust that grandmother left to a spring cataclysm.'

Labour-saving devices were introduced to the home with tremendous fanfare announcing their various abilities to speed and ease the work of the woman in the home and improve standards of cleanliness. Never mentioned in the publicity material – and perhaps not even realised by manufacturers and advertisers in the early days – was that labour-saving appliances would only add to the amount of housework, partly by raising popularly accepted standards, and partly because these devices were to become the 'domesticated monsters' whose operation was a one-woman job. So while a woman may have been able to enlist the help of children in hanging up the wash, the correct operation of the dryer largely fell to her; while husbands may have assisted with washing the dishes, the care and maintenance of the new dishwasher was, on the whole, the woman's job.

Ruth Schwartz Cowan points out in *More Work For Mother* (1983) that not only have labour-saving devices failed to reduce significantly the number of hours spent in housework, they have also enabled one isolated person to do all the work in a home. In the first decades of the twentieth century in America, a middle-class woman of reasonable means who 'did her own housework' was really a euphemism for a woman who did not have a live-in maid but who did some housework herself and oversaw the rest which was done by hired help. The 'appliance revolution', as Christine Frederick called it, enabled such a woman really to do all the work herself. Within a generation of the introduction of major cleaning appliances like washing machines and vacuum cleaners, both of which emerged on the mass market in the first two decades of the twentieth century, these appliances were in most well-off American households. Then the middle-class housewife had no excuse, she was truly on her own with her wondrous machines, and she was busier than ever in trying to achieve and maintain the standards of household perfection which, she was assured on all sides, were easily achievable to a modern woman such as she in possession of such machines.

The outcome of all this progress is described by Betty Friedan: 'Each labor-saving appliance brought a labor-demanding elaboration of housework. Each scientific advantage that might have freed women from the drudgery . . . instead imposed new drudgery, until housework not only expanded to fill the time available, but could hardly be done in the available time.'

Critics spotted these problems almost at once. As early as 1933, Hazel Kyrk commented, in her book *Problems of the Family*, that 'we have shown a tendency to use the time freed by labour-saving machinery not for more leisure, but for more goods or services of the same general character. The invention of the sewing machine means more garments . . . The invention of the washing machine has meant more washing, of the vacuum cleaner more cleaning.' And the *Journal of Domestic Appliances* in 1934 declared that 'Women are tired of labour-saving devices. They would rather go back to the Stone Age than be bothered with these innumerable labour-saving machines.' By 1956 social historians in Britain were noticing that the amount of housework had not been reduced at all by increasing numbers of domestic appliances, that instead what had happened was a labour-intensive raising of standards. And as Christina Hardyment aptly shows in *From Mangle to Microwave*, this argument can be applied to most of the labour-saving kitchen gadgetry in and out of fashion over the past century. It has largely been a waste of time and energy: ingenious lemon squeezers and food choppers and knife cleaners have come and gone in regular procession, leaving the woman of the house no better off, and with yet another appliance to keep clean.

Elizabeth Roberts's surveys of the domestic history of women in the north of England illustrate how, in the industrial setting of Barrow in the 1950s, the cleaning schedule of a housewife had become more than demanding. One woman describes how she tried to vacuum and dust every day, washed some floors daily, washed the others, plus the doors and windows and outdoor yards at least once a week, washed and changed the curtains regularly, washed down the paintwork twice a year, for Christmas and for the spring. Earlier in the twentieth century in this kind of setting, every room and its contents were, at most, cleaned once a week – by the 1950s, once a day.

Elizabeth Roberts suggests that this increased amount of housework was in part to compensate for a sense of frustration, or even guilt, about the easier life new machines brought to a home. Though women wanted these machines as signs of status and affluence, they did not quite know what to do with the leisure the machines offered and so they cleaned more and more. Their work became more demanding, not less, in the face of all the supposedly liberating technologies at their beck and call.

The negative observations about labour-saving equipment become self-evident if you stop to think about your own behaviour around the home. That you wash clothes often because you have a machine is absolutely true; that you keep the carpet passably clean because you have a vacuum cleaner is also absolutely true. If you did not have these machines, both clothes and carpet would be much dirtier: most of us do not possess the energy or the will or the time to do all that washing and sweeping and rug-beating by hand. For myself, I *like* the standards I can achieve with the help of domestic appliances and I would never willingly give them up, shocked though I might be to learn how they determine my behaviour. Ruth Schwartz Cowan recognises the facts:

> However much trouble these technologies may be, however much they may cost to obtain and then to maintain, and however much they may induce us to engage in amounts or forms of work that are often irritating and sometimes infuriating . . . the daily lives that are shaped by washing machines and electricity are so much more comfortable and healthy than the ones that were shaped by washtubs and coal . . . that we will probably not give them up.

The new appliances that poured into the home both responded to and fed the ever increasing concern about domestic cleanliness that marked the early decades of the twentieth century. Sociologists puzzle inconclusively over the chicken-and-egg question that arises here. Did a new desire for cleanliness create new products, or did new products create an increased desire for cleanliness? Clearly a change in public and private perceptions about cleanliness occurred, almost certainly in response to better understanding of germs and disease. And so a ripe and ready market for products promising newer and higher standards appeared. As conditions improved and higher standards of cleanliness came within the reach of more people, being clean about the house was no longer an option; it became a moral and social obligation. At the same time, cleanliness was also an aesthetic pleasure, an eagerly sought quality conferring status and rank and even beauty on those pursuing it. 'Beauty must be Spotless' says a 1929 cleaning fluid advertisement in the *Ladies' Home Journal*, and increasingly it was becoming possible for things to *be* spotless, in a way that would not have been possible fifty years earlier.

While the logical outcome of many domestic improvements may have been to isolate women at home with their 'domestic monsters' and to imbue them with unrealistic desires for ever higher standards of cleanliness, there was at the beginning of all this no conspiracy afoot. Not by a long shot were all the advisers and manufacturers lining up to make the housewife's life more labour-intensive; far from it. Another of the aggravating ironies about household cleanliness is that the improvements that have come our way were initially introduced as means of enhancing and simplifying our lives. That some of these developed into monsters making formerly impossible standards now possible and generally creating more work is not a disembodied process having nothing to do with us; the annoying truth is that we have participated whole-heartedly in setting ourselves up in ever cleaner homes and we have done so by buying and using ever more mechanisms to clean our homes, little reckoning the hidden cost and the high irony involved.

10

BUYERS AND SELLERS

DOMESTIC CONSUMERISM AND THE POWER OF ADVERTISING

In the beginning was soap. The first and the most revolutionary cleaning product to be mass-produced; the product whose history is so intertwined with the history of advertising that the two can seem indistinguishable; the product that has sold longer than any other cleansing agent, and the product whose beneficial qualities still seem beyond reproach. Who, after all, would choose to live without soap?

After soap came the deluge. Then came masses of other cleaning products and appliances. Then came the outpouring of proclamations about disinfectants and polishes and cleansers, about mops and machines and magical potions that would ease housecleaning beyond belief. Then came the ever more sophisticated manipulation of the purchaser, the new cult of consumerism, the vast amount of buying and selling that the twentieth century has witnessed in connection with everyday efforts to clean the house.

But first comes soap. The history of soap manufacture and soap advertising has filled many volumes, a complex and fascinating subject. Having read many books of household advice describing the process of soap-making at home, what strikes me most forcibly is that when commercially produced soap became easily available, it must have come as an unspeakable relief.

To be quit of that hideous job of soap-making meant saying farewell to saving all that old fat and those ashes for lye; it meant eliminating all that boiling and skimming of the foul-smelling mess that resulted. By the second half of the nineteenth century, soap-making was a task long gone from most homes. It was by then becoming a huge commercial success taken up by several large companies both in Britain and in America.

These soap manufacturers were the earliest of large industries to realise the impact and importance of advertising. From 1869, soap advertisements appeared in American magazines, most notably for Sapolio, somewhat later for Ivory and Pear's. In Britain soap advertising was fairly low-key until the 1880s when Sunlight soap burst on to the marketplace, aggressively announcing its virtues in newspapers, on roadside hoardings and at railway stations.

Results were fast and gratifying; soap consumption increased tremendously during the final decades of the nineteenth century. This increase coincided with the early years in which the germ theory was being discussed by home economists, and with increasing awareness of the importance of sanitation, both public and private. On all sides the public was getting the message: keeping clean was an unequivocal good.

The chief agent of this unequivocal good, as the manufacturers all insisted, was soap. As Henry Ward Beecher put it in 1885, 'If cleanliness is next to Godliness, soap must be considered as a means of Grace.' Not only a means of grace, the liberal use of soap was also a sign of advancement and self-improvement. In America liberal use of soap became an almost patriotic duty. According to the authors of *The House and Home* (1896): 'It has been said that the quantity of soap consumed by a nation would be a fairly accurate measure of its degree of civilization.'

Vincent Vinikas points out in his book *Soft Soap, Hard Sell* (1992) that while a great demand was successfully created for soap, by the 1920s the trick was to sustain such a demand. He describes how, in America, the consumption of soap was beginning to fall off because living conditions were generally becoming cleaner. More roads were being paved, more people were travelling in motorcars, domestic heat and light were producing less dirt, fashions in clothing and home furnishings were changing, and less soap was needed in these improving conditions. At this juncture the soap manufacturers of America, worried about the downslide in the market, joined forces and ganged up on the unsuspecting public, deciding to pull together in a concerted effort 'to stabilise the appeal of soap and water as the primary agencies of cleanliness, thus providing a basic and constant background for brand exploitation'.

In their determination to maintain soap sales, in 1927 the American Association of Soap and Glycerine Producers established an organisation called the Cleanliness Institute. Its entire purpose was to remind Americans that they needed soap and water, needed them badly, to improve and maintain their standards of living. No substitutes, no cosmetics, no deodorisers, no new-fangled cleaning agents must be allowed to get the upper hand on good old-fashioned soap and water.

The Cleanliness Institute developed an extraordinary campaign of advertising to promote public awareness, drumming into the American mind the importance of keeping clean with liberal use of soap and water. Through radio talks, schoolroom propaganda, magazine ads, the Institute preached a relentless message designed to sell soap, but a message cloaked as a public service to improve the nation's health and welfare. Keeping clean was a ticket to social and commercial success, a guarantee of feeling good, a way to improve oneself and to ensure one's children were successful. In the ambitious world of America in the 1920s who could resist such blandishments as this one, from the *Ladies' Home Journal* of August 1928: 'Any way you look at it, clean habits, clean homes, clean linen have a value socially and commercially ... In any path of life, that long way to the top is hard enough – so make the going easier with soap and water.' The picture accompanying this text shows masses of people striving to reach the top of a mountain where a triumphant light blazes forth across the sky the words 'Heart's Desire'. 'For health and wealth use soap and water' says the large caption at the bottom of the page.

The Cleanliness Institute aimed most of its work at the classroom, and produced countless curriculum aids, posters, stories, competitions and hand-washing incentives for children. A cleaner-than-ever, soap-consuming generation of American youth was firmly indoctrinated in this fashion. But the mothers at home were not overlooked; their role as overseer of this clean new generation was emphasised in glowing terms, and their function as the keeper of the home rosily romanticised in one advertisement after another. 'Surer than the appearance of the robin or the tender crocus leaves as the first sign of spring is the woman's urge to clean house from attic to cellar,' crows the Institute's Department of Public Information. 'With the first warm zephyr she throws open the windows, hums a glad little song, and reaches for the broom.' Improving booklets with such titles as 'A Cleaner House by 12 O'clock' were available on request. The message to the housewife was clear. 'Her home', as Vinikas puts it, 'could never be clean, only "cleaner".'

For several years in the late 1920s and early 1930s no one could escape the influence of the Cleanliness Institute. A ceaseless barrage of ads appeared in magazines: thousands of schools participated in carefully orchestrated campaigns to keep hands and homes clean. And soap sold and sold and sold. 'Manufacturers', writes Vinikas, 'had to let Americans know, not just that they were still soiled, but that they could never be sanitary enough. As the country became cleaner than ever before, manufacturers had to dig up dirt.'

As the soap trade unearthed ever more dirt for Americans to chase, it instilled ever higher expectations of cleanliness, and always in the name of public good. The influence of the Cleanliness Institute clearly illustrates the complexities inherent in much advertising of cleaning products and shows the degree of powerful commercial interest that can underlie protestations of public interest. During the first half of the twentieth century, the buying and selling of goods of all kinds to keep the home clean developed into a massive and convoluted industry specialising in an unfailingly hard-sell approach to its customer, the housewife – and always for her own good.

One particularly interesting twist in this tale is how home economists came actively to aid and abet the industry. The role of home economists began as that of disinterested educators, passing on new concepts about the household, suggesting ways and means for women to achieve happier, healthier and more efficient homes. Yet this role of disinterested educators rapidly took on new dimensions: within only a couple of decades of its inception, the home economics movement was deeply embroiled in the new consumer culture.

Books of household advice by leading home economists clearly show how this process began. In 1915, Mary Pattison made the following announcement in her *Principles of Domestic Engineering*:

> An unconventional feature included at the end of the book is a list of approved household articles and where to procure them. Because these are questions constantly asked, and because the author feels that the educational and commercial interests should have closer co-operation, she has seen fit to include this partial list of Business Houses.

Pattison's list of recommendations includes Hoover Junior Vacuum Cleaners, Sanitary Toilet Tongs and 'All Off' paper, and Scott Paper's roller paper towels.

Even earlier, home economists had not shied away from recommending products, although in the 1890s when the home economics movement began, far fewer commercial products were available. The author, identified only as 'An Experienced Housekeeper', of *Washing, Cleaning and Removing Stains*, published in London in 1892, issued warm endorsements of such products as Sunlight Soap, Monkey Brand, Hudson's Soap, and Sanitas disinfecting solution, and says firmly that 'The table used for regular cooking must be scrubbed every day, after dinner is over, with Sunlight soap and a little Sanitas'.

This seems harmless enough advice, the sort one might receive from a well-meaning and kindly aunt. Equally understandable is that as new products and appliances came on to the market, women needed advice about how to use and care for them. The home economists took that task to heart. They were an earnest bunch, and for decades produced ream upon ream, volume upon volume of such advice, detailed and worthy in tone. The workings of modern household equipment had to be explained to the unlettered housewife, how vacuum cleaners work and what kind of washing machine to buy. In short, the housewife needed education in the skills of consumerism.

Purchasing and maintaining the proper refrigerator merits a whole chapter of concern to the home economist Sarah Macleod in her *Housekeeper's Handbook of Cleaning*, published in 1915. She discusses the proper outside finish, favouring a polished hardwood, but acknowledging that the new enamelled surfaces are increasingly popular. Inside the refrigerator, the 'common linings are galvanized iron, tin, tile, porcelain, glass, and especially prepared enamels. The white linings are desirable because they show the soil so readily and therefore dirt does not have a chance to collect.' These refrigerators were not electrical devices, but high-tech insulated ice boxes. Their drain pipes had to be kept clean with a solution of hot soda water, for apparently these pipes often had a 'disagreeable collection of dirt from the impurities of the ice'. As for the inside, Mrs Macleod is adamant that the shelves and floor of the refrigerator be washed every day with a soda solution, and that the whole apparatus be thoroughly cleansed every week. Such advice seems, on the face of it, both frank and useful, if over-anxious.

A generation later, Sarah Macleod's successors in this business of advice-giving about appliances were more heavy-handed. An oft reprinted text entitled *Household Equipment*, by Louise Peet and Lenore Sater, appeared first in 1940. It sets out to educate girls in tireless detail about how and what to buy for their homes. Its tone is patronising, its statistics dubious, its aim clear: girls should buy every possible bit of household equipment and use it properly.

In the section on vacuum cleaners we learn that 'studies indicate that 85 per cent (sometimes as much as 97 per cent) of all the dirt that accumulates in a room is in the carpet'. Then we consider carpets, their structure, their woof and weft and tuft and pile and weave, and again we are to heed a warning that the average carpet has 'an enormous capacity for storing dirt, which other home-furnishing fabrics do not have'. The point is driven home by a glum little illustration on the facing page – Figure 10.1: 'Analysis of Rug Dirt', it is called, and attributed to the Hoover Company – a much magnified drawing of four tufts of carpet, looking for all the world like clumps of seaweed, in which different shades represent different kinds of carpet dirt. 'Visible debris and dust' lie on top, then there is 'Floating pile dirt' a bit further down, and still lower lurks what is termed 'Infiltrated pile dirt', followed by 'Top furrow dirt'. At the very roots of the tufts lurks the darkest dirt of all, 'Pocketed furrow dirt'.

This whole silly exercise, the solemnity with which it analyses carpet dirt in order to stress the importance of having a vacuum cleaner, typifies many home economics texts. To what end was this kind of information passed on? It does not, after all, take the genius of Einstein to figure out that carpets can become thoroughly dirty, right down to the bottom of their little tufts, if not cleaned occasionally. Girls stuffed with such nonsensical 'education' in home economics often found it blatantly ridiculous. One woman recalls being taught, in mind-numbing detail, 'The Six Basic Strokes of Effective Vacuuming' as part of her home economics curriculum in small town midwestern America in the 1960s. These strokes, she recalls with embittered relish, included the 'Long Draw' (a graceful out-and-in sweep, in a 'feather' pattern), the 'Short Brush Stroke' (quick, choppy strokes layered one over the other), and the 'Edger Sweep' (smooth, unbroken strokes with the 'edging tool', neither 'digging' nor 'dragging' the tool). The girls in the class were required to practise these strokes, earnestly comparing the efficacy of different strokes as performed by different machines. In this kind of setting, with this kind of domestic indoctrination being regularly inflicted on girls, understanding vacuum cleaners and carpet tufts and cleaning products and refrigerators becomes a cardinal virtue. Such knowledge and expertise, we are led to believe, will enable the student or homemaker to work with grace and good humour, in an 'educated' and intelligent fashion.

Home economists who engaged in this sort of discussion and instruction were doing little more than exhorting their audience to become consumers. They were playing right into the hands of the manufacturers. Generation after generation of school-leavers have been instructed to think that certain devices and products are essential for doing a proper job around the house, ensuring that these school-leavers will go forth and buy these devices and products, and probably buy them repeatedly over many years.

From the very outset, therefore, with their insistence that housework was a serious endeavour demanding education, commitment and efficiency, home economists helped to feed the desire for household change, for new services, new gadgets. Manufacturers and advertisers actively sought out such educators to work as consultants, to advise them about the needs of the consumer, and in turn home economists advised consumers about their need for new products. Thus the home economist became the self-styled mediator moving between that modern phenomenon, the middle-class-housewife-with-no-servants, and the manufacturers of household items.

Christine Frederick is the home economist best representing this new cult of domestic consumerism. She had no scruples about the consumer culture, as she makes clear in her book *Selling Mrs Consumer* which appeared in 1928, dedicated to Herbert Hoover. By then, Frederick was well known both for her insistence on efficient and scientific housekeeping and for her excited enthusiasm about the purchasing power of women. She had written about both in the *Ladies' Home Journal* earlier in her career.

In an article in the *Ladies' Home Journal* of November 1913,

Frederick sets out to show women the important responsibility they bear in learning how to buy for the home:

> Our purchase of one little cake of soap may seem small and unimportant, but the manner in which we buy it, the price we pay for it, and the loyalty and intelligence we show in studying soap values and repurchasing satisfactory quality and service – all these affect the entire soap world, as each of our other little purchases affects its world of trade.

'Consumptionism', as Christine Frederick called it, was 'the greatest idea that America has to give to the world'. She supported the industrial goal of 'progressive obsolescence', became a key proponent of the notion of buying more and more mechanisms for the suburban home, and she knew just how to target the buyers in those homes: 'Every business day approximately 5,000 new homes are begun; new "nests" are constructed and new family purchasing units begin operation.'

As the feminist scholar Dolores Hayden sadly comments about Christine Frederick in *The Grand Domestic Revolution*: 'Housing units did not imply shelter to her but rather endless possibilities for sales . . . This was the final corruption of home economics, representing not women's interests but businesses' interests in manipulating women, their homes, and their families.'

When she stopped writing for the *Ladies' Home Journal* in 1920, Frederick began her career as a consultant to various manufacturers, actively endorsing their products: Thor washing machines and irons, Vollrath cookware, Stahl-Meyer, Hershey. She advised manufacturers of women's 'needs', at the same time telling women what they 'needed' to buy. Her belief in the beneficial effects of advertising was absolute: 'Through advertising, you hear very quickly now when something new and good appears; whereas without advertising you might never hear of it . . . Advertising is the more modern, clean, direct, and straightforward way of going right to the "ultimate consumer" and telling about the goods.'

Christine Frederick was not alone in her enthusiasm for this exciting economic role of 'consumer' for the modern woman.

Mrs Julian Heath, founder and national president of the House-wives' League, wrote in the *Ladies' Home Journal* in January 1915 that housewives must recognise their importance as the 'buying agent for the home' and 'Recognize our economic function as the spenders of the family income', and that 'We women must realize that we are occupying a new economic position'. The domestic efficiency expert Lillian Gilbreth made comparable pronouncements, and like Christine Frederick also ended her career as a consultant to manufacturers about selling household products to women.

Christine Frederick stands out not only in her blatant encour-agement for the modern woman to buy, buy, buy, but also in trying to persuade her to believe what she is told about her purchases. In tones of warm approval Frederick writes that the modern woman 'has developed a "consumer-acceptance spirit" – a readiness to follow where she is led – that has had an immense bearing upon the American industrial prosperity and standards of living'.

Not only was the American home front radically transformed by the new cult of consumerism, but also the British, although considerably later and on a less flamboyant scale. As the years of wartime rationing petered out, more and more consumer goods became available in Britain, and the 'pressures to earn more, spend more and consume more were becoming irresistible', according to Elizabeth Roberts in *Women and Families: An Oral History 1940–1970*. Her research into working-class areas of the north of England indicates that as women bought more appliances and more possessions for the home these women also began to move away from traditional working-class streets, into larger homes. To maintain such a home meant spending more time indoors servicing the place, and women became increasingly cut off from their neighbours. Gone were the days of friendly chatter while whitening the front steps of small terraced houses.

When feminist critics analyse the way in which women have been manipulated by manufacturers and advertisers and encour-aged to buy, buy, buy for the home, there is invariably a bitterness of tone. These tales are not attractive. Women appear to have been easily led, and often easily led by *by other women* into this realm of excessive consumerism and trumped-up 'needs'. Initially, by domestic scientists like Christine Frederick and Lillian Gilbreth; later by whole flocks of 'corporate home economists'. An article in *Sales Management* in 1959 sums up the role of this breed of home economist:

> Certainly only the bravest, or most foolhardy, of the stronger sex claims to grasp the workings of the female mind . . . Hence the growing importance of the home economist in marketing . . . She has the touch of the sociologist, a creative temperament, a background in natural sciences – and the vaunted feminine touch. She is the Home Economist in marketing . . . a woman to convince women.

Not surprisingly, Betty Friedan has nothing good to say of Christine Frederick, Lillian Gilbreth and their ilk, condemning them as little more than agents of their corporate masters. In *The Feminine Mystique*, Friedan points out forcefully how women have been trained to be uncritical consumers: to buy furniture and appliances; to shore up their lives with gadgets and gizmos, to retreat into their 'thing-ridden houses' and then to buy more products in order to care for all their things. She describes how the 'seller of things' can work on a woman's attachment to her home and possessions, encourage exaggerated care of them, and make the cleaning of the home more and more complicated by putting out more and more products with increasingly difficult directions. This creates in the housewife an illusion of having expert knowledge, just because she is the only one who understands how to use the washing machine, or which kind of cleaning product to use on the rubber mats: in truth, far from being an expert she is the gull of every salesman.

Friedan famously quotes market research reports that discuss ways of ensuring that a woman be appropriately enslaved to the idea of cleaning. Amongst other tactics, encourage her to buy lots of different products for different purposes to give her the illusion of expertise. Encourage her to feel anxious and guilty about dirt she cannot see. Having achieved these aims, and having assured her of her role as a killer of germs, protector of the family, and expert household technician, the woman is then ripe for suggestions about what to buy. Chances are that a nice new product will come to the rescue of this guilty, needy, responsible, health-conscious housewife. 'For, it seems', writes Friedan, 'there's a growing wave of housewives who look forward to new products which not only decrease their daily work load, but actually engage their emotional and intellectual interest in the world of scientific development outside the home.'

In other words, if advertisers and salesmen issue solemn scientific warnings about germs and dust mites, about salmonella and viruses, responsible women are likely to be so impressed and concerned and interested that they will immediately buy the new product. 'One gasps in admiration at the ingenuity of it all,' says Friedan. 'The housewife can participate in science itself just by buying something new.' And if the advertisers have done their job well, the woman believes that buying this product is not only a duty, but a pleasure because 'a *new* cleaning appliance or product increases a woman's feeling of security and luxury'.

Bright promises of security and luxury, hints of embarrassment and guilt, sly innuendo and social pressure: such is the stuff of advertisements for cleaning products. 'A job you can do in your evening gown!' declares an advertisement for Gillett's Lyc. 'No more messy scrubbing out of toilets . . . everything sweet and odourless.' 'Is only *half* your lavatory clean?' sternly demands an ad for Harpic cleaner. 'The *Hoover* takes the dirt you can't see!' promises another ad. 'I thought my frock was clean,' one girl sadly declares to another, 'until I saw your Persil-bright one.'

Welcome to the never-never land in which the cartoon creatures of the household swing into action, where the slut and the superwoman compare floor cleaners and laundry, where Mrs Brown looks out from behind her curtain and overhears her neighbour's little Susie saying 'Mummy says I can't play at your house any more!' And all because Mrs Brown is not using the appropriate toilet cleaner. The implicit message has remained the same for years: that women genuinely need all the help they can get in their homes; that the liquids and polishes, powders and potions, machines and appliances are providing honest benefit, a cleaner, safer, happier home benignly administered by a woman who knows what to do and what to buy to keep it that way. Usually the message is also a promise of more free time in the bargain. And all the housewife must do to acquire or achieve all of this immeasurable benefit is to buy some product or other.

In *Objects of Desire*, Adrian Forty points out how every attempt to spread the word about cleanliness has employed two kinds of arguments. One is based on 'science' and quotes experts, often doctors, home economists or unspecified 'scientists'. Using vaguely expert vocabulary, replete with words no one fully understands, these experts provide comments or quotations that help instil graphic ideas. The other is entirely emotive and relies on raising levels of anxiety and guilt about dirt – a technique of emotional blackmail.

An ad of 1928, for example, claims 'Old Dutch' will safeguard your refrigerator with 'HEALTHFUL CLEANLINESS'. There follows a lengthy warning of the danger of contaminated food phrased in a manner designed to encourage the housewife to worry, and the ad then goes on to demonstrate the scientific prowess of this cleanser by describing its active ingredient, a mysterious and impressive substance called 'seismotite': 'Through the microscope you see it as thousands of flaky, flat-shaped particles. There is nothing else like it for removing dirt. With the visible uncleanliness it takes away impurities you cannot see.' The basic message here, as in so many advertisements for cleaning products, is that the purchaser should be reassured by the 'scientific' promises made by the advertiser. And the purchaser's anxieties, purposefully heightened by the advertiser, are simultaneously allayed by the soothing promises inherent in using the product in question.

Advertising for cleaning appliances and products is often crude; the lowest common denominator of the advertising world. The familiar split-screen ads that test one type of soap or washing powder over another are offensively simplistic: advertisements for germ-killing cleaners are no better; little cartoon germs on the toilet seat run off screaming when the toilet cleaner is pointed at them; floor cleaners cut effortlessly through the dirt and kill the germs on the kitchen floor with one clear shining line of a mop. In a world of increasingly sophisticated advertising, that for cleaning products remains for the most part a primitive life form.

Yet however wise we may think we are to the wiles of advertising, there is little doubt that it gets under our skins, and little doubt that it sells products. Think of the dazzling arrays of fluorescent lit bottles of cleaning fluids and powders and potions that declare themselves to us in every supermarket, that proclaim their own virtues in misspelled superlatives, like Kleen, Klear, Fantastik. The relentless parade of the new cleaning products always being added to the shelves would not be there unless we bought them, and we would not buy them unless at some level we believed or wanted to believe their claims.

Rarely has the common consumption of cleaning materials been so well described as in Judith Summer's novel *I, Gloria Gold*. As she contemplates the past thirty-six years of her married life, the narrator Gloria counts her days of scrubbing and cleaning and reaches a flashpoint of angry self-awareness. Why has she been doing this? What *is* all this junk under the sink?

> Thirty-six years of three hundred and sixty-five cleaning days. How much detergent have I flushed down the drains in that time? How many scouring pads, mops and J-Cloths have I worn through? How many containers of Persil and Daz, Domestos and Mansion Polish, Fairy and Pledge, Flash and Ajax, Silvo and Brillo, Oven-Kleen and Windolene have I used up and thrown away. Poured together they would form a vast ocean of germ-fighting, sterile, whiter-than-white suds. And where has all my hard work got me?

All that dutiful cleaning has merely estranged Gloria from her family. She has, however, been most faithful to her brand-name cleaning products and made a solid contribution to the well-being of the manufacturers involved. Like so many of us, she has travelled hopefully down the shining aisles of the supermarkets and she has bought, bought, bought.

On first reading her list of cleaning products I felt pity for Gloria; imagine being such a committed consumer of so many cleaning products. She seemed rather pathetic. But on impulse I looked under my own kitchen sink, only to find that of the thirteen brand-name products Gloria listed, I had nine. Three of them I had not bought myself – they were left behind by various tenants and visitors – but none the less I had nine of these products. That I also had five others Gloria does not even mention meant I had fourteen bottles or boxes or tins under the kitchen sink, *eight* of which I never or hardly ever used. Another cupboard revealed even more: laundry powders, bleach, ammonia, vinegar, trisodium phosphate (TSP), and a few suspicious bottles with shredded labels.

Since looking under my own sink I have asked many people to look under theirs, or in their cupboards, to see what they have. Almost always, rarely used cleaning products lurk in the back of the cupboard, items bought on impulse, or in response to a long-forgotten need. Almost always, the list of anyone's cleaning products is much longer than expected, and often the reasons for purchasing the products in the first place sound remarkably lame.

'My mother always used it' is a much repeated phrase. 'I like the smell' is another. 'I've always used it' is another common response, counterbalanced by the people who say 'I like trying new things'. A few people have confessed 'I have no idea why I bought the damned stuff' adding that they've never used it, or they tried it once and it was useless. Some buy on the recommendation of friends. Some admit that advertisements have influenced them. Many say 'Because it's supposed to kill germs'. My favourite responses are the ones that refer to the pictures on the products. 'Because I like the bald guy with the earring', referring to the famous Mr Clean, pictured muscular and smiling, bald and be-ringed, on every label of the liquid floor cleaner bearing his name. 'I've always liked that little yellow chick' says my mother of Bon Ami scouring powder which chirpily claims that it 'hasn't scratched yet'.

Clearly, when looking closely at the claims of any array of

household cleaners on supermarket shelves, we are not far removed from the domain of the snake-oil salesman. Are we truly expected to believe that one brand of bleach 'kills all known household germs', or that the 'blue-magic-whitener' of a particular stain remover will whisk all stains away effortlessly, or that a household cleanser will leave the house 'spotless and germ-free'? Most of us know better than to believe such nonsense, and yet, dazed and bemused by the sloganeering, we continue to roam the supermarket aisles and we continue to buy, willingly suspending our disbelief. We have been truly and deftly manipulated and encouraged into such purchasing behaviour, and for a very long time too. But no hand other than our own puts an item into the shopping trolley.

Even the least critical and suspicious amongst us can readily understand that if people are trying to sell us something we should not believe everything they say. Throughout the last century and a half, the increased pursuit of household cleanliness has been accompanied – indeed paralleled – by the buying and the selling of innumerable products and appliances. Some of the efforts to sell now seem outrageously blatant, the efforts of the Cleanliness Institute to sell soap, for instance. Some of them are more subtle, like the implicit encouragement many girls received in home economics classes to go out and buy certain appliances. We can be absolutely certain that coming clean around the house has always been costly, not just in terms of money, but also in the effort required to stay alert to all the pressures involved.

When Catharine Beecher wrote, in *The American Woman's Home* (1869), that 'a woman who has charge of a large household should regard her duties as dignified, important, and difficult', however we might argue with that premise, at least we can be sure that Beecher is not trying to *sell* us anything, at least not directly. Further, when Mrs Beecher advises that one should have no fewer than three dishcloths hanging over the sink – one for greasy dishes, one for cleaner dishes, and one for greasy pots and kettles – to ensure that the lady of the house 'will not be annoyed by having her dishes washed with dark, musty and greasy rags as is too frequently the case', we can rest easy, for at least she is not recommending the type of cloth we should use. For this reason, if no other, the earliest domestic advisers can be straightforwardly entertaining to read. Their concern for the 'woman of the house' is transparently honest.

And yet is it? Once a new ethos was in place and housekeeping emerged as a 'science' to be seriously pursued by informed women, moments of transparent honesty are difficult to find anywhere in the trade. Home economists quickly became as thick as thieves with manufacturers and advertisers, with women being encouraged to buy as never before. So while Catharine Beecher stands at the beginning of the period when domestic science began to become a serious business – the age of innocence, in terms of consumerism – she is none the less implicated in all that followed.

Take her apparently innocent suggestions about dishcloths. In subsequent years a staggering number of pages have been filled in advice manuals about dishcloths and cleaning cloths; deadpan articles in women's magazines have rejoiced in such headlines as 'The Virtues of a Damp Cloth'. Solemn advice has been issued about the best type of fabric to use, where to buy it and how to sew the cloths; the virtues of disposable cloths and paper towels have come under intense and lengthy scrutiny. And for all the modern housekeeper like myself might be concerned about dishcloths and cleaning cloths, all of the hype has clearly been taken to exaggerated lengths. Don Aslett, in *Is There Life After Housework*, goes so far as to advise that only professionally designed cloths available in specialist cleaning outlets should *ever* be used for cleaning, and never, *never* old rags.

'The ease with which you do your housework and seasonal cleaning is in direct proportion to the equipment and supplies you have on hand. It matters little what you're cleaning; you'll do it better if you have the right supplies.' So said *The Good Housekeeping Housekeeping Book* in 1947. Take this insistence on having the right stuff around the house to its logical conclusion, and several decades later Don Aslett is laying down the law, telling us what we simply must buy. Most of us need new vacuum cleaners, he declares firmly, so just get rid of the junky old ones, and buy the best. Only the highest quality doormats are really any good, so go out and buy one *now* and no more of those ratty old bits of used carpet, thank you. If something we own is frayed or worn it is probably hard to clean or inefficient, so get rid of it and buy a new one. If a lampshade won't come clean with a few gentle wipes and a vacuuming, toss it out and buy a new one.

Has domestic consumerism gone mad? Nevertheless such exaggerated suggestions are strangely helpful: they put the whole business of chasing dirt in perspective. Because cleaning the house should be a fairly simple undertaking, and it should make life liveable, not unbearable. To deny people their quirky cleaning habits, or a home its imperfections, is pure nonsense. Without old rags many a floor would never be wiped, without worn doormats many feet would not hesitate at the door, without happily shabby possessions many homes would lose their charm entirely. The service of cleaning and tending for our own homes and possessions is just that: a service, not a god. Yet if we believe the blandishments of every adviser or advertiser, cleaning becomes infinitely demanding and extremely expensive; if we buy everything or do everything that is recommended we not only spend too much money, we make complete fools of ourselves.

SEARCH AND DESTROY

THE WHYS AND WHEREFORES OF GERM-KILLING

The lust to kill, the grim determination to eradicate invasive life forms in the home, has always been part of housecleaning. The targets include things visible and invisible, ranging from beasts to bugs to germs. The killing fields of domestic life are many, and the anxious aggression that takes over our cleaning habits is often extreme if we believe our homes have been invaded by hostile creatures great or small.

Germs must be considered first, because destroying germs in the household is such a compelling preoccupation for many people. Indeed, almost everyone has a bash at killing germs, at least from time to time. Much of the fear of visible intruders in the home, bugs and beasts alike, is inspired by the fact that these creatures bear invisible germs on their little feet and whiskers. Killing flies, for instance, became a near-patriotic act in the American pursuit of cleanliness earlier in the twentieth century, because flies carry germs. Rats are a particular source of horror because they are known to carry disease germs. Dust was greatly feared for several decades because it was believed to harbour so many dangerous germs.

The encouragement to kill germs is powerful and insidious, as Marcia in Robert Irwin's *The Limits of Vision* knows well. She becomes entranced by the germ-killing power of the cleaners in

her home: 'Have you looked at the detergents you are using –
how some of them eliminate the dirt, really kill it, while other
detergents lift the dirt off from the fabrics, separating but not
actually killing that much? It has quite a psychological effect on
me which one I use. It's really interesting.' She engages in a
'discourse of detergent power', musing on its hidden violence,
its ability to kill, speaking of its 'power to thrust and drive out,
to lift off dirt; in the fight for family hygiene it kills germs – both
known germs and unknown germs – and breaks down bacteria, it
smashes, beats and bites. Soused with water, it combats dirt like
a mad Lascar. The only language detergent power understands
is violence. Together I and my powder, we conquer.'

Marcia finds this potent language and these powerful promises
on the packages of the products she uses. This back-of-package
propaganda sets her fevered imagination off at a gallop, indulging
in an orgy of violence against germs. Clear in everything she says
is that it does not much matter if she is really wreaking havoc with
germs, what is important is that she thinks she is because it makes
her feel better. This is true for far saner people than Marcia.

Trying to discover what people know or believe about germs
and how to 'conquer' them with lethal powders and potions is an
eye-opening exercise. Like any scientific information that affects
a wide audience, such knowledge reaches the general public in
a form that is over-simplified and often muddled. It was ever
thus. According to Christine Frederick, few homemakers really
understood about germs in the early years of the twentieth
century but 'they meticulously act upon the assumption that
germs must be outwitted'. Little has changed in the seventy-five
years since then.

Whether or not any real understanding is at work, germs are
a hot topic once any group starts talking about housecleaning.
'What is the germiest place or thing in the house?' I asked,
time and again. The dishcloth, said some people immediately
– or the sponge, or the J-cloth, or whatever else they used for
wiping surfaces in the kitchen. No, no, said others, and offered a
seemingly endless number of 'germy' options. The toilet, fridge,
drains, or kitchen counters, suggested some; the kitchen table,

the can-opener, the conjugal bed, insisted others heatedly. The children's toys and the dog's bed were mentioned by a few; also the oven and the basement or cellar.

Why the oven, I wondered, when Yvonne came up with that suggestion. 'Because I only clean it every five years or so. It must be absolutely *thick* with germs,' was her response. Why the fridge? 'It sometimes smells so bad,' said another woman, 'and there's food in there that goes off, and spills of milk. The whole inside of the fridge seems contaminated sometimes.'

This particular conversation took place in an office, attracting a small crowd. 'I don't understand,' declared a new arrival. 'Why the fridge and the oven, for heaven's sake? The cold or the heat will kill any germs that are there, surely.'

'That's not what my mother told me,' said one of the older women. 'When my children were growing up in the 1960s, I disinfected the fridge every week. I used a bleach solution, and washed every single square inch of the inside. Everyone did, it was just part of the weekly routine. Now it seems mad, looking back. Don't ask me if the fridge was really so very germy. I don't know, but I believed it was at the time.'

At this point in the discussion another woman firmly announced that the basement was the germiest place in a house. Why? 'Because', said the basement-basher firmly, 'I've always lived in houses with unfinished basements, with slimy drains in the floor and window sills that were never dusted. The basement is never cleaned like the rest of the house. Also it has things like furnace filters, clogged with dirt, and it's dark and creepy and dank, and there's mice poop down there in dark corners.' 'I felt the same about the stone cellar in the old house where I used to live,' chimed in someone else. 'Damp and filthy and full of stuff I couldn't bear to look at, and it absolutely reeked of germs.'

Such casual and unscientific exchanges of opinion would not have impressed Ellen Richards. Her passionate belief that women should have scientific training to run a household was, in part at least, inspired by her belief that we must understand germs. Grim warnings of how 'a pin-point of dust' could yield 'three thousand living organisms, not all malignant, but all enemies of health' inspired Richards and her fellow home economists to spread the word to other women, telling them to be aware, to be informed, to be achingly conscientious about the nature and ways of these invisible menaces. That so many of us, to this day, have such imprecise knowledge of germs would probably make these determined educators flinch.

I have encountered few people in charge of households who are fully confident of their knowledge about germs. When questioned, many admit that their information is woolly, that it is half-remembered from what their mothers said and did, or from advertisements, or from home economics or health education classes at school. Some are refreshingly blunt about their own level of information: 'I haven't a clue about germs,' one woman declared. 'I know enough to tell the children to cover their mouths when they sneeze and to wash their hands, and I'm scared to death of cooking chicken because of all I've read about salmonella, but no – I don't know much. I buy disinfectant sprays, and I use them here and there, but who knows if they really do any good. They make me feel better, though.'

'I only use disinfectant in the toilet,' said another woman, one of a small group gathered in my kitchen. 'Or if someone in the house is sick then I disinfect doorknobs and the telephone – that's what my mother used to do. And I use exactly the same stuff she used, that pine-scented disinfectant. Just the smell of it makes me think I've done something positive.'

'I think it's a complete waste of time – I never disinfect anything,' declared a third woman.

'You mean you don't even have disinfectant in the house?' asked the toilet-disinfector. 'Not a bit,' was the confident reply. 'Not even bleach?' 'No, not even bleach.' Clearly, this came as a shock to the woman who had put the question. She had never imagined a household could be run without disinfectant. 'What do you do about the toilet?' she inquired in hushed tones. 'I just wipe it with a damp cloth,' the other replied, unrepentant. 'I don't believe those disinfectants do a bit of good – and who needs those ridiculous toilet-cleaners with contorted necks and kitchen sprays with huge nozzles that claim they do all the work and kill all the germs? It's just another gimmick.'

'I agree,' a fourth woman announced. 'Don't any of you remember biology lessons? And looking at scrapings of your skin under a microscope and seeing how it's *crawling* with germs? I know they're all over everything I eat and touch. It's just stupid to think you can kill all the germs in your kitchen or bathroom. And why would you want to anyway? All I ever use is dishwashing detergent and hot water – for everything.'

'Well, you say what you like, but I *always* use disinfectant sprays in the kitchen and bathroom *and* bleach, and I think we *should*, especially on gross and germy things like dishcloths. I mean they just spread germs *everywhere*.' This outburst came from the quietest woman in the group; she had not said a word to this point. She looked upset. 'I change my dishcloths once, sometimes twice a day *and* wash them separately with bleach to kill the germs, *and* I pour bleach down the toilet to kill germs, and I disinfect kitchen surfaces every day, and I use disinfectant in the water when I wash the floors.' *And*, she went on to point out, she has a full-time job. 'It's not that I have nothing better to do, but this is really important.'

Such passionately held beliefs about using disinfectants and killing germs are deeply rooted. Disinfection has been a persistent topic in domestic advice books and in home economics texts; a major theme in advertising; an important part of the dictates passed from mother to daughter. For decades women have been encouraged to think of themselves as the vigilant defenders of the household, keeping dangerous germs at bay. As an advertisement for the 1898 *International Health Exposition* in New York proclaimed: 'Women are born sanitarians, and abhor dirt, darkness and disease.' Affirmation came from all quarters, this from the *Daily Times* in Victoria, Canada in 1899: 'Women are the real sanitarians, and it ought to be their province to keep themselves clean and free from the diseases of dirt, to keep their homes clean, to keep their streets clean, to keep their towns clean.'

Advice about disinfection has resounded far and wide over the past century. 'To be clean nowadays means to be free from germs and all such mischief-making things!' exhorted the *American Kitchen Magazine* in September 1900. 'Keep washcloths fresh and sweet by disinfecting them each day,' intones the *Good Housekeeping Housekeeping Book* in 1947. 'Wash your shower floor and bath mats with disinfecting solution, so that other members of the family will not step where infected feet have been.' The passion for disinfection went to such extremes that an article in *Good Housekeeping* in 1932 provides information about how to disinfect picture frames, should you so wish. 'With a hand spray, sheltered places like mouldings, picture frames, etc., can be properly disinfected.'

In *Housewifery: A Textbook of Practical Housekeeping*, published in 1936, Lydia Ray Balderston is characteristically stern about disinfection. 'Every housewife should be acquainted with disinfectants and fumigants, because drains, garbage cans, and ice boxes need them; and cellars must be kept free from chance causes of odors or sickness.' Balderston recommends periodic cleansing of the 'flush closet' with strong doses of washing soda, chloride of lime or potassium permanganate, and daily cleaning with soap and water and a brush. Dishcloths should be washed after each dishwashing, kitchen towels should be boiled two or three times a week for five minutes, with soap.

A gritty determination to control pests and keep food free from contamination accompanies Balderston's concern about germs. Hence her disdain for the then-popular notion that linoleum should be cleaned with milk: 'Milk, which has sometimes been recommended as a cleaner gives a sticky finish and leaves a sugary covering on the linoleum to attract flies and insects, perhaps vermin.' Keeping flies away from food, keeping privies clean, keeping vermin at bay, disinfecting garbage cans, scalding towels, scrubbing kitchen surfaces thoroughly and repeatedly with soap and water or with washing soda, such are Mrs Balderston's basic dictates. People on farms are assigned extra tasks; they must whitewash chicken coops and outbuildings every spring, and also the cellar, in order to 'sterilise' them. Valid enough advice; properly employed, all of these methods of disinfection could indeed kill at least some disease germs.

Book after book, article after article recommends ways and means of killing germs. The earlier methods included disinfection with carbolic solutions and chloride of lime, with formaldehyde (formalin) and coal-tar compounds, with corrosive sublimate and sulphur fumes, not to mention disinfection by boiling, and soaking contaminated fabrics in strong solutions of lye soap. Most of these methods were probably effective. Lye, for instance, being powerfully alkaline, certainly has anti-bacterial qualities. The disinfectant powers of sunlight are also repeatedly recommended. 'Dry air and sunlight are foes to germs,' Lydia Ray Balderston declares. 'Moisture and filth are their best friends', or as the 1932 article on disinfection in *Good Housekeeping* proclaims even more eloquently, 'light is the eternal enemy of pathogenic germs . . . [they] will live for long periods in dark places'.

Elizabeth Scott is a microbiologist specialising in household matters. She believes that many of our beliefs about germs and many of our disinfecting practices are misguided. 'Often people believe they are disinfecting when all they are doing is getting rid of smells by replacing them with nicer smells. The enthusiasm for disinfecting drains and toilets has far more to do with smell than with actual germ-killing. Because just because a smell has disappeared, the bacteria creating the smell haven't necessarily been killed. Even if an effective disinfectant has been used the surface will not remain uncontaminated for long.'

For decades, products have been on the market claiming to deodorise and sanitise and purify and kill germs all at once, particularly in the bathroom. 'It's a social blessing,' declares an advertisement for Cromessol Fragrant Disinfectant in 1932. 'It destroys odours and infection . . . this powerful disinfectant that smells like flowers.' The picture shows a smiling maid gently wafting an aerosol spray over a toilet; an action that would have had virtually no effect on a self-respecting, odour-causing germ.

The indiscriminate dread of all germs promoted in so many advertisements is often just fearmongering nonsense. Elizabeth Scott advocates knowing what we are up against. 'Most house-hold germs are harmless and of no concern, but there are potentially pathogenic germs carried on food, especially on raw meat and poultry, and on pets, and in human excreta and mucus. These more dangerous germs include the wide range of food poisoning bacteria like salmonella, and also staph and *E. coli.*'

'You have to be very rational about cleaning,' she points out. 'You have to assess risks and priorities. If your child is outside playing, eating handsful of dirt, there isn't much point in disinfecting the toys and the kitchen floor on his behalf. But if there is a diarrhoeal illness in the house, you do take extra precautions about the spread of germs.' According to Elizabeth Scott, these precautions mean ensuring that there is no cross-contamination with food. To reduce this danger, hand-washing should be scrupulous and both kitchen and bathroom surfaces carefully cleaned. 'I do not advocate routine disinfection of anything unless it has been in contact with raw foods, or in the case of infections transmitted by hand-to-mouth contact or the presence of highly vulnerable individuals,' she says.

The basic lesson is that germs from the toilet should be kept out of the kitchen, a seemingly obvious dictate that is often disregarded. A survey done in Britain showed that as late as 1971 fully one-third of mothers poured the soak water from their nappy pails down the kitchen sink, a splendidly effective way of introducing the bacteria from human excreta into the kitchen.

Until recently most household germ-killing activity was directed towards the bathroom, but the major killing field is now the kitchen and food preparation areas. Only in the last decade has the true extent and danger of food-borne diseases been fully realised either in Britain or America. Given the increasing prevalence of salmonella, kitchen cleanliness – especially of work surfaces and dishcloths – is taken far more seriously than ever before.

If raw meat or poultry has been handled, either of which can carry not only salmonella, but other potentially dangerous bacteria including campylobacter and *E. coli*, all contact surfaces should be cleaned with care. Many food safety advisers recommend regular disinfection of all surfaces, warning also of the hazards of dishcloths or kitchen sponges. Because anything used to wipe surfaces can rapidly spread dangerous bacteria around a kitchen if it is used on a contaminated surface and then re-used elsewhere, these cloths or sponges should be treated with caution.

Elizabeth Scott, along with many other experts in food hygiene, recommends bleach as a household disinfectant. 'It's both cheap and effective. Many people are cautious of using it in the kitchen – it has traditionally been confined to use in the bathroom and laundry, but increasingly it is being recommended for kitchen use. Because it works – a dishcloth soaked in a bleach solution will not be a lethal domestic weapon crawling with salmonella, and bleach can safely disinfect sinks, knives and cutting boards.'

Cutting boards have attracted much attention in recent years. What should they be, wood or plastic? Which surface is the more hygienic? Dean Cliver of the University of California at Davis has been involved in studies of both kinds of boards. Before his studies began, he advocated plastic boards in a food safety booklet he was writing; after all, plastic was recommended by the US Department of Agriculture's Food Safety and Inspection Service. But then Dean Cliver began to ask *why* plastic was preferred and he discovered the reasons were at best flimsy. He began his own research into the question, and his findings strongly favour wooden boards. He found that although new plastic boards are easy to clean and to disinfect, they soon become problematic; knife-scarred plastic boards can retain food contaminants for considerable lengths of time, deep within the plastic. On the other hand, wooden boards seem able to 'suck in' bacteria, leaving the surfaces free of contamination, even if the boards were coated with chicken fat. In a normal domestic setting, Dean Cliver recommends simply washing cutting boards with hot water and detergent, regardless of the kind of bacteria on them. 'We've steered clear of using household chemicals on the boards. I'm just not comfortable about using bleach on them.' Other experts on household hygiene disagreed here, quite commonly recommending bleach as a disinfectant for most surfaces.

The use of bleach is inevitably a divisive topic. People have strong feelings about it, and strong beliefs, to the point that I would maintain there are two types of people in the world, bleachers and non-bleachers. I am a non-bleacher, even though it is evident that bleach is a highly effective substance. It disinfects, it whitens, it removes stains, it even smells powerful – and it terrifies me. Not only because it can have the most peculiar effect on fabrics and surfaces if too much is used, but because of its questionable effect on the environment.

Any powerful disinfectant, bleach included, will destroy more than we intend when we pour it down our sinks and toilets. No disinfectant product disappears into thin air once it is used. It may indeed kill the germs you wish dead, but it will go on to kill other micro-organisms as it passes into the sewage systems, rivers and oceans. 'If you must use chemical products,' says Professor Sayed Sattar of the University of Ottawa, 'remember it's a double-edged sword. The product may kill the germs you want to kill, but it probably is toxic and it probably causes environmental damage. I don't know of any truly effective product that is totally safe to use or totally safe to store, that also kills a broad spectrum of bacteria and kills them fast.'

In the domestic market, disinfectants sell on the basis of their self-proclaimed effectiveness, their ease of use, their smell. They vary in their ability to kill germs; some are limited to only a few types of bacteria, the more powerful ones are 'broad spectrum', and will kill a far greater variety of germs. From the supermarket shelves these many and varied types of disinfectant join a single chorus, promising peace of mind and freedom from germs, often with minimal effort. While such claims may contain grains of truth they never merit uncritical acceptance. Disinfectants promising instant results, effortless application and which claim to be non-toxic are probably not effective. Killing germs is not that easy. Usually effort and prolonged contact-time are required, and strong poisons.

Independent scientists who have examined the germ-killing powers of household cleaners are cautious in their assessments of domestic products. Broadly speaking, in order to lay claim to loosely defined terms like 'disinfectant' or 'antibacterial', household products must pass the in-house testing of the manufacturers and must also satisfy outside watchdog agencies in order to prove that the product does indeed do what it claims. The claims made on product labels are trustworthy in so far as they comply with the test standards of the countries in which they are sold.

In the United States, these standards are set by the Environmental Protection Agency; in Canada by the Pest Management Regulatory Agency of Health, Canada. Each agency has the power to request information about product performance and to inspect the laboratories and testing practices of manufacturers. If products comply with the agencies' requirements, the products are issued with registration numbers denoting their status as 'disinfectants'. In both America and Canada, these registration numbers are printed on product labels. Such registration is significant: if a product is registered as a disinfectant in America and has received an EPA number, it has by definition undergone an impressive battery of tests and, as one scientist cautiously ventured, 'it probably works'.

In Britain, standards for labelling and defining household disinfectants have been less exacting than in North America. Claims made on product labels in Britain are often more daring than in North America, for example, 'Kills all known household germs', the claim made by a best-selling bleach. 'What an outrageous claim!' fumed one American researcher. 'I doubt that would be allowed in the States.'

In the European Union, a new Biocidal Products Directive is currently being enacted. This directive will require all germ-killing products to be licensed, thereby harmonising standards in European countries which until now have not been in accord. In the UK, this Biocidal Products Directive will take over from the British Standards Authority and the Trading Standards Authority, until now responsible for proving or disproving the efficacy of product claims when questions arose.

The real problem with household disinfectants is not, however, the nature of claims made on product labels. The problem is that consumers of these products are using them in domestic settings, not in laboratories. Carefully controlled test conditions in laboratories may produce the declared results, but home use is an entirely different matter. Consumers often apply the product haphazardly and hurriedly; as a result, the product may not work properly. Worse still is the 'cleaning cocktail' habit of householders, that optimistic and ignorant habit of combining one or more products together in the hope of creating an effective mix. Not only can this be dangerous if acid and alkali products are mixed, sometimes releasing toxic or even explosive fumes, but this practice also usually neutralises and inactivates the disinfectants involved. The habits of householders are, in short, often the despair of manufacturers.

I use household disinfectants rarely and sparingly, more often than not ignoring the directions on the label about how to dilute the product. Assuming that manufacturers cynically encourage overuse of their products, I generally use much less than the recommended dose. Such wilful disregard for directions is common. Many other consumers behave in the same way, or err in the opposite direction, assuming that if a little works well, a lot will work extremely well. Either reaction undermines the product's efficiency. Industrial researchers and independent researchers all concur; if these disinfectant products are to be even remotely effective they must be used as directed, no more and no less. Even then, their germ-killing powers are open to domestic sabotage, for the effectiveness of household products is at the mercy of many variables: the kind of cloth or sponge used, the nature of the surface being cleaned, the concentration of the dilution, and the length of time the product is allowed to remain on the surface.

While the system of disinfectant registration has merit, even those in the registration business do not make extravagant claims on its behalf. Zig Vaitusis of the Environmental Protection Agency in America offers his opinion that despite all the marvellous products on the market, the best way to keep a kitchen clean is with soap or detergent and water, occasionally using diluted solutions of bleach if a disinfectant is required. Karen McCullagh, of the Pest Management Regulatory Agency of Health, Canada, says that the consumer's relaxed approach to following directions, plus all the variables of how the product is applied, make it difficult to have complete confidence in even the most rigorously tested product. 'Microbial pests are persistent,' she says. 'They're not at all easy to get rid of for any extended period of time.'

Germs are not easy to banish, nor are germ-killing habits and beliefs. No one wants to hear that his or her disinfecting practices may be ineffectual, or unnecessary, or that the product they fondly use is of little or no real value. Yet this is often the case. I discovered this to my cost, because many of my own cherished beliefs and practices have been damned with very faint praise by the professionals.

For many years I have had great faith in vinegar, fuzzily believing that because it changes Ph levels it kills germs, or at least inhibits their growth. Having now talked to a number of microbiologists, I am forced to concede vinegar does little more than remove odours. Having always believed – like Lydia Ray Balderston – that strong sunlight kills germs, I have regretfully learned that although ultra-violet rays kill some micro-organisms, sunlight is not a reliable disinfectant. Equally, I have had to abandon my fond assumption that the heat of the clothes dryer kills all germs – it does not – and I have had to give up my belief that a dry dishcloth is free of germs. Most micro-organisms do need moisture to multiply, but not necessarily to survive. Salmonella and *E. coli* bacteria can survive on apparently dry surfaces for several hours, and a dry dishcloth can hold other types of micro-organisms for several days.

Elizabeth Scott has tested many domestic cleaning products, including disinfectants. 'Some are excellent, particularly some of the new multi-surface disinfectant sprays, but you do have to follow the directions, and it's extraordinary how few householders really do. You can't expect these things to work if you use them any way you like. But more importantly you should try to be clear about *why* you are using them, and what you want them to do. Otherwise you can waste a lot of time and money doing completely unnecessary housework.'

Above all, in any germ-killing quest, you have to know what

is appropriate for your own home, given the health and age of everyone in it. Bear in mind that a home need not comply with institutional standards. Hospitals and restaurants must be infinitely more vigilant about disinfection than anyone in a domestic setting for the obvious reason that these institutions deal with more illness and more potentially contaminated foods than a home ever could. Similarly with nurseries: just because your child's nursery disinfects all the toys that the children share, you need not do so. True, bacteria and viruses can be transmitted on toys, but the risk in the home is infinitely less than at a nursery. If you are unfortunate enough to have upwards of thirty children smearing germs on your children's toys every day, you would need to be more vigilant. In that case disinfectant would be a good idea. So, mind you, would a tranquilliser.

In talking to many different women about their household practices, what stands out, when it comes to killing germs, is a general state of vague anxiety. This applies to almost everyone: to those who strive to zap every possible germ in their bathrooms and kitchens and also to those who are blithely, even scornfully, dismissive of the whole subject. For even the dismissive doubters, if they are closely questioned, are rarely absolutely confident of their position. For them too, when a serious problem of hygiene arises in the house – be it a grave illness, a case of food-poisoning, a flooded basement, a burst sewer line near the house, a backed-up septic tank – the germ-killing conditioning of the past century tends to surface.

On the face of it, this conditioning, in its more extreme mani-festations, seems easy to dismiss. Because so much germ-killing behaviour around the house arose in the pre-antibiotic era when contagious diseases, once contracted, were far more likely to be deadly, many household practices discussed in older advice books or passed on by our grandmothers seem incongruously arcane. Who would now dream of disinfecting picture frames or disinfecting entire rooms with burning sulphur? Probably no one, for there is no doubt that our vulnerability to certain diseases, and our need to be defended against them in the home has been radically eased by modern medicine. At the same time, however, it takes a rash – even a foolish – person to declare absolute indifference to potentially dangerous germs in the household.

As concerned experts like Elizabeth Scott tirelessly point out, new considerations continue to arise in connection with household hygiene. The increasing prevalence of food-borne diseases and growing resistance of many micro-organisms to antibiotics are two extremely worrying trends. Each of these throws much of the responsibility for disease prevention back into the realm of household and personal hygiene. Similarly, the growing number of young children in day care facilities (by the year 2000, 80 per cent of children in America under the age of six will be in day care) means more youngsters are exposed to contagious illness at a vulnerable age and will carry these illnesses back into the home.

While many of us may be cynical about the whole subject of household disinfection, and are repelled by what seems an unnecessary and fear-inducing hard sell of disinfectant products for the home, most concede that at times such cynicism is not appropriate. If we are responsible for a household in which there are infants or frail elderly people; if there is someone in our care whose immune system is seriously depressed; if we know we are handling anything that is likely to carry dangerous germs that might contaminate our food, then there is little option. Extra care is needed in keeping our surroundings and ourselves clean, and this quite likely will involve some kind of effort to kill at least some potentially dangerous micro-organisms. For when the chips are truly down, most households, in self-defence, develop their own search-and-destroy strategies and do carry out some kind of battle with germs.

12

PURGE AND PURIFY

BUGS, BEASTIES AND OTHER HOUSEHOLD INTRUDERS

Getting rid of the unwanted, the intrusive, the sometimes frightening creatures invading our homes doesn't stop with the mere urge to kill germs. Many of us who are philosophical about entire armies of germs respond quite differently to other invaders. These exist in great number: 'However secure and well-regulated civilised life may become, bacteria, protozoa, viruses, infected fleas, lice, ticks, mosquitoes and bedbugs will always lurk in the shadows ready to pounce.'

This comment from the American bacteriologist Hans Zinsser does nothing to soothe the savage housecleaning breast. The disquieting notion of something lurking in the shadows ready to pounce brings no comfort. While it is entirely possible to develop a tolerable level of co-existence with some of these lurking and pouncing creatures, others call for drastic action. The deciding factors are health, comfort and aesthetics. If we are convinced that some creature is a danger to our health, that creature is usually doomed, be it beast, bug or bacteria. If we are made uncomfortable, or if something looks repellent, or if its very presence embarrasses us, again, the offending creature is doomed. All of us have different levels of tolerance, different ways of understanding the menace posed by various bugs and beasts, and different ways of responding to this menace.

Recalling how I have behaved when faced with various invaders, both large and small, reminds me of Mary Douglas's classic definition, in *Purity and Danger*, of dirt as *disorder*. On the whole, I can leave germs to their own devices, for they do not visibly *disorder* my home. But if I know there are fleas in the carpet, cockroaches in the corners, or mice in the kitchen cupboard, here lies true disorder. My home must be cleaned and cleaned well. Worse still, on the occasions when hostile human invaders – burglars and vandals – have been in my home, the sense of outrage and desecration has been overwhelming. For the place to be my own familiar domain once more, I have to purge and purify the entire house in a drastic cleaning frenzy.

In *The Sacred and the Feminine*, Kathryn Allen Rabuzzi ponders at considerable theoretical length the feelings within 'the housewife's' heart when her home has been invaded; invaded by anything. Rabuzzi stresses that the creation and maintenance of a home provides a safe world, a known cosmos, and that 'an ever-present threat to this creation of cosmos is the incursion of chaos'. She continues:

> An invasion of cockroaches, for example . . . is devastating when perceived as an intrusion of chaos into order. Besides the obvious association roaches have with filth and the implication that they are present because the priestess of the home performs her task inadequately, there is an even more disturbing element present in such an invasion. First, it is likely to be a shocking surprise – something that might happen to someone else, but never to me. . . . Still more threatening is the need to dismantle the kitchen so that the exterminator may spray his smelly poisons. Then to discover that one, two, and even three applications at weekly intervals may not suffice, is to be forced to acknowledge the overwhelming strength of antagonistic chaos.

Rabuzzi goes on to discuss the intense feelings of fear and outrage if a home is invaded by humans who have no respect for the order of the household or who come with evil intentions, to steal or to destroy. The threat to the housewife is terrible: 'Her own inner space has been violated, making her feel almost physically ill. It is as if she had been raped. The inevitable cleaning up which follows any such major sign of chaos helps relieve her anxiety as much as it returns her home to order.'

Before examining the impact of large human invaders, think first of the little, non-human ones: the little bugs and beasts familiar to so many homes. The list of these is long and luscious and revolting: bedbugs and carpet beetles, fleas and dust mites, cockroaches, flies, beetles, weevils, ants, silverfish and moths, not to mention mice, rats and, depending where you live, various rodents and reptiles that choose to take up residence under your roof.

Any infestation of bug or pest can find us cleaning as we have never cleaned before. Because over the years I have lived in houses featuring many, if not all, of the small creatures listed above, I know well the frenzy of cleaning and of killing that follows their discovery. My skin still crawls remembering the horror of returning after a holiday to find food carelessly left out on the counter crawling with hundreds of roaches, although even worse was seeing large rats on my front doorstep day after day. Weevils in the flour, mouse droppings in the bread bin, ants in the kitchen cupboards, clumps of spiders' eggs over the baby's crib, earwigs in the fridge, moth larvae in hidden corners, all of these, in my experience, instantly banish any carefree insouciance about household cleanliness.

The urge to kill these intruders, however, is never enough. It is accompanied by the wearying knowledge that if you really want to get rid of them, prevention is the only answer. Unfortunately, my mother was right: if a place is kept scrupulously clean, chances are most of the horrid little beasts will not stand a chance. Household advice books all agree: 'Scrape out cracks. . . . Wipe up spills. Clean out garbage pans. Clean under the stove and refrigerator and between the cushions on the couch . . . Dust and vacuum often and thoroughly – in corners, under things, behind things – to keep pests from nesting.' So says Mary Ellen, in *Mary Ellen's Clean House.*

Once you have dealt with any kind of infestation, such earnest and regular housecleaning, dreary as it may sound, seems like a merry lark. The only other options are to throw out the infested object if it is detachable from the house, call in professional exterminators if the pests are serious enough, or panic completely and move away to a nice new house, preferably in an extremely cold and dry climate like the High Arctic where nothing but the ice worm thrives.

To do justice to all the invasive bugs and beasts is impossible; their number is too great. So consider a chosen few who have created great housecleaning havoc over the years: bedbugs, flies and dust mites. Start first with bedbugs. Of all these invading creatures the bedbug has the longest and best-documented history. The amount of fear and disgust inspired by the bedbug is impressive; it has been killed and killed again with awesome ferocity and determination.

The history of housecleaning has been dramatically affected by the common bedbug – *cimex lectularius* – 'those creatures which it is impossible to name, but which are very dreadful'. About a quarter of an inch long, wingless and shiny, the bedbug feasts on the blood of mammals, preferably sleeping humans, and hides cleverly in every nook and cranny in a household. Caroline Davidson, in her history of housework in Britain, *A Woman's Work Is Never Done*, maintains that the increasing prevalence of bedbugs – probably due to foreign trade – had a great influence on housecleaning in the nineteenth century. After about 1820, cleaning 'ceased to be a peripheral aspect of housework and became one of central importance'. 'The bugg', so engagingly misspelled in some accounts, was at least in part responsible.

Only regular and meticulous household cleaning routines could control the spread of bedbugs; trying to deal with them once the house was infested was, if not a losing battle, certainly a never-ending and demoralising one. Poisons and fumigations and traps and lime-washing and attacks with blow-torches simply could not cope with the ubiquitous bugs. They lived in floorboards and hangings, in walls and ceilings, in every crack and crevice of wooden bedsteads, in mattresses, pillows and bedding, behind wallpaper, in upholstery, in plaster work, in luggage. They gathered in great battalions and fell from the ceilings into food and onto people's heads; they hid in every drawer, shelf and cupboard; they drove whole households to distraction. Maids and mistresses alike, poor homes and wealthy homes all shared the same horror of bugs. Many an efficient housekeeper was defeated by them. Almost without fail, nineteenth-century domestic advice books include lengthy and colourful passages about how to deal with 'the bug'. The anonymous author of *The Housemaid* concludes with a sigh:

> Everything has its use throughout the whole range of creation, but it is not an easy matter to determine the precise utility of this filthy insect. It may be, however, that its presence, especially in the crowded houses of large towns and cities, may be with the view to provoke acts and habits of cleanliness which otherwise would not be insisted on, and thus tend to check accumulations of dirt which might lead to outbreaks of disease more frequent and disastrous in their consequences than those which swell the bills of mortality in the present day.

Destroying bedbugs was a horrible process. '*Ach Gott*, what disgusting work to have to do!' declared Jane Carlyle in 1843, describing the various ways she drowned, poisoned, boiled, squashed and recoiled in dismay from a never-ending infestation of bugs in her Chelsea home. Finding a servant's bed crawling with over two hundred bugs, Mrs Carlyle had to get rid of the wooden bed and buy an iron bedstead, a conclusion reached by many people and one which helps explain the increasing popularity of iron and brass bedsteads and the decreasing popularity of hangings as the century advanced.

No effort was too great in this battle of the bugs. Strong poisons were commonly applied to every inch of wooden bedsteads in the spring; a task which prolonged the work of spring cleaning incalculably. Sometimes the bed was taken to pieces completely and soaked in tubs full of poisonous solutions for days on end, before being reassembled. More typically, the poisons would be applied generously with a feather or with a fine brush capable of getting into the smallest cracks of the bedstead. Either way the smell must have been overpowering, as the lethal concoction was usually made up of corrosive sublimate, spirits of naphtha, oil of turpentine and camphor. Warnings are repeatedly given about the danger of these bug poisons.

Servants were always suspected of bringing bugs into the house. Time and again mistresses are put on their guard and advised to protect themselves from their new employees. Some advice books forbid any luggage to be brought into the house by servants, and insist that everything be fumigated. *The House and Home* (1896) is typical of many in its concern about bug-bearing servants.

> The greatest care is needed in the servant's room ... A servant's room should be cleaned once a month, at least, until the mistress is sure that the servant is perfectly cleanly in all her habits ... No boxes should be tolerated under the bed, nor bundles, and it is wise to insist that all clothing in the room should be exposed to the outside air at least three times after the outside temperature demands closed windows.

Ridding a home of other bugs and insects was comparatively easy. *The Housemaid* makes this clear: 'A whole houseful of fleas may be soon got rid of by good scrubbing with lime and sand, mixing one-fourth part of lime with three parts of the sand used in cleaning. The floors, and any woodwork about the walls, being well scoured with this lime, and the beds being kept thoroughly dusted, aired, and rubbed, there will soon be not a flea left. But bugs are very difficult to dislodge.'

Bedbugs continued to be a major plague in Britain until well into the twentieth century, particularly in older and over-crowded working-class housing. One of the women interviewed by Elizabeth Roberts in *A Woman's Place: An Oral History of Working Class Women 1890–1940* recalls how her mother strove valiantly against bugs. In their neighbourhood in Lancaster before the First World War, 'every house nearly had bugs in. My mother tried her best . . . [she] spoiled beds without end, because she used to take them down . . . and get these bugs out . . . They had all sorts of powder, but they did it more with creosote. They reckoned green paint got rid of them better than anything. All the bedrooms were painted green, walls, woodwork, everything.'

This green paint almost certainly contained arsenic. My father was on several different ships of the British Merchant Navy during the Second World War, and he recalls that the bunks in the cabins were painted this poisonous shade of green, below mattress level, to deter bedbugs. Not that this paint always produced the desired effect; on more than one occasion he had to de-bug his mattress by treating the mattress with kerosene. 'I was so embarrassed about having bedbugs I would have done anything to get rid of them,' he says. 'Thinking about it now, I imagine that most of us on board had them – we just didn't discuss them.'

A woman living in old back-to-back housing in Preston before the Second World War is quoted by Elizabeth Roberts, recalling the persistence of all kinds of vermin in her old house, and how she was encouraged to use DDT. 'I nearly killed myself with this DDT,' she comments drily. Fortunately for her own health she preferred other killing methods. To get rid of bedbugs she cleaned her children's beds with boiling water and paraffin every spring. 'I didn't want to be talked about. There was another woman down the road and she was a bit queer, and she used to put her bedding out the window to shake it. This other woman used to shout, "Take them in, we have enough bugs of our own."'

Bedbugs, so hard and shiny, are unsatisfactory prey, being hard to squash and so dreadfully smelly. Flies are far more satisfactory victims because once they are smacked or swatted, they have the decency to die quickly and easily. A lot of smacking and swatting has been directed their way over the years.

BITING THE DUST

In badly serviced cities in the nineteenth century, flies were in their element, thriving in the glorious dirt. Their potential danger was little understood. In a memoir quoted in Sandra Gwyn's *The Private Capital*, Coly Meredith recalls clearly the flies during his early years in Ottawa in the 1870s:

> As there was no collection for garbage and nearly everyone kept horses, the flies simply multiplied and thrived. They were simply taken for granted as one accepts rain or snow; the danger from them as carriers of disease was not understood. I have no recollection of ever seeing a wire fly screen . . . even in the best regulated households, flies were frequently passing away in the soup or the stew, or getting into the milk.

A few decades later, 'Kill the Fly' became the watchword in early twentieth-century America. As Aunt Polly chillingly announced to the unfortunate child Pollyanna, trying so hard to be glad in the book that bears her name: 'Flies, Pollyanna, are not only unclean and annoying, but very dangerous to health. After breakfast I will give you a little pamphlet on this matter to read.' Pollyanna had broken all the rules by opening her windows and allowing flies into the sanitary refuge that was Aunt Polly's home. Gladly, Pollyanna reads her educational pamphlets, later referring enthusiastically to 'those germ-things' on the flies' legs. She is severely reprimanded; such indecent things were not to be discussed openly.

As Mary Pattison explains in her book *Principles of Domestic Engineering*, the fly 'carries to our food the sickening substance that ends in a list of digestive disorders. From stomach complaint and "ptomaine poisoning" to intestinal disease and typhoid fever, and in fact there exists strong evidence that tuberculosis and smallpox are even carried by the same house fly, as well as many other less known and unnamed disorders.' She speaks of the 'dirty fly' as a creature soon to be eradicated; the mosquito, too, would be brought under control, both of them passing into extinction thanks to modern campaigns of sanitation.

180

Ellen Richards deals with the distasteful fly in her book *The Cost of Cleanness*:

> Just now the war against dirt includes the fly, which has been proved to be as universal and as dangerous a carrier of typhoid as the mosquito is of malaria. The fly that does not wipe its feet is not to blame for the filth it walks over. That danger is of man's own causing. Man himself permits excreta from diseased persons, stable manure, and garbage heaps to become breeding and feeding places.

Thanks to Ellen Richards and other early home economists, such fear of the fly was instilled most rigorously into the minds of mothers. For the sake of the children, mothers must learn to be responsible; they must kill flies and keep them at bay. Advertisers were quick to capitalise on this motherly concern, mercilessly emphasising how flies could endanger children.

'A Fly in the Milk one second carries Death for your Baby' announces a 1913 advertisement for Nestlé's Baby Food. 'Look out for flies and look out for open milk bottles', the ad continues, concluding that the purity of milk is always in doubt. 'But you *can* rely on Nestlé's Food that comes to you packed in an airtight can – clean – pure – that has been watched every minute – that no hands have touched.'

Manufacturers of flypaper advertised their wares constantly. One ad heralds 'The War on Flies' and issues an invitation to 'Meet the Fly Invasion with Tanglefoot', a flypaper which '*Kills the Germ*. When a fly alights on Tanglefoot it is coated over with a varnish that *destroys the germ* as well as the fly . . . *Poisons are dangerous*. The poison does not kill the germ on the fly. Poisoned flies drop into your food, into baby's milk, are ground to dust in the carpet.'

Once flies were known to be germ-carriers, keeping them away from the home and from food became something of a blood sport. In *Chasing Dirt*, Suellen Hoy describes the spectacular 'Swat the fly' campaigns in America in the early twentieth century when the fly was being blamed – wrongly in some cases – for the spread of specific diseases. Fly-killing fervour was fuelled by public education leaflets telling citizens of their duty to 'Swat the Fly . . . Kill Him'. The Boy Scouts in Weir township in Kansas divided the area into districts and assigned a corps of scouts to each district. 'They constructed fly-traps, distributed them among the citizens, covered manure piles, screened the privies, and before the end of the season they boasted that Weir was the cleanest district in the United States.' Flies became a public enemy; referred to as 'dealers in deaths' and 'germs with legs'.

The notion of *swatting* something offensive was clearly popular. Gold Dust Washing Powder invites its customers to 'Make your Refrigerator sanitary with GOLD DUST'. The 'Gold Dust Twins', two little black golliwogs who appear in all Gold Dust ads, smilingly announce 'Another National Campaign'. This campaign was called 'Swat the Dirt'; a challenging notion by any estimation, even with the Gold Dust Twins to help.

'Swat the Dust' would have been more to the point. No household activity has been more tirelessly described than dusting. Nothing has generated so much advice. No substance has been so roundly abused. Dusting was recognised as one of the primary sanitary responsibilities of the woman of the house. After all, as 'An Experienced Housewife' warned in *Washing, Cleaning, and Removing Stains* (1892): 'Every particle of dust is a particle of danger. Never forget this. . . .' Given this solemn fear of dust, a home must be purged of dust as if it were alive and dangerous, which indeed is just how dust was perceived.

Such fear of dust did not become widespread until after the germ theory was popularly accepted, although even before then dust was much mistrusted. Florence Nightingale had strict notions about the importance of dusting. She once warned that the dust from certain wallpapers could be deadly: 'In colouring certain green papers arsenic is used. Now in the very dust even, which is lying about in rooms hung with this kind of green paper, arsenic has been distinctly detected. You see your dust is anything but harmless.'

In *The House and Home*, a full chapter is devoted to 'The Noxious Broom and Feather-duster'. Great is the horror of sweeping with a dry broom; greater still the horror of the feather duster.

Dry sweeping is bad enough, but the most pernicious of all household ceremonies is that which is called dusting. It would be a great thing for mankind had the feather-duster never been invented, and it would still be a great blessing if all those implements could be destroyed . . . The feather-duster does just what, if you come to think of it, it is meant to do. It scatters dust far and wide through the air of a room so as to spread it over a larger surface . . .

Dusting was far more of a challenge in the late nineteenth century than now. A great deal of dust eddied around homes heated by coal fires or by wood stoves; anyone who has ever cleaned a coal fire grate or removed ash from a wood stove can attest to that. And the ornate furnishings, the cornices, the draperies, the ornaments and knick-knacks beloved of the period attracted this dust like magnets. Yet dusting was much more than an aesthetic pursuit to enhance the appearance of knick-knacks and furniture, for dust was considered a vehicle for transmitting disease, a source of serious contamination. As Ellen Richards ominously pronounced in *The Cost of Cleanness*, 'House dust is always liable to be infected dust . . .'

A small article in the *American Kitchen Magazine* of March 1900, splendidly entitled 'Brooms as Germ Breeders', quotes the *Scientific American*: 'The common house broom is both the habitation and breeding place for whole colonies of bacteria, and cases of disease have been traced to this apparently inoffensive article.' The case could not be put too strongly: 'Dust is the greatest source of danger with which the housekeeper has to contend. The danger is twofold: first, because it so frequently carries in its particles the germs of infection, and secondly, because it is so very easy to scatter dust around a room and to make the latter look clean when it is not.'

So, 'How to Vanquish the Dust Enemy?' inquired another article. Simple. Burn the dust. 'When the dust collected by sweeping has been burned and the cloths laden with the wiped-up dust have been washed in hot, soapy water and dried, when possible, out of doors in the sunshine, the housewife may rest assured she has vanquished two detachments of the dust-enemy's forces.'

In the fear of dust, advertisers spotted yet another grand opportunity for sales. 'Watch the Dust in a Beam of Sunlight' declares an advertisement for the 'B-B Dustless Mop' in 1913. For: 'That is what you breathe all the time if you sweep and dust the old way. A War Dept. analysis proves that *ordinary house dust contains every form of disease germs* (my italics), also particles of sand, soot, ashes, street sweepings, hairs, scales, plant pollen and fibres, lint, remains of flies and waste material of endless variety. Dust spreads tuberculosis. It is the most dangerous form of filth.'

Given this state of affairs, the modern housewife had no choice; she *must* welcome new and improved ways of cleaning her home. As Ellen Richards pointed out firmly in *The Cost of Cleanness*, 'The dampened duster and the vacuum cleaner are the twentieth-century helps in getting rid of fine dirt in the house. That the feather duster is a thing of the past is shown by a recent order for its banishment by the War Department, on the theory that tuberculosis is largely traceable to dust.'

The perceived connection between dust and tuberculosis is the real key to understanding the fear of dust. As the incidence of tuberculosis increased in the early decades of the twentieth century, so did the dread of dust. In *How To Be Healthy* (Toronto, 1911) the author describes inhaling dust in the summer on the prairies, how 'filth and even disease microbes will be picked up by a strong wind', and points out ominously how dust from the street comes from where 'men expectorate'. Disease, we are told repeatedly by the author, is carried by dust. A special broom with a screw-top chamber containing coal-oil is recommended, to keep the bristles of the broom moist and to control dust. As in all advice books of this era, any mention of the feather duster brings on an attack of the vapours.

This lively fear of dust was voiced for decades. As late as 1937 an advertisement in *Woman* for Lifebuoy Soap declared: 'Dust

Germs Travel like Bad News!' 'Are your doors dustproof? You know they're not! The door isn't made that can keep dust out. Can you separate germs from dust? You know you can't!' The only solution, this ad declares, is to wash every possible floor and surface with 'hot antiseptic Lifebuoy lather', for 'A baby *is* safer after Lifebuoy has taken away the germs in its all-purifying lather. The scientists who proved the dust danger of air currents proved this too!'

Such advertising disappeared as tuberculosis slowly came under better control and the spread of the disease was more fully understood. Dust was not, and never had been, the major villain in spreading tuberculosis. The fear of dust fed on itself for decades, fuelled by advertisers of products claiming to banish 'germ-breeding dirt'. One Hoover advertisement from 1921 is typical, describing how this machine 'minimises the danger of sickness', getting rid of 'germ-laden, nap-wearing grit' and promising an 'ever-clean home'.

As the repeated warnings about infected dust lost their currency in household advice books and in advertising, dusting – for a while at least – was permitted to be an aesthetic undertaking, no longer an exercise in de-contamination. And if some witnesses are to be believed, it reverted to being a pleasantly ruminative pursuit.

'Dusting makes me happy. It always has. When I was a little boy, I would beg my mother to cede that household chore to me . . . Then, as now, dusting engendered in me a pervasive, meditative calm.' So says Caedmon, cleaning-and-handy-man extraordinaire in Bill Richardson's *Bachelor Brothers' Bed and Breakfast Pillow Book*. Caedmon goes about his work with a lizard in his pocket and an unabashed feather duster in his hand, whistling operatic arias and occasionally falling into a vacant daze.

Contemplating the origins of dust has had a profound effect on Caedmon; in the past a still small voice enchanted him with tales of the motes dancing in the air: 'Chaff, born on the wind from Samarkand. Sand, risen from the baked expanse of the Gobi. Ancient skin and dander from Eden, pollen from Babylon's hanging gardens, fragments of pyramids, shattered bones, beaten feathers, pulverized tusks from Hannibal's elephants.'

Alas for Caedmon's vision, the truth about dust is more prosaic. Although some household dust comes from dramatic sources such as volcanic eruptions and meteorites and some comes from obvious outside sources like building sites, concrete, and roads, most of it comes from our own homes, from dead insects, from our pets and possessions, and from our very selves. Everything sheds little bits of itself every day: paint, wallpaper, wood, plaster, bricks, clothes, papers. As Florence Nightingale explains in her *Notes on Nursing*, 'there is a constant *degradation*, as it is called, taking place from everything except polished or glazed articles'.

Every person 'degrades' in the same way; shedding hair, dandruff and skin. The *stratum corneum* – our outermost and lightest layer of skin – is shed completely every three days, letting loose some seven billion scales of skin, or about one gram, every day. In any home, countless tiny bits of dead skin float around with gay abandon, making up a huge amount of household dust: up to 90 per cent in some estimates.

And so, alas, enters the dust mite. Feasting happily on all these flakes of human skin are hosts of tiny eight-legged creatures that resemble hairy tortoises with pinking-shear jaws. *Dermatophagoides pteronyssinus* by name, the dust mite loves company. Up to two million of these creatures inhabit the average bed; they also find homes in stuffed furniture, in carpets, in any kind of mattress. Microscopically small, the dust mite is capable of wreaking havoc in the lives of asthmatics or of anyone prone to allergies, for its pollen-sized faeces cause an allergic reaction. Dust mites are not readily banished. Anyone afflicted with an allergy to the faeces of the dust mite may have gone through the misery of trying to keep the home as free of dust as possible. Purchasing expensive vacuum cleaners promising to remove the mites and their faeces is one option; purchasing 'dust-free' mattress and pillow fabric is another; the salesmen are, as always, lining up to sell new ways of keeping clean.

Although dust mites were unheard of until the late 1950s,

their presence richly affirms the long-standing suspicion of dust, although for new reasons. Knowing that the mites are there, feasting on our cast-off skin, causes some people immeasurable anxiety; understandably so, if they are asthmatic. Yet in talking to women about their household practices I have been struck by the number of women who fret about dust mites for other reasons, not because anyone is asthmatic, nor because of known allergies, but because the idea of thousands of little creatures invading their beds simply repels them.

'I never used to do this, but now I vacuum the mattress every time I clean the bedroom. I wash the bedding more often, I throw out pillows when they get old because I read that they are full of mite faeces. I just can't *bear* thinking about all those tiny little bugs in my bed,' one woman told me ruefully. 'And I know it's ridiculous, because I was perfectly happy before I knew about them.'

'That is more than ridiculous – it's stupid. You're just making work for yourself,' said another woman listening to this confession. 'Just stop thinking about them. Save your energy for the things that matter.'

'But I know they're there – I know if I do nothing they'll keep multiplying,' the first woman replied. 'I can't do *nothing*.'

When Marcia in *The Limits of Vision* sees flakes of white scurf on her sheets, she too is mesmerised and horrified:

> Every flake of scurf will have a tiny army of mites toiling over it – they are that small, but I can't see them. I can only think about them and marvel at their infinite littleness. I marvel at them, but at the same time their silence, their invisibility and their mystery terrify me, but that is by the way. . . . It would be a fearful thing to talk of. The silence of those tiny mites terrifies me.

Such repulsed fascination for invisible enemies like dust mites or germs is an acquired reaction; a sophisticated response to information difficult to believe. With larger creatures, basic instinct comes into play. If something visible, buzzing or scuttling invades the home, and if that something eats your food, or bites you, or frightens you, then that something must go. Swat it, smack it, squash it, poison it, or show it the door in a more genteel fashion, but that something will have to go, whatever it is. The worst possible level of invasion is reached if your home is taken over, disordered, or upset by hostile human beings.

When a home is vandalised or burgled, the drama and fear and outrage are unequalled. Cleaning up after such an event becomes an urgent necessity for most victims. One of the few times I have used great quantities of disinfectant followed a burglary. My home was devastated. Every room had been – to my eyes at least – ripped apart; everything I owned seemed ruined, contaminated. The mess was extreme.

I cleaned for days; I could not do enough to purge every trace of 'them'. Everything about the invasion outraged me, even the footprints on the carpet left by police officers and the strange silver dusting on the doors left by the fingerprint man. As for the impact of the burglars themselves, I tried to imagine every possible item they might have touched, and I cleaned it; every drawer, every cupboard, every box, every doorjamb, every doorknob and windowsill. Weeks later when the sense of outrage had subsided and my home seemed safe once again, I opened a rarely-used sewing basket and found that even its contents had been ripped apart and turned topsy-turvy. To discover I had missed something in my purging of the house was extraordinarily upsetting; despite my efforts my home still bore traces of the invasion.

On a less dramatic level, I have frequently reclaimed my own home from tenants. I once owned a flat in London which I would rent, fully equipped, for short periods; also a cottage in Canada which I would rent for longer periods. I usually found the places in reasonable condition when I returned to reclaim them, but irrespective of how I found them I always, always, without exception, spent a day cleaning when I took up residence once again. At times this cleaning took me to strange extremes.

On one occasion I was discussing the pros and cons of renting my flat with a group of women gathered in my kitchen. A strained silence fell when I described how once, when I was living in

London, I returned from a two month stay in Canada, arriving back at my flat in the evening, very tired. To my relief, everything had been left in good condition by my tenants. On the surface the place was clean and shipshape, discounting the inevitable buildup of limescale on all the bathroom fittings. As an aside, I often wondered who was responsible for installing dark blue bathroom fittings in that flat, in a city where every single drop of chalky London water leaves a white stain. A young male renovator of Thatcherite persuasions, I later discovered. Not surprising. Only a person knowing nothing about cleaning bathrooms would install dark blue fittings in London.

Safely back in my flat, I sat down to have a cup of tea before doing anything else. Opening the cutlery drawer to find a spoon I groaned aloud. Next to dirty dishcloths, I hate dirty cutlery – spoons with dark brown stains on the back where the handle begins, forks with gook between the tines, stainless steel flatware dulled with accretions of hundreds of meals, silverware black and tarnished. All the cutlery in my drawer was dull, dirty, filthy looking, clearly unfit for human lips. Before I knew what I was about, before unpacking, before hanging up my coat, before opening my mail or calling anyone, I attacked the cutlery; scrubbing the stainless steel with abrasive cleansers and soaking it in a solution of bleach; dipping and polishing all my silver-plated forks and spoons; washing everything twice in hot soapy water; polishing it dry; cleaning out the cutlery tray, and at last putting everything away. When I had finished, I finally had my cup of tea, stirred it with a shining teaspoon, and sat down to read my mail.

One of the women hearing this story gave me a look: 'Oh come on. It *can't* have been that bad, you were over-reacting.' I assured her it *was* that bad. 'Well, if you were so tired, why didn't you just clean one or two spoons and forks and leave the rest till the morning?' I was struck by this comment. Such a solution had not even crossed my mind. All I knew was I had to purge that cutlery drawer, get rid of the tenant's influence, and I went ahead with a kind of dogged stupidity. I remember the activity was soothing, calming me down after a lot of travelling; polishing and scrubbing the cutlery became a way of re-establishing myself in my own territory. Cleaning only one or two forks and spoons would not have been the same, I explained. 'You're mad,' my friend sighed.

No, not mad. Surely not. Just possessed by a mild cleaning frenzy, an urge to purge, familiar to many of us. Not mad. Or – perish the thought – *does* that way madness lie?

13

CLEAN FREAKS AND CRAZIES

THE EXTREMES OF HOUSECLEANING

'You *are* a clean freak, aren't you?' A visiting teenaged girl was eyeing me suspiciously. The washing machine was out of order and for some unfathomable reason I was on my hands and knees scrubbing the shower curtain which was laid out on the lawn in the sunshine. The girl clearly thought I was making an unseemly spectacle of myself. She'd never seen the like.

'My mum isn't a clean freak, not like you,' she said.

What was all this about? Clean freak? Me? 'But you *are*,' she insisted. 'You're always commenting on how easy or difficult things are to clean. You go mad if the dishcloth is dirty. You're always wiping the inside of your fridge.'

How is such behaviour freakish? Of course I buy things that are easy to clean. And when it comes to dishcloths, surely I'm absolutely *right* in replacing them when they are grubby and unsanitary. And as for the fridge – I admit that the egg section annoys me, the way grit and grunge lurks in the bottom of each little round depression. Washing them out is a regular, near-daily, ritual. To be challenged about it and called a clean freak came as a shock.

Others tell similar stories. Jean has often been called a clean freak. 'It annoys me because I'm not sure I even *like* cleaning, but yes, I do clean a lot. I clean to relax. My job can be very stressful. I'll sometimes come home and clean up a storm because it is something I can master. I clean especially when the job threatens to spiral out of control – at the oddest hours, too.' Her husband points out that she becomes most unpleasant during these cleaning sprees as, with nostrils flared and lips pinched, she scrubs shower door tracks with a toothbrush and examines mugs for stains. 'Mean Jean the Clean Machine' he has nicknamed her. 'At least it rhymes. It's better than being called a freak,' she says.

Cathy is another. 'I've always been criticised for cleaning so much. One boyfriend once told me my house was so clean it looked like no one lived in it. I ditched him.' Now married to a man who appreciated her standards when they first met, even he has found her cleaning habits to be annoying. He says with astonishment, 'I've found her cleaning at four in the morning – a perfectly clean bathroom, too. And she looked at me as if I'd caught her doing something illicit.' Because Cathy doesn't like being criticised for how much she cleans she has developed her own means of coping. 'I do what I call sneak-cleaning. I clean things when he's out, or away, or when I think I can get away with it. Sometimes it's so hard *not* to clean something. He wants to sit and chat, and I'm dying to get up and wipe the stove or something.'

While women like Jean and Cathy may fail to arouse much sympathetic understanding as they clean and clean again their already clean homes, in different circumstances assiduous cleaning can elicit active sympathy. Caroline Davidson, in *A Woman's Work Is Never Done*, describes the squalid and over-crowded conditions of urban Britain in the nineteenth century that sometimes drove women to extremes:

> No matter how hard they worked, they never ended up with clean homes. Housewives in these miserable circumstances (and even in slightly better ones) often became hysterical cleaners. They wore their lives away in an endless round of scouring, scrubbing, and polishing, much of which was completely unnecessary.

Davidson tells of a woman who used to polish the coal shovel and scrub the coal cellar floor every day, and of another who polished her dustbin with metal polish and her front gate with furniture polish. Such brave efforts to create clean havens despite the filthy conditions all around were largely futile, but given the circumstances they indicate a kind of desperate pride that cannot be lightly dismissed.

When the outside world is hostile and chaotic and a dirty mess, many try to hold the disorder at bay by whatever means possible. Stories abound of strained and pitiful attempts to keep a home clean in impossible circumstances, like the apocryphal tale of the woman whose house was completely destroyed in the Blitz in London, and although only the front wall was left standing, she was discovered carefully polishing the brass door knocker on the front door that led to nothing but rubble. Or like the impoverished housewife in Peter Hoeg's novel *The History of Danish Dreams* (1995), who, as her slum tenement sinks into a sea of mud, chases dust particles with a magnifying glass.

Creatures like Simone de Beauvoir's 'maniac housekeeper', in *The Second Sex*, however, elicit no sympathy at all. She is a caricature, epitomising all clean freaks and crazy women who, in de Beauvoir's jaundiced view, clean only for cleaning's sake: '. . . the woman is so busy she forgets her own existence. A household, in fact, with its meticulous and limitless tasks, permits the woman a sado-masochistic flight from herself.' The words sweep on, de Beauvoir dismisses housework as the demeaning fate of women, who, deprived of better judgement and insight, accept their role as the burden God and man have handed them. Rather like childbearing, housework is the cruel punishment of Eve.

Seen like that, who but a maniac or madwoman would *ever* do such work? De Beauvoir leaves me with the strong impression I would be better off slitting my wrists in a warm bath. And because of my own occasional outbursts of zealous cleaning I am forced to wonder if there could really be some eye-gleaming harridan lurking within me, punishing my nearest and dearest with anti-social and unnecessary standards of cleanliness. Is there some sado-masochistic flight from myself involved here? Some addictive, mean-minded, half-mad behaviour reflecting a warped personality? I am bound to say no, of course. But then fanatics have never been renowned for self-knowledge.

Until recently I assumed that my own cleaning behaviour was entirely reasonable, perhaps because I rarely discussed it with anyone. Once I began sharing my experiences as a means of encouraging others to tell me of theirs, I realised that many people find my cleaning habits decidedly odd. But so are theirs, quite often.

I don't think, for instance, it can possibly be necessary to clean the toilet twice a day – and with baking soda – as Jan does. I think it downright peculiar to vacuum the lampshades every day, as my neighbour in Birmingham did. I also think it is more than a bit odd to care about a clean oven as my mother does, so that she almost never cooks anything in the oven without a lid. 'I hate things that *spit* on my clean oven,' she says, with feeling.

Yet having been accused more than once of being a clean freak (although never by my mother) I must state a case for the defence here, or at least to point out that unjust accusations of excess are often levied at those of us who have nothing more than a certain – and in my case sporadic – gusto for cleaning. There may be unbalanced behaviour in *some* of what we do *some* of the time, but on the whole we are mostly harmless. Odd, perhaps, but harmless.

The hostility towards zealous housekeepers is consistent and striking. Turn to fiction, to Gloria Gold. In *I, Gloria Gold* she is a clown, a blind fool, a figure of fun, dangerous in her lack of self-knowledge and in her cocoon of domestic security and she must be brought to see the error of her ways. The novel opens with Gloria shampooing the hall carpet at midnight, reflecting that although the pale beige carpet is seven years old it still looks as good as new. She moves on to consider with satisfaction her pale-peach Dralon upholstery, clean as a whistle, as well it should be, sheathed in plastic dust covers. Her husband objects to sitting on plastic, and this perplexes Gloria:

I do not consider myself to be fanatical about cleanliness. I simply take my role as wife and mother seriously enough to be concerned about protecting those I love from disease. God knows what germs they could pick up in the street, when any passer-by might be riddled with typhoid, hepatitis, or even worse.

Gloria struggles whole-heartedly against germs and against the insanitary habits of her family. She is convinced that she is right as she engages in her daily battle against dirt. Books, for instance, those unclean things her husband leaves lying around, are for Gloria simply 'depositories of germs' and, with perfect logic, she decides that the only place for books is in a dark cupboard under the stairs.

Poor Gloria is set up to take a tremendous fall. Her pride must be humbled, her standards cracked. What other fate can await a comic heroine who cleans? Accordingly, as the book progresses, Gloria reluctantly tastes the bitter fruit of self-knowledge. She realises woefully that her whole existence could probably be summed up in six inadequate words: 'I Came, I Saw, I Cleaned'.

At the end of the novel, Gloria is a reformed character. Through a series of increasingly improbable adventures she discovers herself, learns to understand and accept her children, finds a lover, rediscovers her husband's true value, and embarks on a job outside the home. She stops both cleaning and cooking, reaches ringing conclusions about the nature of love and about her own place in the world, and as the novel ends she is proclaiming, 'life is both too short and too exciting to spend the whole of it scrubbing things clean'. Thus one respectable clean freak of fiction is cut down to size, more's the pity. She was more powerful, more lethal, far more interesting at the beginning of the novel when in her unreconstructed state.

Elizabeth Gaskell, in her novel of manners *Cranford* (1853) has the good sense *not* to reconstruct or reform her strange little collection of characters. They retain their oddities intact. These are the ladies of the village of Cranford, women of limited means and interests, utterly absorbed in the minutiae of village affairs, precise and neat as pins in their household habits, and very frugal. The ladies take both thrift and cleanliness most seriously.

When a new carpet arrives at the home of the Misses Jenkyns, the virtues of cleanliness and thrift combine. After spreading newspapers on the new carpet to keep it from fading, the ladies of Cranford get down to the serious work of protecting the carpet from marauding feet, 'stitching together pieces of newspaper so as to form little paths to every chair set for the expected visitors, lest their shoes might dirty of defile the purity of the carpet'. At the end of this account, Mary Smith, the far from guileless narrator, neatly points out the peculiarity of Cranford by enquiring blandly of her unnamed reader: 'Do you make paper paths for every guest to walk upon in London?'

Perhaps not, but in the fictional community of Avonlea, on Prince Edward Island, a character is similarly obsessed. L.M. Montgomery writes of this small, god-fearing, law-abiding community in her *Anne* books. Here in the early years of this century there are countless house-proud women, erect in stature and morals, each running a better household than the next. But Mrs Theodore White, in *Anne of Avonlea* (1909), goes too far. Anne and her friend Diana encounter Mrs White as they are canvassing for the village hall:

> Mrs Theodore appeared at the front door with an armful of newspapers. Deliberately she laid them down one by one on the porch floor and the porch steps, and then down the path to the very feet of her mystified callers.
>
> 'Will you please wipe your feet carefully on the grass and then walk on these papers?' she said anxiously. 'I've just swept the house all over and I can't have any more dust tracked in.'
>
> The papers extended across the hall and into a prim and fleckless parlour. Anne and Diana sat down gingerly on the nearest chairs and explained their errand.

No sympathy emerges for the fastidious Mrs White, but in the same book the peppery perfectionist Mrs Harrison fares better. Her husband has been living alone in Avonlea pretending to be a bachelor and fooling all the good ladies of the town. But one day Mrs Harrison appears and takes her husband's slovenly establishment in hand once more. He is sheepishly delighted to have her back, despite the previous problems her standards had caused him. Some years of them had driven Mr Harrison to shake himself like an angry bear and lumber off to Avonlea to live as a bachelor; a clear warning to all maniac housekeepers.

Mr Harrison tells Anne a little of his early life as a married man, describing the night he and Mrs Harrison returned, a young married couple, from their wedding trip.

> We got home at ten o'clock at night, and I give you my word, Anne, that in half an hour that woman was at work house-cleaning. Oh, I know you're thinking my house needed it . . . but it didn't, not that bad . . . I'd got a woman to come in and clean it up before I was married and there'd been considerable painting and fixing done. I tell you if you took Emily into a brand new white marble palace she'd be into the scrubbing as soon as she could get an old dress on. Well, she cleaned house till one o'clock that night and at four she was up and at it again. And she kept on that way . . . far's I could see she never stopped. It was scour and sweep and dust everlasting, except on Sundays, and then she was just longing for Monday to begin again . . .

Most husbands in fiction are more long-suffering than Mr Harrison. They stay home murmuring 'Yes, dear' in a meek manner, passively accepting the role of the put-upon husband, never arguing, allowing themselves to be reduced to nothing more than potential makers-of-messes as the enthusiastic housewife polishes everything to an intolerable degree. Marriage is portrayed as an institution with rigidly defined roles played out in a way that is partly comic, partly tragic and governed by a fierce domestic terrorism. A perfect example is Mrs Ogmore Pritchard in Dylan Thomas's *Under Milk Wood*, the waspish Welsh housewife who has driven two husbands into their graves and now shrilly demands that if the sun comes into her house it must wipe its feet.

Clearly, single-minded devotion to housecleaning can get out of hand. Humourless germ-killers, spreaders-of-newspapers, and those who, in Simone de Beauvoir's words, spend their days 'ecstatically viewing . . . highly polished taps' are simply not fun to be around. They sacrifice the ease and comfort of the home to achieve what Ellen Richards called a 'pizen clean' home, and even she, a passionate believer in high standards, is firm that 'pizen clean' is a state deadly to live with. Equally, for all her scientific moralising about how to achieve the perfect, efficient household, Christine Frederick, in *The New Housekeeping* (1913), takes care to cover her tracks when it comes to women aiming for impossibly high standards:

> I would feel very badly about it if my earnest plea for a more efficient attitude of mind should result in nothing else but increased slavish devotion to work . . . But it doesn't, please believe me. Its very purpose is more liberty, more leisure, a shrewder sense of values, and the elimination of wasted energy.
>
> I once knew a woman who dusted the back of every picture in her home every day. She believed this was real efficiency.

There seems to be a kind of invisible boundary with cleaning, a boundary between what is socially acceptable and what is not, between what is psychologically healthy and psychologically dangerous. Our attitudes towards the cleanliness of our surroundings range from very lax to highly anxious, from downright sloppy to rigidly meticulous; most of us live within this range more or less comfortably while occasionally raising our eyebrows disbelievingly at others' activities and preoccupations. Those who lie at the outer edge of the boundaries are the ones labelled clean freaks and crazy people, but even they mostly remain within this loosely defined range.

Beyond this range lies a rabid concern for ultra-cleanliness that is by any standard alarming: a truly manic obsession with hygiene and purity that can destroy life, health and sanity. This does not mean housewives who merely make their families miserable by imposing impossible standards, or who indulge in excessive polishing or rug shampooing; this means an unusual psychological disorder that can completely dominate and ruin lives; a dreadful fear of dirt; an all-consuming, Lady Macbeth-like preoccupation with driving out contamination. Psychologists define this as obsessive compulsive disorder, or OCD. It takes many forms.

One of the more common manifestations of OCD is compulsive hand-washing or cleansing of the body. Another common expression is in cleaning one's surroundings. What these behaviour patterns have in common is an exaggerated horror of contamination by dirt or germs, sometimes in a specific form like fear of faeces, or fear of a younger brother or a mother's germs. Compulsive washers can spend hours each day showering or washing their hands, sometimes to the point that their hands bleed; compulsive cleaners can fill their days by repeatedly washing floors, wiping tables, cleaning sinks, doing laundry. Here is one woman's testimony:

> I cannot touch anything I think is dirty. It is mainly the toilet, but then when you come out of the toilet you bring the dirt and the germs out into other parts of the house. . . . I nearly died when once a young man who came in to fix something used my toilet. He just came out and went on touching things, and walking about the place, as if everything was fine! . . . I cleaned and cleaned all over the house after he left. I used disinfectant on the things he touched, even the things he went near. I don't like people coming into my home, not even friends, any more. My bedroom I somehow keep clean. Every other part of the house is really dirty, however much I clean . . . All the clothes I wear for outside, I never bring into the bedroom without first washing them. If the bedroom also got dirty then I would be finished. Where could I go? That is the only clean place I have.

Obsessive compulsive disorder is a serious and frightening condition. It reduces to mild name-calling such terms as clean freak and maniac housekeeper. It takes us into quite another realm in which daily existence is entirely crippled. A regular working life is virtually impossible for people suffering from OCD because contact with the outside world is such a fearsome challenge. Public toilets and telephones become dreaded sources of pollution, other people are carriers of filth and corruption, the germs floating in through an open window can contaminate an entire household beyond redemption.

Few of us, however exaggerated our cleaning habits, come anywhere near this realm of obsessive compulsive disorder. On the whole we manage to carry on with our normal lives, to do other deeds and think of other matters between our little orgies of cleaning. The slimy messes inside the fridge can completely disgust me one day and I simply *must* clean them up, but new ones will pass unnoticed the following week and be allowed to fester happily for days and days until I have time to deal with them. Yet sometimes it is tempting to wonder if someone else's psyche – always, note, someone *else's* psyche – is seriously disturbed when we are faced with reports of extreme cleanliness. Take the stories about Joan Crawford.

According to her disenchanted daughter Christina, author of the biography *Mommie Dearest* (1978), Miss Crawford was maniacal, dangerous even, on the subject of cleanliness. The mania would hit her in tidal waves of insane, almost violent cleaning, both of her own body and of her home. Not content with repeated showers and hand-washing, she would attack every nook and cranny of the house, dragging all her staff and her children into what her daughter terms 'these voyages into cleanomania'.

> Together we moved tons of books, boxes, furniture, and clothing. In teams we cleaned out closets, scrubbed down and repainted lawn furniture. We moved trunks from one storage basement to another. We hauled and swept and pushed and pulled and mopped and rearranged until she was satisfied or until her own craziness subsided, whichever came first.

Christina Crawford tells of her mother's 'night raids': uncontrolled outbursts of anger when she would storm into her children's rooms and haul them out of bed for some obscure infraction of discipline. One day nine-year-old Christina had been asked to clean her mother's dressing room. That same night, sometime after midnight, she was awakened by her screaming mother, who dragged her into the dressing room, demanding retribution because the floor had soap streaks on it. Joan Crawford's anger climaxed in a bizarre beating of the little girl with a can of Bon Ami scouring powder. 'She beat me over the head with the Bon Ami until the can burst open with a small explosion. A cloud of white scouring powder filled the entire room, settling over every square inch of mirror and glass and linoleum.' At this point Joan made her grand exit, and left young Christina to clean up the mess, a task that took all night.

Cleanliness as a form of terrorism continued to dominate Miss Crawford's children's lives for many years. According to her daughter, there was no satisfying Joan Crawford, though one of her later homes came very near to perfection:

> Everything was new and modern and plastic. Even the flowers and plants were plastic. Mother preferred them because they could be kept sparkling clean and were regularly washed in soapy water. There were plastic covers on all the upholstered furniture that crinkled and stuck to you when you sat on them. All the windows were sealed. There was no fresh air . . .

Joan Crawford's insistence on cleanliness is borne out by another of her biographers. Bob Thomas, in *Joan Crawford: A Biography* (1978), tells how friends would arrive to find Joan cleaning on her hands and knees with a scrubbing brush. One friend rashly offered to help:

> 'Sure,' said Joan. 'You can clean the bottom side of the dining table.'
> 'The bottom side? What for?'
> 'Someone might drop a napkin and look up at the bottom side. I'd be embarrassed if it were dirty.'

Interestingly, in an age when so many kinds of peculiar personal behaviour are recorded in tiresome detail, preoccupations with cleanliness are not much discussed. Clinical journals carry academic papers about the extreme problem of obsessive compulsive disorder, but that type of discussion, as well as the problem itself, lies beyond the realm of most people's daily experience. On a more mundane level, those of us who fixate doggedly – at least from time to time – on the ordinary concerns of cleanliness and cleaning are not overwhelmed with self-help articles and true confessions in women's magazines, nor is there much in the way of reference material or case histories if we go searching in a library.

In novels, though, we do meet our counterparts, our shadow sisters, the Gloria Golds, the Mrs Harrisons, the Mrs Ogmore Pritchards. The doyenne of all of these is Marcia in *The Limits of Vision*. Marcia provides a fantastic first-person narrative of one woman's day spent alone in her house with all its dirt:

> The carpet is alive with activity and its undergrowth rich in smells . . . small clouds of bluish gas break free from decomposing fragments of food, mites toil through the pile forest looking for stain pools to browse beside, tiny eggs are being laid and hatched, at every moment more tiny particles of dust descend from the upper air to land in the forest.

Marcia perceives herself 'engaged in a struggle against dirt that ranges across all time and space'. This struggle drives her mad and the novel takes us deeply into her weird tangled fantasies. Spots of mildew become malignant personal enemies jeering at her. The enzymes in laundry soap take on heroic proportions as they destroy bloodstains: 'They crouch over the reddish brown stuff, tearing, chewing, ripping, breaking up the surface of the stain.' Every germ, every speck of dirt is a personal threat to Marcia, and many are alive and sentient. Typical is the extended conversation Marcia has with a spot of fungus that has become to her the 'spirit of uncleanness'. She threatens to kill it with her foaming carpet cleanser, and the fungus menacingly replies:

> Small white spot though we are, we have been elected to speak to you on behalf of dust, fermentation, dry rot, iron mould, the moth, grease, understains, soot, flies, dandruff, fluff, excrement, bedbugs, mites, rising damp, draught, rust, stale odours, cockroaches, scorch marks, rattles, creaks, bangs, cracks, kettle scale, leaks, rips, mice, rats, scratches – in short – the whole *grimoire*.

In the middle of all this imagined, terrifying filth and decay within her own house, Marcia's solace is a picture on the living room wall, a print of Pieter de Hooch's *A Woman Peeling Apples*. This clean, sane, seventeenth-century Dutch interior eases Marcia's household terrors. The woman peeling apples is her heroine, calm and organised. No dust dances in the light beams of the painting, the black and white tiled floor is clean enough to eat from. But then the painter, de Hooch, comes alive for Marcia. He gloats about the cleanliness of the household in his painting, claiming that 'Dutch culture is not germ culture. But you I can hardly see for dirty germs.'

Trust a Dutch painter to launch such an attack. The reputation of the Dutch as clean freaks is legendary and long-standing. They are an uncannily, uncomfortably clean people, 'perfect slaves to cleanliness' as the eighteenth-century writer Thomas Nugent declared sniffily when he was on his Grand Tour.

The cleanliness of Dutch housewives has been acclaimed throughout Europe for centuries. Well documented accounts from the seventeenth century indicate the rigid regime of household cleanliness followed in all respectable Dutch middle-class homes. Shoes were always removed, smoking and spitting prohibited, the floor inspected inch by inch for insect eggs, and laundered sheets folded in such a way that the end used for the feet would never accidentally come in contact with the head. The front hall, the steps, the path were all washed every day, and keeping the public sidewalk in front of the house clean was a civic duty enforceable by law. Travellers coming fresh from the reeking streets of London and Paris noted with awe how 'the smallest filth in the streets would be declared a reproach . . . to anyone that would suffer it to lie at his door'.

Why did the Dutch adopt such rigid, outstanding standards of cleanliness? The historian Simon Schama is convinced that more lies behind it than a fear of contagion and disease. A moral code verging on idolatry might be perceived to be at work here, a code by which the Dutch set themselves apart from their grimy, unenlightened neighbours. To be clean was patriotic and vigilant, a militant defence of nation, religion and family.

The Dutch poet Pieter van Godewijck has one of his female characters describe her soldierly attitude towards dirt:

> My brush is my sword; my broom my weapon
> Sleep I know not, nor any repose
> No labour is too heavy; no care too great
> To make everything shine and spotlessly neat
> I scrape and scour; I polish and I scrub . . .
> And suffer no one to take away my tub.

As Witold Rybczynski points out in *Home: A Short History of an Idea* (1986), the Dutch word for clean is *schoon*, which also expresses purity and beauty, and this word, the very language, may reflect something of the Dutch spirit: a delight in the neat and the orderly. His discussion of the Dutch preoccupation with cleanliness also takes into account the easy availability of water, the dustless marine atmosphere, and even, perhaps, a conscientious preventive maintenance against the damp air. He quotes William Temple, English Ambassador at The Hague in the late 1660s, who explained the 'brightness and cleanness' of Dutch homes: 'The same moisture of Air makes all Metals apt to rust, and Wood to mould; which forces them by continual pains of rubbing and scouring, to seek a prevention or cure.'

Insistent cleanliness was a way of being separate, superior and distinct when in Dutch history the nation was emerging as a republic and when Calvinist doctrine was working to establish acceptable norms of social behaviour for godly people. External purity was a reflection of internal purity, and women were the guardians of both on behalf of their families. Those who cleaned well and persistently were illustrating their virtue and righteousness.

> These womenfolk, neat and clean from without, mop and scrub, wash and scour and polish and wipe all the walls, the beams, and the pillars that hold the building up. While their hearts and souls shine from their ardor for this work . . . *for the impure heart can never be freed from dirt.*

That passage, quoted in Simon Schama's *The Embarrassment of Riches* (1987), comes from a seventeenth-century misogynist Dutch satire, *The Stock Exchange of Women.* As Schama points out, the only women in the satire who are above reproach are the cleaning ladies. By virtue of their work, their purity of heart is self-evident.

In *The Limits of Vision* Marcia senses, tantalisingly, the absolute purity, outward and inward, of the woman peeling apples in de Hooch's painting. No image, in her opinion, can equal this one, not even other more famous Dutch domestic interiors, like those of Vermeer. Marcia doesn't rate Vermeer at all because she feels his interiors are messier, the tablecloths rumpled, things like cups or letters or half-eaten fruit lie around and, as Marcia puts it, 'though the place looks perfectly clean, I always suspect his women of having swept the dust under the carpet'.

Marcia never stops trying to achieve the standards of the woman peeling apples. She clings to the belief that in her good moments as a dispeller of dirt she is powerful, effective, achieving something great and worthwhile. She revels in her power as she cleans. Washing the dishes, she waxes lyrical about the streaks of silver gushing from the tap, the tongues of steam, and she is exultant and joyful as bubble mounts on bubble of detergent.

This proscribed and limited power that cleaning offers does offer us the opportunity to impose order, however limited, upon disorder. And while powerless to influence the great disorder of the surrounding world, we *can* do the dishes, clean the windows, polish the stove. We can ignore the greater chaos around us by concentrating furiously on whitening our socks and dishcloths.

And although sometimes exaggerated and freakish, such behaviour can have a truly helpful role in our lives at times, particularly to those people one might term the heartbreak cleaners – those of us who clean feverishly, often pointlessly, for a short period of our lives when something has gone wrong. Such cleaning helps to deal with the heartbreak of the situation.

Many of us have been heartbreak cleaners for a period of time. Moira, for example, who has a black and white linoleum floor in her kitchen. Over the years, she has developed an intense relationship with this floor because despite her best efforts it never looks clean. Sometimes for days or even weeks it does not bother her, and then she'll have what she calls a kitchen floor attack. When her brother was critically ill the attack was spectacular. For four days she cleaned the floor repeatedly, waiting to hear news from the hospital. She bought new cleansers and floor brighteners and wax strippers, and one evening her husband came home very late to find her in tears, down on the floor on her hands and knees applying yet another magic remedy to restore original shine. Gently, he took the mucky sponge applicator away from her saying, 'You know, I really don't want to be visiting you in the psychiatric ward next week, knowing that the floor has finally won.'

Such behaviour is not uncommon. A friend of mine, after the suicide of her son, went into a state of emotional paralysis. Unable to shed a tear, not wanting to talk to anyone, she stayed up all night before his funeral, and she distracted herself in a frenzy of polishing. Through the dark hours, she waxed and shone not only all the wooden furniture, but the banisters and all the hardwood floors in the house – floors and furniture that were already gleaming. A similar story came from a woman who begged her disturbed daughter to seek psychiatric help and all through the conversation she cleaned the racks from the oven, scouring, scraping, jabbing at them as she pleaded with her daughter to listen. My own reaction after the breakup of a long-term relationship? I found myself at midnight cleaning the stained coffee mugs and then all the cutlery in the friend's house where I had sought refuge. And Annette, who turned cleaning the shower stall into an all-day job when her father was dying. 'I'll never get it clean,' she told me distractedly, scraping at hidden corners with a toothpick and digging out another minute speck of slime. Such cleaning excesses have very little to do with getting rid of dirt; they are distractions offering a manageable focus when the bigger realities around us are too terrifying to deal with. But like all such behaviour, it appears to be exaggerated, anti-social, and somewhat mad.

There are many degrees and types of exaggerated cleaning. Some, like the heartbreak cleaners, are easy to understand sympathetically. Others are not. But in all cases, terms like 'clean freak', 'mad housewife', 'maniac housekeeper' are too unforgiving. Such language is unhelpful, accusatory and damningly negative. Excessive cleaning behaviour in one person is normal in another. In the end, the choices we make in how we clean our houses are ours to make, and make freely. We may not understand each other, we may disagree with or disapprove of another's behaviour, but on the whole we leave each other alone with a shrug, acknowledging that people are free to behave as strangely as they wish. And usually, *usually*, no harm is done.

In *The Sacred and the Feminine*, Kathryn Allen Rabuzzi puts forward an array of ideas about the *spiritual* role of housework in the lives of women. According to Rabuzzi, when cleaning we are *not* generating negative and destructive energy, in the way described by Simone de Beauvoir. Instead, we are creating a sensible, positive world order for ourselves, carving something ordered and pure from the chaos around us. Rabuzzi points out, however, that this activity can be easily corrupted into something else: 'these sacred processes of ordering and purifying . . . are frequently carried to extremes. When that happens, the results, instead of being holy and self-affirming, are demonic . . . Instead of being alive, the overly ordered environment is lifeless: a tomb instead of a cosmos.'

Rabuzzi goes on to speak of this 'demonic' tug of housework, as opposed to the freeing and, as she calls them, the 'sacred' rituals of housework. The loftiness of her language disguises a cheerfully sensible message: that when carried to extremes cleaning habits can be lifeless and deadening, but at their best they are creative and affirmative, a way of honouring ourselves and our surroundings. That is how I like to think of my own cleaning behaviour. Who wouldn't? But the balance between what Rabuzzi calls the 'sacred' and the 'demonic' is, undeniably, a delicate one.

14

LOOKING FOR MR CLEAN

IN FAIRNESS TO MEN . . .

Women have dominated this book so far; necessarily so, for the obvious reason that women clean more than men – far, far more. No dispute exists here; all statistics, all surveys agree. Yet, to be fair, some men in this world do shine; they clean rigorously and often; no task is too small for them, no dirt too dirty. Take Bob, for instance, hero of Bill Richardson's poem 'Queen of All the Dustballs':

> Once – not very long ago and not so far away –
> Lived a man called Bob who, at the dawning of each day,
> Vowed to rid the world of grime and keep it all pristine.
> He'd dab his dainty wrists and lobes with Vim and Mr Clean,
> Then don his starched and ironed jeans and freshly laundered shirt,
> And stride out in the germy world to vanquish filth and dirt.

The Bobs of this world are above reproach. They bleach and polish and scrub; they insist on doing the dishes in particularly pure ways, using special brushes for glassware, others for plates, and still others for pots and pans; they sweep their front doorsteps and clean their cupboards even more often than my mother; they shudder at the sight of mildew or slime, and shine bathroom taps with vigour. Such men really do exist.

But I admit to a prejudice here, having never lived with a man like this nor having been close to one. No 'Mr Clean' has ever

come my way. Trying to understand men and how they clean –
or fail to clean – is an exasperating challenge, down among the
women. Equally exasperating – some might say, futile – are the
unceasing efforts made to try to change the behaviour of men and
women alike so that household labour is more equally divided.
An old and angry set of arguments opens up with the subject of
men and housework; arguments in which no participant, male or
female, is ever entirely innocent.

Looking for Mr Clean, for a heroic, dishcloth-literate man in
one's life who understands intuitively and meets effortlessly a
complex set of largely unarticulated standards of cleanliness is
not a solution here. It is part of the problem, giving rise to
much domestic grief for women. We make the same mistakes
time and again, unthinkingly expecting men to share, or at least
respect, the household standards we assume to be normal. My
own experience is typical of many. The men I have known best
have neither shared nor conformed to my standards. I have tried
not to mind – and failed miserably. Battles have been engaged,
tempers have been lost, relationships have been frayed. These
men can relax with a book, chuckling heartily over the funny
bits, happily oblivious to disorder and dirt and largely unaware
of the churning resentment emanating from their partners. 'I am
not your skivvy,' I have declared time and again, all the while
cleaning as I complained. 'When did you last clean the toilet?'
'If you spill it, *you* wipe it up.'

The truth is, though, men *do* clean, sometimes well. But
for many women, myself included, the problem is that they do
not clean the way we do, not as often. In my own home, the
toilet, for example, has never been cleaned *regularly* by anyone
but me, yet once every three months or so a lather of bleach
and soapsuds and virtue emanates from the bathroom and the
whole room is mercilessly scrubbed, right down to the slime in
the shower stall. And every now and then an excess of energy
and righteousness has been evident in the kitchen, also, and lo!
the kitchen counters are not only cleaned, but bleached, the floor
washed, all surfaces polished, and even the windows cleaned. As
for dishes: 'Just ask and I'll do them', says the genial man on

the scene. Through gritted teeth I explain that I do not want to have to *ask* – can't he see they need doing? And then when he *does* the dishes, something is always left, some totemic offering on the countertop beside the sink, usually something out of the ordinary like the thermos, a yogurt pot, a large jug perhaps. Or the stove is unwiped, or the frying pan forgotten. At such moments, men like Bob, who see all and do all, take on positively mythic proportions:

> Let's hearken back to Bob and to the story that's at hand:
> His mission was to purge the scourge of dirt throughout the land.
> He'd travel through the countryside and challenge every mess,
> He had a thousand solvents to alleviate distress.
> If gallant lords and damsels couldn't cope with rampant dustballs,
> They never had the slightest doubt that it was Bob they must call.

Bob is equal to any cleaning challenge, able to defeat any mess, conquer any dustball. But along comes the massive and malignant Queen of All the Dustballs, who challenges him to mortal combat:

> He smelled her ere he saw her and he gaped at what he saw:
> A tangled mass of clinging dirt around a gaping maw.
> She had a tumbling swagger and she had a taunting sneer:
> She pulsed and loomed and then she boomed:
> 'HEY BOB! GET OVER HERE!'

Poor Bob is no match for the Queen. He beats her with his mop and douses her with ammonia, but she wins the battle. In the course of many plangent lines she consumes Bob entirely, proving that 'no man's match for dust'.

As Bob discovers, being a hero of housework is a thankless business. For men, as for women, little honour is given for aspiring to superb standards of cleanliness; worse, men with such aspirations are often greeted with mock-comic disbelief or slightly fearful amazement. When a family in which the father does all the cleaning visited my home some time ago, his high household standards, which had amused and entertained his wife before they were married, now seemed to arouse a combination of jittery respect and mild contempt from his nearest and dearest, wife and children alike.

'She's peeing on the carpet!' The cry came, sharp and anxious, from the visiting four-year-old child as she watched my naked baby daughter peeing cheerfully on to the newly shampooed carpet. 'Oh well, let's mop her up and scrub the rug,' was my reply. An all too familiar event. The child stood watching me, rigid with concern. 'My daddy will be really shocked when I tell him,' she said nervously.

This child's daddy is tired of having to explain himself. 'Yes, I suppose I am fussy,' he says. 'But what's *wrong* with that? Why do I feel I have to defend myself? People seem to think it's so strange that I do all the cleaning and that I really care about it. And Pam doesn't seem to appreciate it at all. She gets so offended and so cross about my cleaning.'

'It's a nuisance – a burden for me and the children, that's why,' says his wife tiredly. 'Honestly, he notices the fingermarks on the walls and the stains on the carpet before he even says hello at the end of each day. I've known him get the Hoover out within thirty seconds of coming through the door after work. When I took the children on holiday he had the rugs shampooed *twice* while we were away. Every little crumb, every little spill, every handprint on the window is a major event. He can't relax at all he's so obsessed about keeping the place clean.'

Finding a woman who feels victimised by the excessive cleanliness of her husband is unusual, at least on such an all-encompassing scale. More often, women who live with over-bearingly fastidious husbands or mates tell of cleaning behaviour that is directed not towards the entire household, but towards a specific target. A prized object like a car, a motorbike, a bicycle, a boat, a computer, a collection of CDs even, regularly receive scrupulous attention from their male owners. In some sense the cherished object is specific to the man in question, an extension of himself or a public statement about himself, and keeping it immaculate provides much ego gratification.

Within the home, however, many men who are not generally good cleaners can be strikingly single-minded in their pursuit of definite goals. 'The kitchen sink – I think my husband believes every kind of disease lives in the drain of the kitchen sink,' Sally says. 'He is a mad bleacher, he'll get up even when we're still eating and start to pour bleach down the drain. There we'll be at the table, eating our pudding, with bleach fumes rising from the sink and catching us in the throat.'

'Tile grout,' declares Judi. 'With us it's tile grout. Perhaps because he installed those tiles himself. The house can be just filthy, mud all over the floor and the cooker all sticky with food, and there Rob will be with his little tile-grout-cleaning-brush scrubbing his little white lines of grout. I never even knew you *could* buy special brushes and cleaners for tile grout.'

Stories abound of men who excel at keeping mirrors, or stove tops, or garden tools, or even underwear clean. 'Have you ever found men's underwear in the microwave?' one woman asked breathlessly. 'Seriously. My brother cleans his underwear in the microwave. He puts it in a bowl of water and turns the microwave on and boils it. He says it kills the germs. When we lived together I couldn't believe it – finding a bowl full of cold wet underwear in the microwave every morning.' The same brother is a devotee of disinfectant spray. 'He sprays *everything*, doors, telephones, computer keyboard – he even sprayed the neighbour's dog.'

Window-washing appears to appeal to many men. Perhaps because they like being on display on chairs and ladders, gaining a minor form of public recognition for the work they are doing. Perhaps there is something vaguely macho about wielding bucket and squeegee at intrepid heights in full view of the street. Yet Peter, who lives alone on a remote homestead on Canada's west coast, cannot be accused of this. Matters domestic do not preoccupy him, the smell of his dishcloth could fell an ox at fifty yards, yet he is perpetually cleaning his windows; great high things requiring a tall ladder and a lot of work. There are good reasons for this, a marvellous view of water and mountains and a great deal of sea spray. 'You have to keep the windows clean here,' he says. 'It'd be a crime not to see that view. I wouldn't bother if I lived in an apartment in the city.' What is so striking about Peter's preoccupation with windows is that he cleans them entirely for his own pleasure, not in response to social pressure, not in keeping with high domestic standards, not because anyone else wants him to, but because he wants to.

'That's how men always clean,' says Trudi firmly. 'They do what they want, when they want. Both my ex-husbands were really good at cleaning, so long as it was on their own terms and in their own time. I think it's because they don't really feel responsible for the state of the house, it's something noticed in passing. But I *do* feel responsible; even after a full day's work I'll find myself doing some little job like the inside of the fridge or the bathroom mirrors. I'm *always* cleaning.' Her husbands cleaned sporadically. 'Neil did the car, the garage, the windows. Derek didn't do as much but he was picky about silly things like cobwebs, he was always knocking them off the ceiling. And he hated dust on the television screen, and bought his own high-tech lint-free static-proof duster for it. But all the ordinary, dull, boring, tedious stuff that had to be done every day – forget it. Neither of them ever really saw it.'

Forcing the issue is difficult when it comes to doing the 'ordinary, dull, boring, tedious stuff'. Many women give up quickly and take refuge in the martyred posture of declaring they prefer to do it all themselves. 'That way we never argue about it – I just do it all,' laughed one woman, good-natured and resigned.

Not Sharon. The veteran of three marriages, each one fraught with housework disputes, she decided she had to approach her fourth marriage differently. She and her husband are both artists, working from home, with erratic schedules and limited resources. 'I told Frank from the beginning we had to sort out the housework issue. I just couldn't stand it, heading into yet another marriage with all these horrible little fights to deal with. I had to act radically, because I know how destructive the resentment can be for me.' Even before the wedding she told Frank that within twelve months she expected him to be doing as much work around the house as she did. They divided all the chores evenly, on the understanding that if Frank was not pulling his weight by the allotted date, Sharon was going to ask him to leave. She was deadly serious and Frank knew it. 'Yes, it was a shock. I'd done almost nothing in my former marriage. My ex-wife seemed to want to do it all, or at least she never said much about it. This was pretty scary.' Twelve months later Frank *almost* made the grade, enough to be allowed to stay on for another year, on a kind of marital probation. 'I think we can manage', says Sharon, 'but organising housework is a conscious effort all the time, and I don't like having to police it.'

The very notion of making such a conscious effort appals some people. Bill will have no part of it. 'Isn't it enough that I love you?' he asks his wife of one year, Danielle. 'I don't want to argue about dirty messes every evening, and make lists and schedules. I just want to spend time with you. Don't nag me about all that stuff.'

'I hate being told I'm nagging. I hate to think I'm nagging. I hate people who nag. But how about doing the damned dishes, how about the laundry, how about the floor, the bathroom – it's your mess, too – it drives me mad.' That is Danielle's response. Over and over, time and again, they argue about housework and chores and cleaning up. 'I am so disillusioned with this marriage,' she says. 'I never expected all this conflict, never, never. It just eats away at me constantly.'

Bill and Danielle are twenty-five, they both work full time, they have no children. They did not live together before marrying, but Bill claims Danielle knew about his ways. 'I thought I did,' she says, 'but he's so much worse than I realised, and it puts such a strain on our relationship. And I don't understand how he *can* be the way he is – his mother is fanatically clean, but I guess she never made him clean up anything. How could she do that to *me* – that's what I wonder – because I'm paying the price.'

Bill completely denies the entire problem, seeing it as neurotic exaggeration on Danielle's part. 'I am the way I am,' he says, 'and it's not so bad. Our place looks just fine to me.'

According to Danielle the place is on the edge of disaster. 'Without me, it would be a complete pigsty. He takes advantage of me, that's what is so maddening. By not *thinking* about cleaning, by not even realising that he expects it to be done. By me. His attitude is so disrespectful. And I won't take any more of it, I just won't.'

New systems are now in place in their home. For a start, Danielle never does Bill's dishes. He piles his dishes on one side of their double sink and she puts hers on the other. She refuses to do his, and he won't do them until they begin to smell or until there are almost no dishes left. 'He can let a week pass before he does them. And I hate looking at them, but I will *not* do them.' Bill also does all his own laundry now; Danielle will not touch it.

'And if I'm the only one doing all the cleaning in the kitchen and bathroom, all the vacuuming, all the floors, then I think he should pay me,' she says. 'What's more, until we agree about housework, I won't even consider having children. If he won't wipe the stove or vacuum or wash dishes even *now*, just imagine the horrible scenes if we had a child to look after!'

Case histories such as Bill and Danielle's are frankly depressing. The division of labour between men and women in the house is no less intractable and awkward a subject for all the efforts of the women's movement. Sharing housework is as much a minefield as ever; an obstacle course of half-truths, evasive answers, ill-defined boundaries and special pleading. The tired jokes continue to be trotted out; the hackneyed sayings persist. 'She who waits for her knight must remember . . . she will have to clean up after his horse.' 'What's a man's definition of house-cleaning?' 'Lifting his feet so you can vacuum under them.'

Periodically, newspapers and domestic surveys turn out articles and statistics proving yet again that yes, men do far less house-work than women. Roughly speaking, these statistics join forces to indicate that women do at least twice the work that men do around the house, usually more. Whether or not both parties work outside the home and whether or not they hire cleaning help, these statistics still hold true. A recent report from the Vanier Institute of the Family in Canada concludes weightily that 'most marriage partners appear to be following traditional patterns of household work allocation'.

Acid voices have long been raised about this 'traditional pattern'. A letter written in 1787 by an outraged American woman fumes with indignation: 'It is the attention and assiduity of the women, that prevent the men from degenerating into swine. How important, then, are the services we render! and yet for these very services we are made the object of ridicule and fun: – base ingratitude! nauseous creatures!' The letter concludes angrily, 'When one is about a thorough cleaning, the first dirty thing to be removed is one's husband.'

A commonly repeated sentiment is the notion that women are put on this earth to save men from their dirtier selves. In Edwin Chadwick's mid-nineteenth-century report on sanitation, men are strongly advised to marry well, since 'the improved condition of the household' is entirely dependent on the woman they choose to marry. Similarly the Reverend J.P. Faunthorpe, in his 1881 book *Household Science,* describes the science of domestic economy and declares that 'every English girl ought to know it well, for upon girls and women depend almost entirely the domestic happiness of men'.

Make no mistake, this attitude still thrives and is fostered not only by men but by women also. How many girls, to this day, move in with their boyfriends and take on the task of cleaning the place up? How many of us, women and men alike, fall into this mutually dependent clean-up pattern, even against our better judgement? At the very least, many of us have learned to watch our domestic behaviour with wry suspicion, fearful of what we might do in an unguarded moment. Take the narrator in Margaret Atwood's novel *Cat's Eye*:

> Jon is big on purity, but only in art: it doesn't apply to his housekeeping . . . His living room floor is like a beach after the weekend. His bedsheets are a moment of process in themselves . . . I prefer the top of his sleeping bag, which is less septic. The bathroom is like the bathrooms of service stations, on out-of-the-way roads, up north: a brown ring around the toilet bowl, which is likely to contain floating cigarette butts, handprints on the towels . . . At the moment I make no moves towards cleanliness. To do so would be to overstep the bounds, and to display a bourgeois lack of cool . . .

Making 'no moves towards cleanliness' can be a supreme effort of will for women visiting the homes of the men in their lives. Twenty-year-old Elizabeth gave up the unequal struggle some time ago. For over a year she regularly visited her boyfriend's home in a city fifty miles away. He would leave all the dishes for her arrival; never clean the bathroom or wash the floors or wipe the stove or any kitchen surfaces. 'I tried not to clean up', she says, 'but I couldn't stand it. I *had* to clean that place. Just doing the dishes took me three hours one Saturday.' After a year of complaining ceaselessly about her boyfriend's standards, Elizabeth decided to move in with him, knowing full well that she would be doing all the housework, probably for the duration of their relationship. Somehow she convinced herself that this move was a step forward in life.

Even though up to fifty per cent of men are reckoned to do little or no housecleaning, those who do clean have impressive tales to tell. Some men have painstakingly learned about housecleaning and dishwashing and laundry, many of them later in life. Marriage, retirement, the birth of a child, the decision of a wife to go back to work, the necessity of living alone: all of these are reasons why men come to grips with cleaning house.

'I just never knew, until my wife made me look, that dust gathered under a bed,' says Paul, now in his forties. 'My mother did all the cleaning when I was growing up – my sister helped her a bit, but I was never expected to clean. I lived at home till I married, and then my wife had to train me, more or less. I really didn't know what needed to be done, except for vacuuming and mopping floors. I'd never noticed the dirt on shower curtains, or the smell inside fridges, or that grimy stuff inside the telephone mouthpiece. Trivial stuff like that wasn't my concern. Now it is.'

'You'd be impressed, you really would,' an ex-boyfriend told me on the telephone. 'I keep this place really clean. And you should see the dishcloths and the towels, they're immaculate.' Dishcloths and towels provided a rich source of dispute between us when we lived together; I was driven mad by the way he wiped his shoes with dishcloths and cleaned the floor with teatowels. Mutual friends claim that his protestations are true, that this man has become positively houseproud. Having lived with two different women since we parted, he is now happily living on his own with his Hoover. A small epiphany has occurred in his life. He has realised that no woman in shining armour is coming to clean up for him, so if he must take care of himself and his surroundings, he may as well do a proper job. Perhaps I and my successors were complete mugs; if we had not done as much as we did, he would have seen the light earlier. Perhaps we were simply up against a problem of evolution; he was not quite ready to climb out of the swamp of his own conditioning and expectations, but when the time was right he was more than able to make the move.

Women impatient with the status quo naturally want more change, and faster, in men's attitudes towards housework, but the change that has already taken place is worth noting. This is evident in the grim tone of some feminist publications. An article in *Spare Rib* in 1976 describes how one couple battled out the division of housecleaning. Here is the usual tired business of a woman trying to force her mate to take responsibility for domestic chores.

'Together, we had to work out a common definition of "dirty" and "untidy". I've read that men *camp*. Certainly, Dave's standards, like most men's, had been lower than mine . . .' The author describes how shocked her in-laws were that she was 'making' her husband clean house; how she was accused of 'not loving' her husband properly. She persevered, teaching him how to use the washing machine, trying not to despair at his passive resistance to the whole process, ignoring his declared inability to sort dark and light colours. 'All this pretence at ignorance, I found, is an exercise in defiance. Men can't really be that stupid. He not only succeeded in making me feel like a tyrant, but also failed to lighten my load.'

After a fashion and after a while, this couple worked out a division of labour that appears to have been livable. Yet reading this article some twenty years after it was written, what stands out like a beacon is that despite all the discussions and confrontations, the husband in question refused point blank ever, *ever*, to clean the toilet. 'I tried all tactics,' the writer claims, 'from asking, cajoling, joking, teasing to bullying and humiliating. None worked.' She gave up. Her husband never sullied his hands with a toilet brush, never went down on his hands and knees and wiped his own urine off the toilet bowl. She did the job for him.

Relating this story to mixed gatherings of women provoked lively discussions. 'Why are men so funny about the toilet?' one woman asked. 'My husband does clean it now, but I've been at him for *years*.' 'I reckon they think they have to stick their heads in the bowl and lick it,' said another woman caustically. 'Most of them don't even know what the brush is for.' 'Oh come on. You're exaggerating,' said a third woman. 'Every boyfriend I've ever had cleans the toilet.' She was immediately asked for their addresses and phone numbers.

No doubt legions of men still refuse point blank to clean toilets, but they are a slightly more alien species than they once were. A man who expects a woman to do *all* the dirty work is a lonelier creature than he once was. A buzz of outrage arose in a group of women when one described how her husband had been ill while she was away. He vomited all over the living-room carpet and all over the bathroom and then he covered the mess with newspapers and left it until she returned a day later. 'He said he felt too sick to clean up, but he was much better by the time I arrived. The whole house stank of vomit.'

Amongst the women listening to that story, the hostile reaction was palpable, and it was not only aimed at the vomiting husband. Several of the listeners could not understand why the woman in question did the necessary cleaning without a battle. 'But I just knew he wouldn't do it,' she said defensively. 'You should have called in a professional cleaner, then,' said another woman in the group, 'and sent your husband the bill.'

Christina Hardyment would probably agree. She tackles the subject of shared housework in *From Mangle to Microwave*, and she points out that in a dual-career household where there are children, even with all possible modern appliances, too many domestic demands exist for a couple to manage easily. Trying to do all the work themselves means someone, most often the woman, has to do more than is reasonable. Hardyment writes: 'It is possible that men need to be congratulated rather than nagged at for their clear-sighted refusal to fall into the trap of trying to be more than one person. . . .' Her conclusion is that neither the man nor the woman of the house should even pretend to be able to do everything demanded of them in a dual-career family home; household labour should be farmed out and 'properly paid professionals can take over the drudgery of domesticity, and leave men and women enough time to make their houses satisfying homes'. Giving up on the strained notion of being a do-it-all supercouple and hiring help around the house is an obvious solution to housework disputes, but this solution presupposes two conditions: that domestic help is both available and affordable. For some couples this is not true.

Yet such a solution is a good deal healthier and more real-istic than the patronising quasi-solutions proposed in so many household advice books. One after another, such books topple over themselves trying to say something helpful about sharing housework, and manifestly fail to do so. Their suggestions make embarrassingly trite reading. In *Is There Life After Housework* Don Aslett sets out to woo the 'woman of the house' by showing how well he understands her frustrations. In a tone of hushed confidentiality, under a subheading 'The root of housework evil', Aslett says, 'Do you want to know what the biggest, ugliest housework problem is? It's that 90 per cent of all housework is caused by men and children – and 90 per cent of all housework is done by women.' Having delivered himself of this fearsome statistic, Aslett reverts to his usual style of grating bonhomie. In a section entitled 'What to expect from your husband and children', a full-page cartoon features a beaming man and two children all wearing haloes, followed by two pages of feeble suggestions about encouraging your supportive family to share tasks and to clean up after themselves. Aslett staunchly vows to help educate the males of the universe. 'There are ever more enlightened men out there who've always wanted to clean but wanted an efficient way to accomplish it ... Cleaning isn't women's work, it's the work of those who created the need for it, and I promise you I won't rest until that truth is taught to all and practised by most.' His ringing conclusion is: 'Help me out; give cleaning books ... to the groom, the athlete, the son, the engineer, the father.' The implication is that Aslett's own cleaning books will guarantee the enlightenment of men. Frankly, I doubt it.

Deniece Schofield, in *Confessions of an Organized Homemaker* (1994), does not demand the conversion of men, she assumes that women make an undue fuss about housework because they are poorly organised. The whole question, in her estimation, revolves around in-depth organisation of an entire household by the woman she assumes is in charge of the home. When you are truly organised, Schofield suggests, everything is easily achievable and nothing your partner does can upset the equilibrium. 'Next time you are faced with another mess, step back, take a deep breath, and say to yourself, "This is the signature of someone I love!"'

In *Superwoman* (1975), Shirley Conran devotes several pages of equally irritating commentary to 'Your Man's Attitude' when a woman goes to work and wants more help around the house. 'Openly or otherwise, men often resent "menial" household chores on principle (except that they're not menial when wives do them, then they are tangible proof of love) ... What you must realise is that he is being *unconsciously* selfish, emotional and unreasonable. It is unreasonable to expect an unreasonable man to be reasonable. Don't try to deal with the situation logically ...' Any man, reasonable or otherwise, could understandably take exception to all this patronising piffle; the only good purpose it serves is to highlight the eternally uneasy nature of the subject of shared housework.

Ringingly unhelpful comments on the subject abound. In *The*

Second Sex Simone de Beauvoir refers briefly and admiringly to how men contribute towards housework:

> It is tiresome, empty, monotonous, as a career. If, however, the individual who does such work is also a producer, a creative worker, it is as naturally integrated in life as are the organic functions; for this reason housework done by men seems much less dismal; it represents for them merely a negative and inconsequential moment from which they quickly escape . . .

A most aggravating comment, by any estimation. Since this was written in 1952, many more women have entered the workforce, and as 'producers and creative workers' outside the home many of us have discovered that keeping house is far from being a 'naturally integrated' process in our busy lives. Some of us may wish housework to be a 'negative and inconsequential moment' from which we can escape, but unless we have extra help household tasks remain inescapable and demanding, requiring a considerable amount of our time and attention. For a great many men, however, Simone de Beauvoir's observations still hold true; basically, they can walk away from housework worry-free.

Women often make it easy for men to walk away, in refusing to let go of their household tasks. 'To keep the world clean,' enthuses Helen Campbell in her book *Household Economics*, 'this is one great task for women.' Writing in 1896, Mrs Campbell concedes that many domestic skills are open to men, but she rejoices that cleaning is a skill that 'can never pass' from women's hands. Cleaning the home has often been understood and represented in this fashion; as a peculiarly female responsibility, a way of staking out domestic territory, establishing authority, declaring self-worth and virtue.

Lying at the heart of any discussion of shared housework is the thorny question of whether women really *want* to throw off such conditioning about the quintessentially 'female' nature of housework. In Elizabeth Roberts's *Women and Families: An Oral History 1940–1970*, she quotes one man describing how his father occasionally tried to do some cleaning in the home in the 1940s

and 50s. 'My mother just didn't believe in men doing housework . . . I mean, if he picked up a duster he was in trouble . . .
he wasn't allowed to do anything in the house. Many a time he
would offer but never ever would he be acceptable. My mother
always thought it was her job and that was that.'

Housework has long been considered unfit work for a man.
This assumption, strong and largely unspoken, has been held
by both women and men. Look at the numbers of mothers
who did not, and often still do not, expect their sons to do
housework. Many grown men speak of how they were never
asked or expected to do anything around the home when they
were young, and while most mothers now expect their sons to
do *something* around the house, a striking number seem to expect
far less of their sons than they do of their daughters in the home.
Teaching one's son to cook is now common; asking one's son to
do the dishes or perhaps vacuum the carpet seems reasonably
widespread. But how many boys are taught to clean the toilet
or the fridge or the oven? How many are taught to notice that
such items even require cleaning? Not many.

The pattern of gender-specific housework has not been broken,
although it has been cracked. 'Men who do housework are
crossing one of the deepest and longest standing barriers in
human society' – so said William Beer in *Househusbands: Men and
Housework in American Families* (1983). A sweeping statement,
and an infuriating one, but one that is borne out by a vast amount
of what we can continue to observe around us.

Elizabeth Roberts understands this 'long-standing barrier'
neither as a product of male dominance nor as an indication of female subservience. She points out that many of
the women she interviewed for her books were far from sub-
servient and powerless; on the contrary, they were exceptionally powerful in wielding their domestic skills to establish
a dominant role in the home, convinced that their strong
control of the domestic setting reflected the natural order of
things and was greatly to their credit. Similarly Ann Oakley,
in *The Sociology of Housework* (1974), found that the women
she interviewed tended to believe in the 'natural' domesticity

of women, and that it was 'unnatural' for a man to lead a domestic life.

Vast numbers of women *have* accepted, and even rejoiced in, domestic work as a 'natural' part of their lives and as their allotted power base. Many have done so with good grace, finding honourable satisfaction in the running of their own homes. 'It is a great blessing, you know,' one elderly woman said gently, 'for women to be in charge of the home. Because we always have a job and something important to do. It may not always seem important, but if something goes wrong, if there is a death, if your husband loses his job or is forced into early retirement, women have to keep going with housework – people rely on us and need us so we're never at a loss like men so often are.'

Yet in recent decades, as the economic dependence of women on men has lessened, countless women have found infinitely broader arenas in which to find fulfilment and through which to establish identity and a sense of self-worth. As a result, domestic arrangements have required rethinking on a most basic level, leading to the predictable and ongoing tensions familiar in many households. Any woman who tries to do it all is probably going to fail, unless her standards drop. Any man who expects everything to be done for him is inviting the anger of the women around him, particularly if he should be so misguided as to be demanding and critical.

Many women are sensitive on this point, having lived with or been raised by men who could be menacingly critical of household standards while at the same time never lifting a finger to help. Not infrequently, petty household tyrants exercise their powers by inspecting standards of cleanliness, thus dominating, controlling, and sometimes humiliating others. Any new recruit to the army, any new prisoner in a jail learns fast how a rigid insistence on cleanliness is part of the process of spirit-breaking subjugation. Many bullying fathers and husbands have been known to use similar tactics at home, and while women also can be remorseless bullies about cleanliness, the added threat of physical violence is, on the whole, peculiar to men.

'Not good enough' is the reprimand still resounding in

Edna's mind, her father's usual denunciation after inspecting the housecleaning she did as a teenager. 'Not good enough', the response of a man who had spent many years in the army, who insisted that beds be made so firmly that a coin could bounce off the blanket, who demanded standards of military spit and polish from his nervous family. Once when Edna had cleaned the house and the inevitable inspection came around, dust still lay under a bed. Her father hit her, hard. 'It has taken me a long time to relax about housecleaning,' she says. 'I was tense and anxious for years – nothing I did was "good enough", ever.'

Similarly, Geoffrey recalls his ex-military father's ferocity about keeping the home clean. 'He never cleaned up himself – he just shouted at my mother and us kids. He'd go crazy about dirt, especially when he'd been drinking. Once he got totally out of control about some dust on a coffee table – he picked the table up and threw it across the room at my mother.'

Cold disapproval rather than violence was the technique employed by Jane's father, dictatorial about even the smallest details of domestic life; his ominous silences and dark frowns sent her mother scurrying. 'Definitely my father set the standards for cleanliness in our home,' Jane recalls. 'He was really rather terrifying about it. He'd do things like this . . .' Slowly and menacingly, she extended her finger, running it the full length of her bookshelf. She paused, looked down at her finger, paused again, raised her head, looked coldly around, lifted her dusty finger, stared at me, and said nothing: an altogether chilling performance. 'That's what he did. Nothing was ever said, but he checked up on my mother's housework all the time, in just that way.'

In the 1950s and 1960s, images from the advertising world strongly supported the notion of a wife keeping her house clean for the benefit of husband and children. During this period, television advertising developed what the trade cynically calls the '2 Ts in a K' school of advertising, code for 'Two Tarts in a Kitchen'. Such advertising endured for a long time, inevitably featuring two women having inanely earnest conversations about waxy yellow build-up or how to remove stubborn stains. In recent years, advertisers have been trying different ploys to sell cleaning products. Now a wife and husband are sometimes shown cleaning the kitchen floor together, with the man doing the work-made-easy, thanks to the product being used, and the wife giving him a grateful kiss for his labours. The recent Mr Muscle advertisements in Britain show no woman in the picture at all. A man who is an unimposing weakling does the cleaning; his power comes entirely from the cleaning fluid.

Some advertisers of cleaning products have been self-consciously daring in their attempts to cross the gender gap. The Ajax 'Beef-cake' ads, launched in the UK in 1993, tried to sell Ajax liquid cleaner by featuring naked-to-the-waist and well-muscled young men busily cleaning kitchen surfaces. The captions declared: 'Cleaning is quicker when you don't have to rinse. Especially when you get him to do it' and 'How to Save Time Cleaning. Get him New Ajax Liquid'. The suggestion was that real-men-with-muscles do indeed clean the bathroom and kitchen, not just women and wimps.

But as anyone with a grain of sense realises, no brawny model from Ajax is about to come to the rescue in any real households. Like my own vague hope for a 'Mr Clean' to share the housework with gallantry and panache, this is pure fantasy: stirring stuff, as long as no one is foolish enough to believe it or to live in vain hope. Few women do, knowing full well that Mr Clean, the Ajax Beefcake or Mr Muscle do not, and never did exist. Similarly, a growing number of men know full well that the women in their lives are muddling by as best they can, juggling the haphazard demands of jobs, children and home, and that these women bear no relation whatsoever to that phantasmagorical creature, the perfect housewife. She never existed either.

We are dealing with reality here, the practical reality of keeping a house clean enough to be tolerably comfortable. Life would be much simpler if everyone in the home pitched in, shared the same standards, did the same kind of work. However, usually they do not, as countless case histories illustrate. So if someone is suffering, doing too much work, feeling ill-used – and if that someone is the woman of the house – she has to blow the whistle and change the nature of the play. All the suffering in the world, however angrily vocal, however heroically silent, will gain her nothing. If she wants change, she has to pursue it. Only two options are really available: lowering household standards or hiring help. Waiting for the man of the house to evolve into Mr Clean is a waste of time, a sure-fire recipe for nasty arguments, a guaranteed way to become a self-styled martyr. Certainly he may evolve, he may change, and more power to him if he does, but counting on this as a realistic option around which to structure domestic life is not wise. The other options at least offer new and different battlegrounds.

PROS AND CONS

PROFESSIONAL CLEANERS AND ADVISERS

Enter the professionals and the mixed blessings they bring with them. Two different kinds of cleaning pros exist in the domestic sphere. First, and most importantly, the housecleaners themselves; the hands-on workers, mostly women, who come into the house and 'do'. The second kind is altogether different: these professionals do not do the hard work, but are the self-styled experts dispensing household advice from the sidelines; strange creatures giving out many conflicting messages.

Without their cleaning ladies – or men, as the case may be – many people would be utterly lost. 'I can't recall when I last cleaned the house,' Sandra claims. 'Not *really* cleaned. Once I had hired a cleaning lady, that was that. I've never looked back.' 'Absolutely,' Gordon agrees. 'I first hired someone to clean in 1967 and I haven't washed a floor or cleaned the bathroom since. I'm bad at it, and slow, and hate doing it.'

By making themselves invaluable, housecleaners often command from their employers a nervous respect, particularly if their employers are working women who feel uneasy about hiring help around the house. 'I've finally broken down and hired someone', is the oft repeated line. 'And I'll do anything to keep her happy.'

'Oh yes, of *course*,' says Christine hurriedly. 'I buy whatever Margarita wants, I fit around her schedule, I never ask her to do anything she dislikes doing. I could never ask her to clean behind the stove; I once found a dead mouse there, and I'm sure she would quit if that happened to her. And I never criticise her work; I'm just so grateful to have her.' This cleaning lady will not do ovens, nor does she do the outside of windows. 'That's not a problem,' says Christine eagerly. 'I do the oven myself, and hire someone else to do the windows.' She paused, adding breathlessly, 'Margarita is *so* wonderful.'

Having a cleaning lady can and does inspire odd behaviour. Many are the stories of tidying up and cleaning before she arrives. One woman confessed to rushing to clean the toilet before her cleaning woman arrives. 'I just cannot ask her to do it. It's too much to expect of anyone.' Listening to this, Joan disagreed. 'Oh no, the toilet isn't a problem – the problem is putting everything away, especially in the kitchen – clearing all the dirty dishes and pots and pans out of the sink and off the stove. If I *don't* she'll just give me one of her *looks*.' A third woman raised the point that now she has professional help, she is 'freed' to do more cleaning herself. 'I clean up for Helen, of course. And now that she does the regular cleaning, I can do all the special cleaning jobs; like getting the limescale off the taps and grease off the tops of kitchen cupboards and cleaning the light fixtures, jobs I'd never have bothered with before, and that Helen doesn't have time for.'

Admitting our need for help and hiring someone to clean leaves many of us swallowing hard. Much safer, much more estimable is soldiering on and trying to do the job yourself, or so it can appear. Letting other people see the mess of your home or your private affairs can be, to say the least, humbling, and some people simply cannot allow an outsider to range freely around their homes.

'I always do our bedroom; I don't want our cleaning lady even to go in there. It's too personal, somehow,' says Eva firmly. Such comments lead to wild speculation about what the bedroom contains; any cleaner issued with such a prohibition would be consumed with curiosity. Certainly I would have been itching to examine the room had I worked there.

I cleaned houses during my school and university years. I

thoroughly enjoyed the work; the independence, the hours, the curious sense of power it gave me as I roamed around other people's homes quietly assessing them and their possessions. I learned a great deal, particularly about the social graces of employers. Some were touchingly tentative and appreciative: 'Would you mind very much doing the kitchen cupboards? I'd be so grateful,' and, 'I'm afraid the dog has left hair all over the sofa. Can you manage?' Others were cavalier to the point of comedy: 'One of the boys threw up for hours last night, it's all over the bathroom and the hall carpet.' 'You do ovens, don't you? It's awful: I've not touched it in six years.' Then there were the supremely fussy ones: 'You used the wrong cloth in the bathroom last week. Use the checked one, not the striped one, and you know the toilet brush holder wasn't cleaned properly.' 'I like the kitchen floor to have two coats of wax every week; you have to let each coat dry thoroughly. And *don't* wax hairs on to the floor.'

The fussy ones were not much fun to work for, particularly if they never left the house. One employer never left me alone for an instant and timed my coffee breaks. Nothing was ever good enough, and I hated the way she checked up on me. Was I rinsing the floor? dusting the lightbulbs? cleaning right behind the fridge? In some places I was under scrutiny every moment of the day; a mistrusted and socially inferior intruder in the home. At one house the two good-looking sons who were about my age never, to my intense chagrin, even spoke to me. They simply did not notice the person who did that kind of work.

Few of my employers seemed aware, or seemed to mind, that as their domestic help I soon knew a great deal about them and their private habits and tastes. I was repeatedly astonished at what people left lying around and what lay inside the drawers or cupboards or under the beds where I had been asked to clean. 'It's true that you get to know a lot about your clients' lives,' says Ian, who runs a domestic cleaning business. 'I'm always struck by how trusting they are, not only with their things, but with the information about themselves that they leave in full sight – letters and prescription bottles and things in the wastebasket. Cleaners have to be very discreet sometimes.'

The redoutable Blanche White is proof positive that a family cannot have domestic help and secrets. Certainly her clients have none from Blanche. She is the black cleaning lady, the amateur detective, and the heroine of the detective novel *Blanche on the Lam* (1992). Nothing escapes her attention, for 'reading people and signs, and sizing up situations, were as much part of her work as scrubbing floors and making beds'. Her ability to assess a household and see through social pretension makes Blanche a formidable presence; little wonder that she is the first to smell a rat when a suspicious death occurs. As the blurb on the book cover suggests, 'Keeping other people's homes clean can be murder'.

At her workplace Blanche first makes clear who is in charge. 'For all the *châtelaine* fantasies of some of the women for whom she worked, she was really her own boss, and her clients knew it. She was the expert. She ordered her employers' lives, not the other way around. She told them when they had to be out of the way, when she would work and when she wouldn't.' Because she is in their homes, her employers are at Blanche's mercy. She does what she wants when she wants, though she occasionally pretends to do what is expected: 'She lugged the vacuum and a bucket holding a feather duster, furniture polish, chamois, sponge, spray cleaner, and a long-handled brush up the back stairs. She had no intention of using all of these items, but it looked good to have them.'

Being black, Blanche is cynically accustomed to her employers' racial attitudes. 'Usually it took three to five cleaning sessions for a new employer of the racist jackass variety to stop speaking to her in loud, simple sentences. It took an additional fifteen to fifty substantive contacts before she was acknowledged as a bona fide member of the human race.' Over the years, Blanche has cultivated a 'bright-eyed and vacant' expression in order to fool her employers into thinking she is under their thumb, while in truth she exudes nothing but acid criticism and silent scorn for most of them.

Every new household tests Blanche's patience. She is infuriated by the disorganised mess in her latest employer's bedroom; the dirty clothes strewn about, the heaps of damp towels, the junk heaped on the dressing table. 'If she were planning to take these folks on as regular customers, she'd tell him about leaving his dirty underwear lying about. She didn't consider picking up people's funky drawers from the floor a normal part of her work ... She pictured herself holding his smelly socks under his nose until he understood that she had some rights, too.'

Intimidating as Blanche can be, she remains loving and warm and human, unlike some of her fictional counterparts. In another whodunnit by Jill Churchill entitled *Grime and Punishment (1992)* the protagonist Jane Jeffrey hires the unpleasant Edith to clean for her. Edith is employed in several nearby houses and she comes highly recommended. But not only is she dour and silent and unattractive, Edith is, in Jane's opinion, a poor worker to boot. Jane can't understand why some women in the neighbourhood praise Edith so highly and she discusses her confusion with a friend.

> 'People have such different opinions of her. Dorothy Wallenberg didn't like her because she didn't clean very well—'
>
> 'Dorothy said that? The woman who had the patio party and didn't notice there was dog shit under the grill?'
>
> '—and Robbie Jones thinks she's wonderful.'
>
> 'Jesus God. You could eat out of Robbie's toilets! I had a salad there once that tasted sorta funny, and after a while I realized it was soap. When she washes lettuce, she *really* washes lettuce. And this cleaning woman meets her standards?'

The dreadful truth soon emerges: Edith is a blackmailer. She snoops around until she discovers disreputable secrets in her clients' homes, and while extorting money from them makes them recommend her to other households containing potential victims. Edith has learned that 'the cleanest house can hide dirty little secrets'. Eventually, Edith gets her just deserts: she is vilely done to death, strangled with the cord of a vacuum cleaner.

No clinically defined term exists for 'fear of cleaning ladies', but the fear certainly exists, sometimes with reason. Anyone roaming freely in a home can learn altogether too much about the owners, and can wield a lot of power. In a decidedly menacing article in the *New York Times Magazine*, Louise Rafkin reveals the extent of inside knowledge open to her. 'As the housecleaner, I know who is having sex with whom, and how often (condoms in the bathroom, lubricant on the bedside table, stray hairs on the pillow). I know who is not having sex (separate rooms, separate beds). . . . I arrange sex toys and dust prescription bottles.' Like Blanche White, Rafkin indulges in hearty contempt for some of her clients. She scathingly questions the upbringing of the couple who admit they have never mopped a floor or pushed a vacuum cleaner in their lives. Another set of clients she nicknames 'The Anal Retentive Boys'; they will spot 'every nick in the woodwork and even the tiniest paint chip knocked off by a dragging vacuum cord will be noted'.

Rafkin goes on to admit that housecleaners themselves are not always beyond reproach. 'I have had sex in a client's empty house . . . but left not a trace of my tryst. I have eaten food and tried on makeup (but never clothes), and even while my clients are home I sometimes read magazines behind closed doors with the vacuum running. . . . I don't steal, and unless I am mad for some justifiable reason, I won't hide things so my clients can't find them.'

Just a little of this kind of talk is enough to frighten employers out of their wits, or at least put them off domestic help for life. Some potential employers require little dissuading. In Robertson Davies's *The Rebel Angels* (1981), the eccentric collector Francis Cornish entertained a profound aversion to cleaning ladies. After his death, his nephew Arthur finds another eccentric scholar, Urky McVarish, trying to sort through the spectacular filth and chaos of Cornish's apartment. Arthur is appalled.

'Good God,' he said. 'I had no idea it was anything like this.'

'I don't suppose it was ever cleaned,' said McVarish. 'Your Uncle Francis had strong views about cleaning-women. I remember him saying – "You've seen the ruins of the Acropolis? Of the Pyramids? Of Stonehenge? Of the Colosseum in Rome? Who reduced them to their present state? Fools say it was invading armies, or the erosion of Time. Rubbish! It was cleaning-women." He said they always used dusters with hard buttons on them for flogging and flailing at anything with a delicate surface.'

No cleaning lady in her right mind would choose to work for such an employer. Suspicious and jumpy people with precious and delicate possessions are notoriously hard to please; even those with only a few prized possessions can be a nuisance. Anne was forced to make a choice. 'Arlene announced she would quit if I didn't get rid of all the family copper and brass: she refused to clean it any more. She knew I didn't much like the stuff anyhow, so I sold it. My mother nearly had a heart attack, but I told her Arlene was far more valuable than all that brass.'

When working as a chambermaid in a small country hotel in Scotland, I first became conscious of the strength and the power that can be exerted by someone who cleans. I worked with an older woman called Alice who had cleaned at the same hotel for thirty years. She was fiercely proud of the place; in her heart she probably believed she owned it. The hotel gleamed; the mullioned windows and the white paint and the brass and the polished furniture and glass doors responded brilliantly to Alice's daily assaults. As for the floors, never has anyone taken so much pride in polishing black linoleum as did Alice. 'I like to gi'it a guid rub,' she would say, sitting back on her heels to admire the shine. Methodical, unhurried and thorough, she found it hard to be paired up with a young lass like me. 'It wasna well done, that flair,' she said reproachfully, having inspected one of my bathroom floors. 'You didna really gi'it a rub.' Even in the early 1970s, when many self-shining, labour-saving products were on the market, we worked on those floors with paste wax, applying it on our hands and knees, afterwards polishing the floors – again by hand – with a soft cloth. Brutal work, all that rubbing, and not easy on the knees if you wore a mini-skirt.

Watching Alice in action gave me an entirely different understanding of cleaning. I admired her dignity, her determination never to be rushed, and most of all her unflinching ability to control our boss. The hotel owner never crossed her, never told her what to do; after all, she had been working there for two decades longer than he; she knew every nook and cranny, every tile and curtain in the hotel and she maintained it all. She never asked what to do, she just did it, heedless of permission or advice. The hotel owner let Alice be and spent his energy in finding fault with the younger staff. As a North American student breezing through the establishment, I provided just the target he needed.

I did everything wrong. 'You do *not* using scouring powder in the tub,' he roared, as I was advancing to the bathroom with the wrong cleanser in hand. He removed the offending powder and presented me with a bottle of cream cleanser – the first I had ever seen. 'We always use scouring powder at home,' I said. 'Perhaps in Canada you can afford new bathtubs every couple of years,' he replied sourly, 'but we can't.' I had never before been told that scouring powders could scratch bathtubs. 'Haven't you ever cleaned a fireplace before?' he said, seeing the dismal results of my labours with the coal fire and fire irons in the lounge. No, I hadn't. 'Do you know what these are?' he asked, holding out a tube of black-leading and a bottle of brass cleaner. No, I didn't. 'Haven't you Hoovered a set of stairs before?' he demanded. Well no, not with a great awkward upright machine that bucked and snorted like a horse.

Looking back, I cannot imagine why he hired me at all. I did not last long, only a few months, but I learned to think highly of my job. Working alongside Alice made me realise how someone who cleans can be a potent figure, a setter and maintainer of standards with the power to dominate and control lesser mortals. We were all in awe of her.

Despite the awe-inspiring dignity of women like Alice, the image problem for housecleaners remains considerable. The job of cleaning is, for so many people, a last resort, the employment sought when all else has failed, an occupation to which people are 'reduced', the only job often available to new immigrants and people so needy they have little choice. This job is the one famously described as the 'task for which society hires the lowliest, least-trained, most trod-upon individuals and groups', in a marketing report quoted by Betty Friedan. When offered an unattractive job, how often do we think 'I'd rather scrub floors'.

Even the buoyantly optimistic American cleaning guru Don Aslett warns would-be cleaners that 'the status you are inheriting may catch you off guard'. Having worked many years running his own large and successful cleaning business, Aslett still confronts the negative image of 'the cleaner', and he describes – with a certain relish – the social hesitations and pauses when he or his family would say that his job was 'janitor' or 'cleaning man'.

'Most people are just fine, but some do still treat you like a fourth-rate servant,' says a housecleaner who has worked for over twenty years doing private homes in Birmingham. 'I work for some large houses where you are expected to use the tradesman's entrance, and never to be seen in the main living area unless you've arranged it all ahead of time.'

'It's true that you encounter attitudes like that, but I just ignore it. I think the trick is to enjoy cleaning and to value it properly.' This confident approach is that of an exquisitely dressed and groomed woman who runs a cleaning business in London. 'I really love cleaning, the dirtier the better, as far as I'm concerned. I like getting things clean and I try to employ people who feel the same. We can't be made to feel second rate because we know we do excellent work, we know we are essential to our employers, and we know they need us more than we need them.'

The wages paid for cleaning services vary greatly. Louise Rafkin coolly reports that in New York she charges between 20 and 45 dollars per hour, well beyond the range of most in the trade. But to receive 15 dollars an hour is not unusual, or about 7 pounds an hour in urban centres in Britain. Many housecleaners earn substantially less than that, however, and employers often assume they should pay the barest possible minimum for this type of work. The shameful lack of generosity shown by employers earns the undying contempt of Blanche, the detective. She thinks with tired scorn of the 'so-called genteel Southern white women for whom she currently did day work. Most of them seemed to think she ought to be delighted to swab their toilets and trash cans for a pittance.'

'It's ridiculous. Just think of what you are getting,' crisply says the glamorous London businesswoman. She knows the real value her cleaning company offers: 'Much more than a clean house. Peace of mind, time to relax, time to work, freedom from domestic arguments about housework. I'm amazed that employers who get so much dare to be mean, and that some housecleaners charge so little. I'm all for charging a hefty fee – it's the only way to be noticed and valued, and if you believe you deserve it, your employer will believe this too. That's true of every other profession, isn't it? The worst thing is to undervalue your own service.'

Hiring a housecleaner offers the only logical salvation to women who try so hard, and often with such self-defeating futility, to do the 'double shift', full-time work and housework. Hiring help is also the only logical course of action for those overwhelmed by household cleaning for other reasons. Many of the elderly struggle valiantly to keep their homes up to scratch and find themselves unable to manage, for as strength fails and eyesight dims, dirt encroaches in a way that can often only be managed by an outsider.

Admitting the need to hire help can be a wrench because so much self-esteem can, unknowingly, be bound up in our household tasks. One elderly lady ruefully explained that she realised she needed a housecleaner when she slipped on the grease on her kitchen floor and fell. The day before, her daughter had visited and had told her that all her glasses in the cupboard were dirty. The elderly lady was devastated by both incidents. 'It felt like such a defeat to admit I couldn't handle it all myself; after sixty years of doing all my own housework, and complaining about it, I became aware that doing the cleaning meant a lot to me. And it was so hard, being told I wasn't doing it well and should let someone else in to help.'

'I feel I should be able to do it all,' says Jo Ann. 'But with a full-time job, a big house and three children, I just can't, and it was such a huge relief to admit it finally. Now when I get back from work on Thursdays – that's cleaning day – I just walk into the house and breathe deeply and feel lighter than air: it's sort of magical to know the place is clean and I didn't do it. This is what liberation is all about, I'm free not to clean now – and I love it!'

The second breed of cleaning professional is a far less essential creature than the housecleaner, although far more vocal. This kind of pro is the advice giver, the purveyor of household lore. Reading countless books of such advice persuades me that the only proper attitude towards the advisers is one of deep suspicion. But, suspicion notwithstanding, as barometers of social and domestic attitudes, household advice books can be intriguing.

Certain kinds of household advice do inspire a kind of dazed admiration, particularly the arcane tips, the impressive solemnity and the calm self-assurance of some nineteenth-century writers. To be told in majestic detail the best manner of cleaning an alabaster Cupid can be peculiarly soothing to the modern woman who does not own and never will own an alabaster Cupid. But as such advice advances towards and into the twentieth century it rapidly loses its charm and becomes positively harrowing, demanding ever more of its bewildered readers, exhorting them to polish their sink taps three times each day, disinfect the drains and garbage pails at least once a day, dust the walls and ceilings daily, polish the inside of the coffee maker each morning, and so on. And although the advice books now available almost all claim to offer far more sensible and practical approaches to housework than their predecessors, they are none the less downright depressing and astonishingly inconsistent. They repeatedly reassure readers that cleaning is indeed a dreadful bore, and yet a few pages later lay down the law about such activities as waxing floors regularly, or insist that you, too, can have shiny bathroom taps for only a small amount of labour.

Home economists no longer dominate the field in the way they did earlier this century when they were responsible for jolly little books like *America's Housekeeping Book,* published in 1941 by the *New York Herald Tribune's* Home Institute. This kind of book gave postwar American homes their impossible reputation. Here polished surfaces are polished again, and every room is dusted daily. If you followed the instructions, you would be confined to the house and forever cleaning; clad in a 1940s shirtwaist dress you would be lashed to the vacuum cleaner with a crazed red smile lipsticked in place, carolling 'Que Sera Sera'.

The authors soothingly croon that 'no one can be dogmatic about the daily cleaning of various rooms in the house', and then provide detailed and dogmatic instructions for cleaning each of those rooms, with daily, weekly and seasonal tasks described. The tone is completely uncompromising. Venetian blinds must be waxed and polished frequently, slat by slat, to prevent the accumulation of dust. Walls must be dusted 'regularly and often' or they will attract a 'film of greasy dust'. Every room should be cleaned every day, in a prescribed order, and that means daily dusting and vacuuming. The preface trumpets that 'This book is unique . . . the only one of its kind, the first ever published which is a complete manual for the housewife.' If this book is unique, the reading public should be profoundly grateful. Unfortunately it is one of many such offerings.

Journalists, professional cleaners, self-declared career women and avowedly reluctant housewives are now responsible for most of the advice books on the market. The authors generally profess to share their readers' dislike or reluctance for housework and claim to know how to make it all easier. In tones of great good cheer, they announce dazzling innovations like dusting a computer keyboard with baby wipes, or scattering cat litter on the carpet to remove smells. They knowingly suggest ways and means of cleaning so that you will have 'much more time to enjoy your life' because 'who wants to spend the day . . . with a mop in one hand and a dust rag in the other?' Terms like 'lazy perfectionism' appear along with assurances that you can save time, money and energy and still maintain a sparkling home if only you wisely employ vinegar and fuller's earth; 'concise and easy to follow' instructions are promised, instructions that never appear; winning ways are proposed to escape the 'old drudgeries' of cleaning, followed by detailed instructions about how to clean chandeliers or cloisonné.

In recent advice books different pressures come into play: to clean less but keep the house just as clean, to feel good about housework, to do it in a flash after an eight-hour workday, to involve the whole happy family. Frankly, to believe the unbelievable and to do the impossible. To make matters worse, a peculiarly repellent form of humour seems to dog many recent books.

'Remember,' laughs Don Aslett heartily in *Is There Life After Housework*, 'where there's a wall there's a way!' Quite enough to put anyone off washing walls for life, if indeed anyone ever felt moved to do so at all. Aslett goes on to reassure readers that the problem in any kind of cleaning is not doing the job, it's the 'procrustination', that's the real problem, and yes, he means leaving things until they are crusty. 'Some people obsess about their housework because it's their only chance to shine' is one of Mary Ellen Pinkham's many witticisms in *Mary Ellen's Clean House*, followed a few pages later by 'Some people define a "natural cleaner" as Mom'. A little of such bonhomous jesting goes a very long way. As occupational hazards go, humour is a besetting one for the current generation of domestic advisers.

The worst, though, is not the humour, but the 'feel-good' assumptions. Don Aslett proclaims that 'You are entitled to a life of love, fulfilment and accomplishment . . . Time – the time to love, to be, to grow – is the most precious commodity on earth. No one's time should be wasted cleaning needlessly or inefficiently.' Still common fare in books of household hints, just as they were in the implausible effusions of the Cleanliness

Institute in the 1920s, are phrases like 'You can become a happier, more cheerful you', and 'The plan works . . . you must sprinkle the magic dust' and 'You can be as much a Wonder Woman as anyone you'll meet or read about, if only you'll learn to harness your own resources'. Despite the smiling reassurances that perfectionism and a completely antiseptic environment are no longer the order of the day, the image endures of a woman who can, if she tires, be spectacularly in control of her household; who can be knowledgeable, efficient, orderly, clean, slim-waisted, and repellently cheerful to boot.

Like so many domestic advisers, Don Aslett sympathises with women who have found that rigid schedules and cleaning systems and sure-fire cleaning tips don't work for them. He then immediately goes on to provide his own version of these tips: 'simple secrets' about how to clean; detailed lists of duties that must be done regularly, including daily chores, semi-weekly ones, weekly, monthly, quarterly, twice a year and annually. A familiar and claustrophobic world of impossible expectations closes in with his recommendations that walls should be washed annually, floors waxed regularly, freezer defrosted twice a year, doormats washed once a month. Almost every other household adviser does the same, dismissing schedules as products of our benighted past, and then suggesting their own.

Like most others Shirley Conran, of *Superwoman* fame, dismisses the need for a regular spring cleaning, yet shortly thereafter she comes up with the sprightly suggestion that the best spring cleaning outfit is a leotard, and that you should do your spring cleaning with a friend. The inconsistencies in domestic advice are many, and in *Superwoman* Shirley Conran provides particularly rich pickings. She begins sensibly enough, suggesting that a woman in charge of a household should learn to disregard what she is *supposed* to do, and to consider what she cannot avoid doing. Conran recommends simplicity in the home and the elimination of extra trouble: '*Don't* keep pets. *Don't* polish floors. *Don't* dry dishes.' Yet, at the same time, she comes out strongly in favour of a log fire in the living room to make the house look more attractive, and she speaks up for having a collection of 'useless old objects, artlessly arranged, on a small table or shelf' to improve the appearance of the living room. Nothing creates more cleaning than a log fire and a lot of arty little objects scattered around the place.

Conran places herself down among the women, acknowledging and sharing all the problems: 'I find routine cleaning tedious at the best of times and clinically depressing at the worst.' Therefore, she recommends, 'Keep it to the minimum and keep it underfoot. No one's going to strangle you if the mantelpiece is dusty. Your man doesn't love you because you can tell the difference between whitest and whiter-than-white. Your children won't remember you with love in twenty years' time because your floors didn't have a waxy yellow build-up.' Yet when writing of cleaning the house, Shirley Conran indulges in detailed instructions about the joys of making your own cleaning products, and she happily recommends washing curtains by hand in the bathtub, the sort of advice that is even clinically depressing to read.

The cult of the domestic superwoman was so named by Shirley Conran, but it has been familiar for generations. Advertisers have long perpetuated the image of happy, productive women with clean floors, buoyant hairstyles, and time to spare for the children and, in recent years, for the full-time job as well. The same superwoman image has also sold, and continues to sell, books of household advice that promise peace of mind, order, cleanliness and house-trained families if only you, as the woman of the house, will adopt certain means and methods. Such stuff is insidious and dangerous.

Reading dozens of household advice books is bad for your mental health; the cumulative effect is both hypnotising and stifling. Whether advising you to boil muslin in milk or to rinse floors with vinegar or to remove rust stains with lemon Kool-Aid powder, the writers' unshakable shared assumption is that you, as the woman in a household, will be preoccupied with matters domestic, that you will in some fashion, to some degree, feel responsible for stains and floors and toilets and germ-bashing, and that you can be cajoled into buying the necessaries for performing these tasks. The only possible response to such assumptions is mulish resistance and deep suspicion.

There are glowing exceptions, however, books that are simple and helpful and sometimes even funny. Peg Bracken, in *The I Hate To Housekeep Book* (1962), has never been bettered for dry humour and practical ideas. 'Don't just do something, sit there' is one of her mottoes, and she provides many ideas about how *not* to clean what you may have thought needed cleaning. 'Who, or whom, are you keeping house *for*?' she demands, pointing out that it is not for your friends or neighbours, because they'll like you all the better for being dirtier than they are, 'it'll make them feel all warm inside . . . You never heard a woman say, "I simply adore Marcia, she's the most *meticulous* housekeeper."' Yet even Peg Bracken, transparently engaging as she is, prescribes a certain lifestyle: no house should be without a dishwasher – 'it hides a hundred sticky little secrets', a self-defrosting fridge – 'get one', and a large jug of martinis – 'Hail, prosit, and skoal! Let the party begin!'

Generation after generation of readers have received more than they bargained for in advice books. From Catharine Beecher through to Mary Ellen Pinkham these are books that in the apparently simple business of giving practical household advice often end up, powerfully and insidiously, promoting ways of perceiving the home, and perceiving the self in that home. When all you want to know is, for instance, how to remove a mess of chocolate pudding from behind the radiator, it can come as a shock to be faced with homilies about the sacred role of the homemaker, with beguiling instructions to buy all sorts of gadgets, with images of a leotard-clad, spring-cleaning, feel-good Superwoman. Such are the unspoken subtexts of household advice; we are to believe certain images, to buy certain equipment, to aspire to certain types.

Never has the potency of household advice been more evident than in witnessing Martha Stewart in action. This 1990s queen of American domestic idealism heads up a huge industry based on her books and magazines and her television show 'Martha Stewart Living'. She seldom deigns to discuss household cleaning; she simply assumes it as part of her cult of domestic perfection. How to store antique table linen comes in for scrutiny, polishing crystal and silver are acceptable preoccupations, but the earthy realities of day to day cleaning she rarely graces with much attention.

Martha Stewart is the epitome of the household adviser who manages to impose a domestic world view upon her audience. No one has better succeeded in bemusing and seducing women into thinking that 'homekeeping', as she calls it, is a near-religious calling. In her world no effort and no expense is too great to achieve the perfect home, meal or garden. Utility and convenience are scorned in the name of beauty and high standards. If and when Martha Stewart does incline her attentions to the skills of housecleaning, she will no doubt attempt to imbue them with the same unreal honour and glory that enshrine all of her other household activities. An unnerving prospect. And for anyone remotely aware of how household advice has evolved, a wearying one. We have seen all this before.

The patterns of the past repeat themselves as Martha Stewart speaks of 'professionalising' the arts of housewifery and domesticity, improving their image, seeing them as part of a precious tradition of housecraft that can be intelligently embraced by thinking, professional women. Over a century ago, much the same message was being delivered to women: to become professionals, to educate themselves properly in domestic matters, to value their role in the home properly. When the history of household advice so clearly shows women being encouraged to follow impossible role models, and so repeatedly having to break free of these role models, watching yet another image being forged – and this time a multi-media one – is fascinating, and watching how viewers and readers flock to this dream-world, wanting to believe is almost shocking.

Most of us know better. In our hearts we know our homes will never be the oasis of moneyed tranquillity, perfect rose gardens, glistening napery and silverware and Italian marble countertops so lovingly depicted in the Martha Stewart publications and programmes. We know. We know just as surely as we know we cannot be Shirley Conran's Superwoman, Don Aslett's happy woman of the house, or that gleaming housewifely creature of 1940s advice books, so avidly dusting walls. All these books really offer is a kind of domestic pornography: they show idealised, impossible images and settings and activities to an audience that knows full well life is not like that, yet we seem to lap this stuff up, generation after generation.

The ever-bracing Peg Bracken is helpful in bringing any discussion of household cleanliness back to earth. She wonders cynically about all of her predecessors in the advice-giving trade, the home experts who 'truly want to be helpful, but they go too far; and in doing so, they set up too many straw men to knock over'. To illustrate her point, she singles out the staggering amount of information available on stain removal. 'According to the manuals, [the bride] must know about oxalic acid and forty other queer things. She must maintain a Stain Removal Shelf too, in order to hold her own . . . Luckily, though, you needn't believe everything you read. For one thing, nice people simply don't go around spilling as much as these books would have you think.' She is quite right; the amount of attention paid to stain removal in household advice books is completely out of proportion to the importance of the subject. Stain removal is only one of many 'straw men' set up in household advice books, one of many that we are free to dismiss or disbelieve. This freedom to disbelieve is essential, especially if the household advisers are promoting some kind of domestic vision that we know to be entirely at odds with our own sense of reality. If or when we choose to follow the siren's calls and strive for an impossible domestic ideal, we have no one to blame but ourselves.

FLAPPERS AND SCRUBBERS

WHICH KIND OF CLEANER ARE *YOU*?

The whole messy business of housecleaning revolves around two kinds of activity, two sets of attitudes and two ways of coping: flapping and scrubbing. Flapping is random and unconsidered; scrubbing is painstaking and conscientious. These two approaches can mix and mingle with each other; they each can free us or imprison us; the routines they involve around the house can be both comical and grim. Neither approach can be dismissed, for together they account for all the cleaning we do.

Rather than being a method, flapping is a philosophy – or lack of philosophy – about cleaning. Totally unmethodical, this kind of cleaning is often done on a whim. It is everything that the inimitable Ellen Richards would have disliked, favouring as she did the kind of housekeeping that is motivated by 'intelligent direction from within'. Flapping involves no intelligence at all. It involves short-lived bursts of manic energy, often at odd moments: getting rid of suddenly-spotted cobwebs on the ceiling by jumping up and down waving a pair of jeans while you are dressing; dusting a picture frame with a grubby tissue when you happen to be passing; cleaning fuzzy-looking chair rungs with a sock from the laundry basket. The frenzied last-minute assault that inevitably occurs before giving a party is a classic form of flapping; dashing from room to room simultaneously tidying, polishing wineglasses, taking a quick swipe at the bathroom sink and mirror, hiding dirty pots and pans in the oven, and blowing dust off the serving dishes.

Every flapper develops odd and interesting habits, like cleaning the bathroom sink only when washing delicate laundry by hand, perhaps even using the treasured pair of tights or the silk scarf to polish the sink. Or cleaning the bath with scented soap and a facecloth because these happen to be nearby, or cleaning the kitchen floor at peculiar hours with window spray and paper towels or with a few squirts of sticky, self-polishing wax – never mind washing the floor first; or distractedly wandering around the house scooping up dustballs and dead insects by hand and stuffing them into a pocket. Being a flapper is not generally a conscious pose; the condition grows on one when time is short and priorities lie elsewhere.

'You can call it flapping if you like, *I* call it crisis management,' says Nancy. 'When my shoes stick to the floor, I wash it; when the toilet looks revolting I clean it; when I can see mildew in the bathroom without my glasses I get out the bleach. I'm always dabbing away at something with a mop or a cloth, but I never seem to be organised about it. The edge of chaos is always near, but I never quite tip over into it.'

Keeping dirt barely under control is what flappers do best, a mysterious and personal process understood only by the flapper herself. Only she knows what her own boundaries are, only she comprehends her own notions of being 'under' or 'out of' control. Flapping is an impressively incoherent way of keeping house, cheerfully oblivious to decades of rational propaganda about domestic performance.

Maria is a prize flapper, periodically launching herself at her house in a state of distracted concern. 'You won't, you *will not* be vacuuming at two in the morning again, will you?' groaned her husband, the night before they were due to go on a long trip. 'I do far more cleaning when I'm about to leave than I ever do when we stay put,' she admits. 'And always, always at the last minute. Or else I decide to clean when both of us are under a lot of pressure with work. I become totally preoccupied with some cleaning job or other – like the kitchen fan or the skylight, something really unnecessary, but I can't rest till it's done.' Her husband washes his hands of the whole thing; in his view such activity is perfectly ridiculous. He fails completely to understand the dazed sense of satisfaction a flapper can achieve with a little frenzied and inappropriate effort now and then. Such lack of understanding is common.

The term 'flapping' was memorably applied to housecleaning by Florence Nightingale, in tones of profound disapproval. 'Flapping,' declares Miss Nightingale sternly in her *Notes on Nursing*, 'by way of cleaning, is only admissible in the case of pictures.' Miss Nightingale understood flapping to be an energetic and inefficient method of dusting. 'The only way I know to *remove* dust . . . is to wipe everything with a damp cloth . . . To dust, as it is now practised, truly means to distribute dust more equally over a room.' Picking up on this theme, countless home economics texts deliver their anti-flapping homilies, advocating a slow and solemn dusting process. Blithe flicks of the wrist with a carefree feather duster or with an old sock or half-used paper tissue are dismissed with heavy sighs.

My mother, of course, is not a flapper; such erratic cleaning habits are foreign to her. She does her cleaning regularly and thoroughly and rejoices in a kind of hand-to-hand combat with dirt; no corner, however dark and unfrequented, ever gathers dust. A committed duster, an energetic polisher, a great believer in getting down on your hands and knees to clean, she is the epitome of a true scrubber – in the most elevated sense of the word, naturally.

In the streets of London scrubbers abound. No double entendre here, no reference to the colloquial use of the word 'scrubber' (meaning prostitute), *these* scrubbers are professional cleaners. More than one cleaning company in London has taken the name 'Scrubbers' over the years; having that name emblazoned on a van is a sure way to attract attention. 'Of course, all it really means is that we're excellent cleaners', the voice on the telephone assures me when I call to ask about the name. True enough. Scrubbing is, after all, the most thorough, the most arduous type of cleaning anyone can undertake. In employing anyone to clean house, a real scrubber is what you want. Flappers are altogether too flighty.

The true scrubber not only does battle with dirt but truly believes that, for a few brief shining moments at least, it is possible to *win*, to vanquish that dirt, to put it in its proper place. Cleaning propaganda has long nurtured this idea of conquering dirt in a kind of domestic warfare. Headlines like 'First Aid to the Housewife' have appeared in women's magazines, along with lists of 'Weapons for the Spring Assault upon Dirt'. Domestic advice books issue stirring statements about 'the daily battle against dirt', and folksongs such as 'The Housewife's Lament', which dates back to the mid-nineteenth century, also celebrate the never-ending battle:

> In March it is mud, it is slush in December,
> The midsummer breezes are loaded with dust.
> In fall the leaves litter, in muddy September
> The wallpaper rots and the candlesticks rust . . .
>
> With grease and with grime from corner to centre,
> Forever at war and forever alert.
> No rest for a day lest the enemy enter,
> I spend my whole life in struggle with dirt.

Flappers know that this war with dirt – if it even exists – cannot be won, so they see no point engaging in battle in the first place. Sometimes this attitude is hard won, for within many flappers lurk vestiges of a scrubbing mentality. 'Your house is much dirtier since my dad moved in.' So announced a ten-year-old girl to her father's new wife, in tones of deep approval. 'I took that as a compliment,' the new wife says with a laugh. 'I consciously decided to do less cleaning when we moved in together, or life would have been unliveable. My place used to be immaculate; it was easy to keep that way by myself. Now we're all together I just look the other way and *make* myself do nothing. I make sure I'm too busy to get worked up about it.'

Some committed scrubbers find that looking the other way is impossible, even when in other people's homes they look around suspiciously for dirt. 'I had a friend,' Deidre recalls, 'who would bring her little girl over to my house, and this child was always dressed in white tights that showed every speck of dirt. This friend said that she used her daughter's white tights to check up on other people's housekeeping standards. I think she really meant it. I wanted to run when I saw her coming to the door.' She paused, adding venomously, 'That woman's house was so clean, she probably put newspaper under her cuckoo clock.'

Scrubbers are in the minority, but not by a great margin. For every two or three people who lay claim to slapdash flapper habits, at least one scrubber can counter with stories of extreme thoroughness, at least in relation to specific activities. I think of the woman, a mother of five, who sweeps her hall and kitchen three times every day without fail. I think of all the impassioned disinfectors, using disinfectants and bleach daily, on toilets, on doorknobs, in kitchen sinks, in drains. I recall the woman with two young children, living in a small suburban bungalow: she is one of those increasingly rare beings who keeps to such a rigid cleaning schedule (dusting Mondays, vacuuming Tuesdays, windows every second Wednesday) that she almost never goes out. I think of the extraordinary shine on everything in my neighbour Cathy's house, how she refuses to use a toilet brush because it doesn't clean the toilet well enough, how she arrived to visit late one evening and announced with evident self-satisfaction that she had just finished bleaching the inside of her fridge. Everyone in the room looked at her in silent disbelief.

'Are you thinking I should have better things to do?' she asked defiantly. 'But I *liked* doing it. I *hate* dirty fridges.' Scrubbers have a hard time socially; their private passion for cleaning – if they are rash enough to mention it – is so often met with blank incomprehension. Like Shelley, in the murder mystery *Grime and Punishment*:

> Shelley regarded her mania for cleanliness as an affliction. 'I know it's shallow of me, but I really love to clean,' she'd said once. 'You know my favorite shopping place in the world? The hardware store – the section with the industrial cleaners and mops and buckets. I sneak in sometimes just to look at the new products . . .'

This particular passion for cleaning pays off. It proves Shelley's innocence to her friend Jane. When the cleaning lady is murdered in Shelley's house, Jane knows her friend is not guilty. 'I knew you wouldn't risk messing your house up. If you were going to kill somebody, you'd do it where you wouldn't have to clean up afterwards.'

To distinguish flappers from scrubbers is something of an art, for they often adopt each other's characteristics. Many people combine the two approaches; flappers can veer off course and become scrubbers for a while: if, for instance, their mothers are coming to visit. Scrubbers may be subject only to sporadic or partial fits of deep-cleaning, and otherwise can lapse into long periods of mere flapping.

Nothing shows the cross-breeding of the two types better than examining attitudes towards dishcloths or kitchen cloths, or sponges, or J-cloths, or whatever is used to *wipe up* in the kitchen. The most fastidious scrubbers can be surprisingly easygoing about these, while certain flappers astonish their friends by speaking in hushed tones of having a bucket of bleach solution always at the ready underneath the sink, especially for dishcloths.

'You do *not* wipe the baby's face with the dishcloth, do you? And don't tell me you use it on the floor too?' Barbara's voice was full of dismay. 'That is *so* disgusting.' This woman claims to be entirely nonchalant about housecleaning, she takes pride in her liberated attitude, often declaring 'I clean to live, I don't live to clean', yet she bleaches her dishcloths daily and never, ever uses them on the floor and cannot bear my own more relaxed approach. Mary is even more rigid. Although her standards in most matters domestic are barely average, she has a collection of *four* cloths hanging above her sink: one for countertops and tables, one for dishes, one for the floor, and one for the baby's face. By contrast, my neighbour Cathy, whose standards are far beyond the reach of most mortals, happily swabs her children's faces and most kitchen surfaces with the dishcloth. 'But I'd never use it on the floor, of course, and I change it every day.' Finally my mother who, with all her passion for scrubbing and shining, is robustly indifferent to dishcloths; she uses them for everything. When I explained that there were *three* cloths in my kitchen, one for the dishes, one for the floor and one for the baby's face, she gave me a pitying glance and said, 'You'll soon be using one for everything.' 'Oh no I won't, you'll see,' was my reply. She did see. Keeping all those cloths separate quickly defeated me. Now I have reverted to one – frequently changed and washed, but only one, and use it for every imaginable surface or spill.

Whether we flap or scrub, the activities of cleaning often signify something quite apart from the business of chasing dirt. For anyone who works from home they provide an unsurpassed means of procrastination. 'I usually sweep the floor five or six times a day when I'm working,' a colleague confided. 'It's my favourite way to put off writing.' Alice Munroe says much the same: 'I was brought up to be a good housewife. . . . But there's apt to be chaos underneath – in the backs of closets or cupboards – and it's the knowledge of this chaos which I use to keep myself from writing. I can get into housework very, very quickly, because I get a whole lot of virtuous feelings not from writing but from cleaning.'

The virtuous feelings aroused by cleaning apply most particularly to a quiet and committed kind of scrubbing, the sort of cleaning I have rarely done unless someone has paid me to do it. In my own home, I am usually too distracted to enjoy the expansive and calm sense of virtuous achievement that I knew when working as a housecleaner. The silent concentration of being on my own in a house, cleaning methodically and without interruption, remains powerful in my memory. My best moments were leaving the houses behind, quiet and clean, shutting the doors and knowing that a small and decent job had been done well. That level of simple satisfaction has rarely been equalled in all my subsequent work.

In *The Sacred and the Feminine*, Kathryn Allen Rabuzzi explores what she calls the 'cultic ritual' aspect of housework. She points out that doing housework can hold meaning in and of itself, quite apart from the ends that may or may not be achieved, and she maintains this meaning can take on near-religious dimensions. Pretty far-fetched stuff, I thought, on first reading Rabuzzi, but then people began to tell me in detail about their housecleaning practices. Now I have to agree with her, having so often heard women talk of the calming effect that cleaning has upon them; the virtuous radiance it sometimes imparts.

'*Faire le ménage, c'est Zen*,' says Céline. One of a large family from rural Quebec, she hated the disorganised mess in the crowded farmhouse where she grew up. Determined to distance herself from this background, she now maintains a discreetly perfect suburban home, paying close attention to details; the chrome rings on the stove always shine, the children's bath toys are free of slime, the tile grout is free of mildew, the perfection of the ordered linen cupboard is dazzling. Cleaning is a soothing, concentrated act for her, something she makes time for every day like a kind of meditation, a way in which peace and quiet and beauty and ritual enter her home.

Zen and the art of housecleaning have been mentioned in the same breath by a surprising number of people, most notable of whom is Ruth. As a single parent without much money, Ruth had been dreading the usual eight-hour blitz on the house that she generally forced herself to undertake before her mother came to visit. In a moment of rebellion she called her mother before the latest visit to say that she could not do the cleaning this time, and her mother would have to bear with a dirty house. A chilly pause on the other end of the phone, before her mother said firmly, 'I will send you money to hire a cleaner'.

Outmanoeuvred, Ruth dumbly went forth to find one. At a local coffee house she found a card announcing, in calligraphic curlicues, 'Zen Cleaner'. Ruth called, explaining that she could only afford to hire the Zen Cleaner for eight hours. The cleaner, a most pleasant woman, agreed, and at the appointed time she arrived, kindly bearing a loaf of homemade bread and a pot of fresh strawberry jam for Ruth. They agreed that she would work for two days, four hours each day, and that most important was to clean the kitchen stove, after which the rest of the kitchen would be tackled, followed by the basement.

Ruth went out and after nearly three hours returned, hopes high, to find her cleaner, with an air of trancelike calm, was still cleaning the stove. After another half-hour the stove was not yet finished. When Ruth nervously asked how it was going, the woman replied dreamily, 'The stove is much quieter now, can't you tell? But it's not Zen yet.'

'Quieter?' thought Ruth. 'The stove is quieter?' She swallowed hard. 'Look,' she said. 'I think we need to talk.' It was time to find out the real meaning of 'Zen' cleaning.

'Going back to the beginning of all things,' her cleaner explained.

'Do you mean going back into factory conditions of cleanliness?' Yes, was the answer. 'I don't think I can quite afford that,' said Ruth humbly.

'Could you ask your mother for more money?' asked the woman, ever patient with her clients.

'I felt I was violating her religious principles in asking her to hurry up,' says Ruth, 'but I had to be quite tough. I said we would have to forget about Zen for now, and I assigned a list of tasks with time limits. Half an hour more for the stove, half an hour for the fridge, twenty minutes for the floor, an hour for the cupboards, and so on.'

When the time was up, Ruth was left with a half-cleaned kitchen, a pot of jam and half a loaf of bread. Yet to her astonishment, she has found that this encounter has transformed her cleaning methods. 'I thought it was such pretentious nonsense, when she talked about how something is so quiet, so calm, when properly cleaned. But now, when cleaning anything, I find I'm almost listening to it. Just the other day I was scrubbing a filthy old door and as it became clean the wood grain shone through, and I began to stroke the door, and polish it, and take real interest in it, and I felt everything becoming quiet. That door had a real serenity about it. Honestly, I've come to believe that if you clean something well it does become quieter. And now I understand my mother better: perhaps there was an unacknowledged spiritual quality to all that cleaning she always did in our house, taking things back to a state of newness, going back to the beginning, to a kind of purity. So I've given up resenting how my mother brought me up – I'm trying to understand it as Zen.'

While all this may sound like an effort to believe far too many impossible things before breakfast, it helps Ruth deal with her mother. 'Now when she visits, I don't even comment if she cleans the kitchen. I just tell her that she is reaching a new plane of spirituality; the very idea has almost scared her off completely.'

To reach an exalted plane of consciousness through cleaning is an achievement beyond most of us. The mundane repetitiveness of household chores, and the sheer volume of them, and our own busy schedules all mitigate against it. 'As I grow older I like order and cleanliness more but because there are more people around me, I have less and less of it. I'm not calmer about it, I'm more frazzled and fed up.' So says Eva, now in her forties with a full-time job and a family. 'In my twenties when I lived alone I actually washed the kitchen floor once a week and enjoyed it. Now I don't even sweep it once a week. When I do clean I use cleaners full of poisonous chemicals and I *know* I shouldn't, but they're fast and they work and I try not to think about it except when I lie in bed at night feeling guilty about the environment.'

As though adding to the burden of women like Eva, advice about appropriate cleaning solutions pours forth from domestic advice books and newspaper columns. Green-cleaning enthusiasts speak of the joys of whitening socks by boiling them with a slice of lemon, of using copious amounts of baking soda, cornstarch and vinegar around the house. Bracing instructions about making your own cleaning compounds, green or otherwise, appear in the most unlikely places.

Superwoman's Shirley Conran is one of the most adamant

about making household cleaners. 'To make a good selection takes less time than baking a cake,' she enthuses, admitting, however, that amassing all the ingredients can take quite a while. She promises that making your own cleaners saves 'wads of money', and that 'you will get an *instant* reputation as an old-fashioned, real homemaker.' She fails to explain why anyone would *want* such a reputation, but let that pass.

Conran's particular favourites amongst her recipes for cleaning products are a window-cleaner that combines kerosene, water and rubbing alcohol and, for furniture polish, a brew of turpentine, linseed oil and water: 'Takes a lot of rubbing, but you get a good shine,' she says cheerily. Hideous as that sounds, it pales alongside her recipe for toilet-cleaner which combines sodium bicarbonate and caustic soda and comes with the Conran warning of 'wear gloves, it's dangerous'. More alarming still is her recommended method of cleaning the oven, invoking a steaming concoction of caustic soda, flour and water, applied with a mop while wearing gloves and, I would assume, a breathing mask and goggles. She emphasises the strength, and the potential danger, of the main ingredients of most household cleaning products, and she provides a list of them: soap, washing soda, trisodium phosphate (TSP), ammonia, alcohol, bleach, caustic soda, vinegar, kerosene, turpentine and paraffin beeswax. A powerful, grim-sounding list it is, many of its components found in the 'receipts' in the back of nineteenth-century household advice books.

'I won't,' objected one woman strenuously. 'I just will *not* go back to mixing up horrible messes like those and using fuller's earth and beeswax and smelly hard yellow soap. I like buying cleaning products in shining plastic bottles with big nozzles, the kind you see on television. I like having *lots* of them, smelling wonderful and zapping the dirt and making things squeaky clean. And I won't feel bad about it!'

Flappers and scrubbers alike struggle with the cleaning solution conundrum. Some dedicated scrubbers whip up their own steamingly caustic oven cleaners without a qualm; they take to baking soda effortlessly, and happily boil their white socks with lemon slices; others cling with religious fervour to the bleach bottle and all the seductive products from the enchanted supermarket aisles. Flappers tend to be confused. Try as they might to make their own products or use politically correct substances, flappers never quite understand how *much* baking soda to use in the toilet, and wonder lamely if the lemon is meant to disintegrate as it does when boiled, leaving bits of mushy pulp all over their socks. Generally they lack the needed dedication.

Hybrid cleaners, part flapper and part scrubber, like myself, often develop stubborn affections for certain cleaning products and persist in using them no matter what anyone says. Vinegar, for instance. 'Dead vegetation can turn into oil and gas faster than vinegar sometimes takes to clean. Better to do something really useful with vinegar, like make Worcestershire sauce.' So says a scathing article in Toronto's *Globe and Mail*. Don Aslett, in *Is There Life After Housework?*, agrees, pointing out that because vinegar is acidic it is useless in combating grease, which is also acidic; vinegar's only proper use is as a rinsing agent. But such arguments often fall on deaf ears.

Because I *like* using vinegar and have developed a touching faith in it over the last twenty odd years, I will not be deterred. Even after reading so many unenthusiastic reports, I continue to wash windows with vinegar, soak pans in it, use it in the laundry and clean carpets with it. Rational critics might prove me wrong, try to dissuade me, but just as my mother likes to shine every bit of furniture in sight, preferably with the hardest paste wax on the market – a purely aesthetic, altogether unnecessary activity – I like to use vinegar. Neither of us is likely to change.

Once any idea about cleaning takes root in a person's head, flapper or scrubber, dislodging such an idea is difficult. A young woman I know comes from a small coal-mining village, now lives hundreds of miles from there, but continues to clean her house as though coal dust were lying thickly on every surface. 'It doesn't seem right *not* to wash the walls twice a year,' she says. 'That's what we all did – my mother, and my aunts and all my cousins. Once in the spring and once before Christmas. We washed all the walls and all the ceilings, too. And everything was turned out, every cupboard, every drawer and shelf; it would all be cleaned and put back. I still do all that.' No one else in the small community where this woman now lives cleans like she does, but she pays no heed. 'People say it isn't necessary here, but for me it is.'

In *Wasting Girls' Time* (1990), her critique of the teaching of home economics, Dena Attar is angered by the imposed routines and artificial labour of housework. She does not like how the women she sees are behaving. 'My own horror story', she writes, 'is of seeing, as I drove into a small town, a middle-aged woman sweeping the road beyond the pavement in front of her house.' I cannot share her horror in this sight. The woman sweeping the road was probably content enough; perhaps she came from a long line of sweepers, stretching all the way back to seventeenth-century Holland where women always cleaned the street outside their homes. Perhaps she is a distant relative of my own mother who is never happier than with a broom in her hand, who even used to sweep the rocky beach in front of the seaside home where she and my father lived. Perhaps the road-sweeper enjoyed busying herself out on a public street, passing the time of day with anyone walking by, and checking up on her neighbours.

To impose one's own horror or dismay on such a simple scene of sweeping is an exaggerated response. Many of us enjoy ordinary repetitive actions, day after day, season after season, small, sometimes unnecessary, but essentially decent routines. Many such routines are connected to cleaning, either cleaning ourselves, our possessions or our surroundings. Think of the small automatic acts of personal care: we clean our teeth, we polish our spectacles, we brush dirt off our sleeves, we take care of contact lenses. Then think of the small automatic acts of housecleaning: we wipe countertops, we clear tables, we mop up spills, we wash dishes and clothes. And some of us sweep.

The middle-aged woman caught sweeping the street is possibly a maddened housewife with time on her hands; a woman with such desperate standards to maintain that she had alienated all her family and was a fearsome legend in the neighbourhood. Possibly she *is* the hapless victim of decades of cruel and unnatural conditioning. But to give her the benefit of the doubt she may have been sweeping simply because she thought the street looked dirty, or because she liked sweeping, or perhaps because she wanted a breath of air and the chance to look up and down the street. Such sweeping has an honourable enough place in our lives, surely, even if we do not care to do it ourselves.

Many domestic critics and dispensers of household advice now choose to turn up their noses at committed sweepers and scrubbers; such single-minded, hands-on, old-fashioned work belies decades of propaganda about housework becoming easier. Don Aslett maintains that if you dirty your knees while cleaning, you are doing something wrong; with the right equipment, like long-handled brushes and mops and the appropriate cleaning solutions and above all the right attitude, such labour, he thinks, is unnecessary. Christine Frederick was saying more or less the same thing in the 1920s and even earlier; in her public lectures about efficient housekeeping she would drop to her hands and knees with a bucket and brush, address the men in the audience in a ringing voice, and ask, 'Does your wife really have to work this way?'

Probably not. With careful planning, the right tools, improved house design and well selected possessions, we can eliminate much of the hard work of cleaning. Yet still, such 'intelligent direction from within' is emphatically, even triumphantly, absent in the way most of us clean our homes. Despite a century and a half of domestic advice, despite the efforts of the home economics movement, despite the new and improved homes and equipment and supplies available to us, housecleaning, and our attitudes towards it, remains buoyantly illogical, while our homes for the most part remain passably clean. The luxury of the era in which we live is that most of us can clean as we please – sporadically, intensely, or indifferently – without risking life-threatening disease, without being reported to social services, without being ostracised by our neighbours.

The way we flap or scrub has a persistence, a stubborn and

enduring kind of glow, that deserves both recognition and celebration. The idiosyncrasies of cleaning have proven that they will not be squelched, and they are far too interesting to be ignored. Flappers and scrubbers alike, we deserve credit for how we get by, for how we muddle through and learn to live with the standards we have set, accepting either the hard labour or the inevitable mess as best we can.

NOTES ON SOURCES

Anyone curious about household cleanliness will probably find that this is a peculiarly awkward subject to research. Not only is material scattered and diffuse, it is also unkempt and unconsidered, the subject being so rarely granted serious attention. Household manuals and home economics books often lurk, unloved, in dark and messy corners of libraries and bookstores; good collections of women's magazines are not widely available; material on microfiche that relates to household concerns, while invaluable, is often incomplete, highly idiosyncratic, and strangely catalogued.

While most of my research took me, predictably, to a number of different libraries, ranging from the British Library to the periodicals library at Colindale to the Woodward Medical Library at the University of British Columbia, a significant portion of my research was anything but predictable. I have spent many dusty hours searching for magazines and manuals in used bookstores and, more entertainingly, in a number of different homes. Crawling through dim attics and damp garden sheds in search of long-forgotten copies of various publications was a rewarding diversion on many occasions. I was also fortunate to receive so much unexpected help with my research; both friends and strangers called me and sent unsolicited letters, faxes, articles and e-mail messages, providing many valuable leads and ideas.

The purpose of the following notes is to show the sources I have used, and to acknowledge my debts to other writers. Because this is not an academic history I have not burdened the book with intricately numbered line-by-line references. These notes are, rather, a kind of map to show the lines of research I followed, chapter by chapter, and to show the origin of quotations not already explained within the text.

Chapter 1: DENIAL AND DEFENCE

This chapter, like many others that follow, owes much to conversations and interviews with many different people. Comments and exchanges have sometimes been edited, but they have not been substantially changed.

The origins of the more pithy quotations in this chapter are: The term 'dusty drudgery' is coined by Betty Friedan, in *The Second Stage* (New York, Summit Books, 1981). Catharine Beecher's comment on 'vulgar people', from her *Treatise On Domestic Economy for The Use of Young Ladies at Home and at School*, is cited by Annegret S. Ogden in *The Great American Housewife: From Helpmate to Wage Earner, 1776–1986* (Westport, Connecticut and London, 1986). The condemnation of cleaning as the 'least desirable of labors' involving everything 'basest and foulest' was made by Charlotte Perkins Gilman in *Women and Economics: A Study of The Economic Relation Between Men and Women as a Factor in Social Evolution* (London, G.P. Putnam's Sons, 1905, first published 1898).

Mary Douglas's *Purity And Danger* (London, Pelican, 1970, first published 1966) has been a helpful and provocative source, transforming and challenging some of my ideas about dirt and cleanliness. See particularly Chapters One and Ten.

Maria Coffey's experiences are described in *A Boat in Our Baggage* (Little, Brown, 1994). Quentin Crisp's famous comments about cleanliness appear in his autobiography *The Naked Civil Servant* (London, Fontana, 1977, first published 1968).

The 'necessary' admonitions about cleaning are taken from Don Aslett's *Is There Life After Housework?* (Cincinnati, Ohio, 1981, revised and expanded 1992), from Ellen Richards's *The Cost of Cleanness* (New York, John Wiley and Sons, 1914) and from Augusta Moll Weiss's book of household management *Le Livre du Foyer* (Paris, 1906), quoted by Adrian Forty in *Objects of Desire* (London, Thames & Hudson, 1986).

Chapter 2: DIRTY WORK AFOOT

Details of all fiction quoted in this or subsequent chapters can be found in the fiction section of the bibliography.

Simone de Beauvoir's *The Second Sex* (New York, Vintage Books, 1974, first pub. 1952) has several splendid and fuming pages on housework, in the chapter tellingly entitled 'The Married Woman'. She is eminently quotable, and spitting mad.

The Diaries of Hannah Cullwick, Victorian Maidservant, edited by Liz Stanley (London, Virago, 1984) remains without any doubt one of the most important books I have read in the course of researching this book. Not only is it an invaluable historical source and richly informative about housecleaning, the personalities revealed within it, particularly that of Hannah, are unforgettable.

Chapter 3: MOTHERS AND MENTORS

The famous quotation 'Cleanliness is indeed next to godliness' origi-
nates from John Wesley's sermon 'On Dress'.

The I Hate to Housekeep Book (New York, Fawcett Crest, 1962) by
Peg Bracken is one of the most robustly sensible books on housework I
have read, if you can overlook her preoccupation with having a pitcher
of martinis at the ready when your husband returns from work.

Despite the sometimes overpowering sociological jargon, Kathryn Allen
Rabuzzi's *The Sacred and the Feminine: Towards a Theology of Housework*
(New York, Seabury Press, 1982) has been a most useful source in this
and in subsequent chapters. In a very different fashion Elizabeth Roberts's
Women and Families: An Oral History 1940–1970 (Oxford, Blackwell,
1995) and her earlier book *An Oral History of Working Class Women:
1890–1940* (1984) have been consistently helpful, citing as they do so
many interviews with women about their daily lives.

Chapter 4: HAPPY AND GLORIOUS

The opening poem appeared originally in the *Chicago Herald Tribune*
and was reprinted in the *American Kitchen Magazine* in September 1899.
'The Happy Housewife's Song' appears in the March 1899 edition of
the same magazine.

Sources for advertisements quoted in this chapter are: 'Wizard
Triangle Mop' ad is from the *Ladies' Home Journal*, March, 1914,
reprinted in Jennifer Scanlon's *Inarticulate Longings:* The Ladies' Home
Journal, *Gender, and the Promises of Consumer Culture* (New York,
Routledge, 1995). 'Masonite Presdwood Products' ad is from *Time*
magazine, 3 March 1941. 'Sapolio' ad is from the *Ladies' Home Journal*,
March 1913. (Sapolio ads were famous for their ditties about 'Spotless
Town'). 'O-Cedar Mop Polish' advertisement is from the *Ladies' Home
Journal*, December 1913.

For my understanding of the history of housework in Britain I owe
much to Caroline Davidson's magnificent book *A Woman's Work is
Never Done: A History of Housework in the British Isles 1650–1950*
(London, Chatto & Windus 1982). It is an immensely valuable reference
work full of meticulous detail. I have also drawn on Barbara Ehrenreich
and Deirdre English's study of domestic advice, *For Her Own Good:
150 Years of Experts' Advice to Women* (New York, Doubleday, 1978),
particularly the chapter 'Microbes and the Manufacture of Housework'.
For an understanding of American ideas of cleanliness, both household
and personal, Suellen Hoy's *Chasing Dirt: The American Pursuit of
Cleanliness* (New York and Oxford, Oxford University Press, 1995)
is an essential book to read. Her research is unequalled by any other
writer in this field; the book is both entertaining and erudite.

Catharine Beecher and Harriet Beecher Stowe, *The American Woman's Home* (New York, J.B. Ford and Co., 1869) is an intriguing and influential source. Later titles by Beecher containing material from this book and from her earlier *Treatise on Domestic Economy* (1841) include *Principles of Domestic Science* (New York, J.B. Ford and Co., 1870), *Miss Beecher's Housekeeper and Healthkeeper* (New York, Harper and Brothers, 1876).

Spon's Household Manual: A Treasury of Domestic Receipts and Guide for Home Management (London, E. and F.N. Spon, 1887) is a splendid example of late nineteenth century domestic advice. Ponderous, thorough, vast and unindexed, it pours forth information about drainage, diseases and laundry methods along with countless recipes for sauces to serve with fish and instructions on how to carve. *The House and Home: A Practical Book*, by Dr Lyman Abbott and L.W. Betts (New York, Charles Scribner's Sons, 1896) is an excellent example of the more down-to-earth American domestic advice of the 1890s.

Adrian Forty's *Objects of Desire* (op. cit.) has been exceptionally useful to me throughout writing this book. I have drawn repeatedly on his detailed critique of how advertising has moulded twentieth century attitudes, and on his analysis of how housework has changed and developed.

Chapter 5: MAIDS AND LADIES

Accounts of the work of Victorian maids are many and varied. Amongst others, I have found the following books helpful: Asa Briggs's *Victorian Things* (London, Penguin, 1990), Caroline Davidson's *A Woman's Work is Never Done* (op. cit.), Christina Hardyment's *From Mangle to Microwave* (Cambridge, Polity Press, 1988), Frank Huggett's *Life Below Stairs: Domestic Servants in England From Victorian Times* (London, John Murray, 1977), and most importantly, *The Diaries of Hannah Cullwick: Victorian Maidservant* (op. cit.).

Household advice books directly referred to or used in this chapter include the following: *Mrs Beeton's Book of Household Management* (London, Chancellor Press, 1982, first published 1861), *Common Sense for Housemaids* by 'A Lady' (London, T. Natchard, 2nd edition, 1853), *The Housemaid* (London, Houlston and Sons, undated), Florence Caddy's *Household Organization* (London, 1887) quoted in Briggs, *Victorian Things* (op. cit.), Florence Stanton's *The Practical Housekeeper and Cyclopedia of Domestic Economy* (Philadelphia, Keeler and Kirkpatrick, 1898), Robert Roberts's *Guide for Butlers And Household Staff* (Cambridge, Applewood Books, 1988, first published 1827), Mrs Mary Eliza Haweis's *The Art of Housekeeping* (London, Sampson Low and Co., 1889).

The quotation from *The Gentlewoman and Modern Life* comes from the 16 January 1926 edition. Rather like a cross between *Country Life* and *The Lady*, this magazine provides consistently rich pickings on the 'servant problem'.

The *Baltimore Sun* article describing happy domestic economists in training at the Maryland State Normal School was reprinted in the *American Kitchen Magazine* in August 1899.

Catharine Beecher's comments about the differences between Britain and America appear in *The American Woman's Home* (op. cit.). Susannah Moodie's servantless anguish in her new Canadian homeland is chronicled at length in *Roughing It in the Bush* (Toronto, McClelland and Stewart, 1962, first published in 1852).

The article 'I am Glad my Servant Left!' from the *Ladies' Home Journal*, November 1918, is quoted in *Objects of Desire* (op. cit.).

Lilly Grove (later Lady Frazer)'s *First Aid to the Servantless* (Cambridge, Heffer and Sons, 1913); Randal Philips's *The Servantless House* (London, Country Life, 1920); E.H. Begbie's *Life Without Servants, By a Survivor* (London, Mills & Boon, 1916); Kay Smallshaw's *How to Run Your House Without Help* (London, John Lehman, 1949) all bear witness to the slow-dawning reality of the one-person household.

Sources for advertisements quoted in this chapter are: 'I've just got a maid at fourpence a day!', Hoover ad in *Woman*, 5 June 1937; 'Come to dinner on Sunday', Dishmaster ad in *Good Housekeeping*, April 1956. The Eubank Sweeper ditty was recited to me by Christine Airey, who recalls her father quoting it from a 1920s advertisement. 'Now you've this, m'am, I'll stay', 1911 Vortex Suction Cleaner ad is reprinted in *From Mangle to Microwave* (op. cit.).

For more on the debatable point of whether there really was a maids-for-machinery exchange, see *Objects of Desire* (op. cit.).

Chapter 6: PUBLIC CONCERN

In this chapter I have drawn freely on Edwin Chadwick's *Report of the Sanitary Conditions and the Labouring Population of Great Britain* (Edinburgh, Edinburgh University Press, 1965, M.W. Flinn, ed., first published 1842) and on the 1865 report by the Citizens' Association of New York entitled *Sanitary Condition of the City* (New York, D. Appleton and Co., 1866, reprinted by Arno Press, 1970). I have also used Stephen Smith's report 'New York The Unclean', reprinted in *Medical America in the Nineteenth Century: Readings from the Literature* (Baltimore and London, Johns Hopkins Press, Gert H. Brieger, ed., 1972).

Dr Southwood Smith's account of the young woman in Rosemary Lane, and his declaration about 'A clean, fresh and well-ordered house', are quoted in Arthur Swinson's *The History of Public Health* (Exeter,

1965). See also Shirley Foster Murphy's *Our Homes and How to Make Them Healthy* (London, Cassell, 1883).

Florence Nightingale's *Notes on Nursing* (Edinburgh, London and New York, Churchill Livingstone, 1980, first published 1859), along with her other writings, became 'a bible to household, as well as hospital hygiene' according to Arthur Newsholme in *Fifty Years in Public Health* (London, George Allen and Unwin, 1935). This is evident in how often she is quoted in household manuals on matters of cleanliness and hygiene.

Sandra Gwyn's *The Private Capital: Ambition and Love in the Age of Macdonald and Laurier* (Toronto, McClelland and Stewart, 1984) is peppered with vivid domestic detail of the lives of early residents of Ottawa, showing the insanitary hell of life in new North American cities as well as any source I have read.

Frank Prochaska's account of philanthropic women at work in Britain's large cities, *Women and Philanthropy in 19th Century England* (Oxford, Clarendon Press, 1980), is a remarkable critical tribute to the charitable women who visited the poor and set about educating, feeding, cleaning up, whose work was important both in the evangelical and the public health movements.

Moralising about cleanliness was standard fare in household management books. *The Encyclopedia of Domestic Economy*, while somewhat more strident on the subject than most, is entirely typical of its kind. At the beginning of Chapter 6, 'Cleaning', of *A Woman's Work is Never Done* (op. cit.) Caroline Davidson has several pages describing attitudes towards household cleanliness, especially in the eighteenth and nineteenth centuries. Amongst many other anecdotes, she cites Francis Kilvert's reaction to the couple who lived in sin.

Chapter 7: GERMS

Both Mary Douglas in *Purity and Danger* (op. cit.) and Adrian Forty in *Objects of Desire* (op. cit.) make it clear how acceptance of the germ theory of disease transformed our perception of dirt. Suellen Hoy, in *Chasing Dirt* (op. cit.), provides an abundance of colourful detail about the public campaigns for improved cleanliness in America that arose in response to growing concern about germs.

Arthur Newsholme's two books describe how understanding grew concerning the spread of disease within the public health movement in Britain: *Fifty Years in Public Health* (1935), *The Last Thirty Years in Public Health* (London, George Allen and Unwin, 1936). For more on the slow acceptance of the germ theory in the medical and public health communities, see Phyllis Allen Richmond's article 'American attitudes toward the germ theory of disease (1860–1880)' in the *Journal of the*

History of Medicine, Vol. 9, 1954, and Lloyd G. Stevenson's 'Science Down the Drain', *Bulletin of the History of Medicine,* Vol. 29, 1955. Also see William Bulloch's *The History of Bacteriology* (London, 1938; reprinted 1960).

To appreciate how much emphasis has been put on the housewife's role in fighting germs, simply look through *any* household manual of the late 1890s or of the early decades of the twentieth century. The message is inescapable. Similarly in almost any women's magazines, where countless articles and advertisements stress the same germ-killing theme. I have found the *American Kitchen Magazine* from the late 1890s a particularly vivid source for this chapter, and the household manuals and advice books I have used include *Home Sanitation: A Manual for Housekeepers,* compiled by The Sanitary Science Club of the Association of Collegiate Alumnae (Boston, Ticknor and Co., 1887); Mrs Harriette Plunkett's *Women, Plumbers and Doctors; Or, Household Sanitation* (New York, D. Appleton, 1885); Mrs S.A. Barnett's *The Making of the Home: A Reading-Book of Domestic Economy* (London, Cassell and Co., undated); *Spon's Household Manual: A Treasury of Domestic Receipts and Guide For Home Management* (London, E. and F. N. Spon, 1887); J. Halpenny and Lillian Ireland's *How to be Healthy* (Toronto and Winnipeg, W.J. Gage and Co., 1911); Mary Pattison's *Principles of Domestic Engineering; Or the What, Why and How of a Home* (New York, Trow Press, 1915); Christine Frederick's *Household Engineering* (Chicago, American School of Home Economics, 1920, first edition 1915).

Sources for advertisements quoted in this chapter are: Platt's Chlorides 'Diphtheria' and 'Consumption' advertisements, both from the *American Kitchen Magazine* of March 1898; Hoover's 'germ-breeding dirt' ad from *Maclean's Magazine,* 15 November 1921; Croydon Electric Vacuum Cleaner ad from *Good Housekeeping,* March 1922; Eureka Vacuum Cleaner ad, reproduced in *Objects of Desire* (op. cit.) from the *Ladies' Home Journal,* October 1928. The Gold Dust washing powder claim of digging deep 'after every trace of germ life' appears in the *Ladies' Home Journal* of June 1913; the Sanitas wall covering ad is from the *Ladies' Home Journal* of September 1913, and the Sani-genic Polish Mop ad appears in the *Ladies' Home Journal* in October 1913. The Lysol 'haunted house' advertisement is reproduced in *Objects of Desire,* from the *Ladies' Home Journal* of April 1918.

Chapter 8: MOVERS AND SHAKERS

For the phrase 'high priestesses of the new religion . . .', see 'The Ethical Value of Domestic Science' by Anna Pollock, *American Kitchen*

Magazine, April 1899. For 'Science is her handmaiden . . .', see Lillian
W. Betts in 'The Principles of Housekeeping' in *The House and Home*
(1896). I have also drawn on the following articles: 'Foes in our own
household' by Anna Barrows, *American Kitchen Magazine*, January
1898; 'Woman's Point of View: Its Effect upon the Home' by Maude
Hanson Lacy, *American Kitchen Magazine*, April 1899; 'How can any
Woman become a Sanitarian' by Mrs Harriette M. Plunkett, *American
Kitchen Magazine*, February 1899.

Quotations from Ellen Richards are taken from *The Cost of Cleanness*
(New York, John Wiley and Sons, 1914), also from 'The Present Status of Domestic Economy and Home Economics', *American
Kitchen Magazine*, May 1899; 'Housekeeping in the Twentieth Century', *American Kitchen Magazine*, March 1900. This March 1900
edition of the magazine also carries a review quoting Richards's new
book *The Cost of Living as Modified by Sanitary Science*. See also
Anna Pollock's article cited above in which she quotes Richards. For
more on Richards, see *Chasing Dirt* (op. cit.), and *For Her Own Good*
(op. cit.).

Quotations from Christine Frederick are taken from *The New Housekeeping: Efficiency Studies in Home Management* (New York, Doubleday
Page and Co., 1913); from the four articles by Frederick that appeared in
the *Ladies' Home Journal* in 1912; from *Household Engineering* (op. cit.).
For more on Frederick, see Jennifer Scanlon's *Inarticulate Longings* (op.
cit.) and Witold Rybczynski's *Home: A Short History of an Idea* (New
York, Viking Penguin, 1986).

For more on Charlotte Perkins Gilman, see Dolores Hayden's
sympathetic and highly readable study of material feminism *The Grand
Domestic Revolution* (Cambridge and London, MIT Press, 1982). See
also Betty Friedan's assessment of material feminism in *The Second
Stage* (op. cit.). Quotations from Gilman come from her *Women and
Economics* (op. cit.).

'Housework-as-we-know-it': Barbara Ehrenreich's comments come
from her essay on housework, reprinted in an anthology of her work,
The Snarling Citizen (New York, Farrar Strauss & Giroux, 1995).

Chapter 9: IMPROVEMENT AND IRONY
I am indebted in this chapter to Forty, *Objects of Desire*, in which
he quotes LeCorbusier and the Electrical Development Association
manual of 1914. I have also drawn on Rybczynski, *Home: A Short
History of an Idea*; Briggs, *Victorian Things*; Roberts's *An Oral History
of Working Class Women: 1890–1940* (Oxford UK and Cambridge USA,
Blackwell, 1984) and *Women and Families: An Oral History 1940–1970*;
Davidson, *A Woman's Work Is Never Done*, Hardyment, *From Mangle*

to Microwave and *Home Comfort: A History of Domestic Arrangements* (in association with the National Trust) (Chicago, Academy Chicago Publishers, 1992).

Both in her *Notes on Nursing* (op. cit.) and *Notes on Hospitals* (London, John W. Parker, 1859), Florence Nightingale discusses absorbent surfaces. Quotations in this chapter come from both sources.

Sources for advertisements quoted in this chapter are: 'Electrical Hands that Wash Clothes', Western Electric Washer and Wringer ad, *Good Housekeeping*, August 1922; 'Swing through Spring Cleaning', Ajax ad, *Good Housekeeping*, April 1965, reprinted in *The Grand Domestic Revolution*; 'You set it and forget it', Bendix automatic washer ad, 1955, 'Which shall it be?', Hoover publicity photo in *The Electrician*, September 1927, 'Beauty must be Spotless', *Ladies' Home Journal*, May 1929, all reprinted in *Objects of Desire* (op. cit.).

Descriptions of laundry day are so numerous and so colourful it is hard to select amongst them. Almost every book of domestic advice chimes in with its own ideas and suggestions for boiling or soaking or rinsing or its own notions of what to add to the washtub; I have drawn on many such books, also on an article entitled 'Memories of My Mother-in-Law' from November 1974, reprinted in *The Spare Rib Reader*, Marsha Rowe, ed. (London, Penguin, 1982). Certainly the best summary of laundry techniques is found in Davidson's chapter on laundry in *A Woman's Work is Never Done* (op. cit.). The quotation from Kate Mary Edwards is taken from *A Woman's Work is Never Done. From Mangle to Microwave* (op. cit.).

Discussions of how labour-saving devices have failed to save much labour can be found in most of the books mentioned at the beginning of this section. See particularly the work of Forty, Hardyment, and Roberts. See also Ruth Schwartz Cowan's *More Work for Mother: The Ironies of Household Technology From the Open Hearth to The Microwave* (New York, Basic Books Inc., 1983), Betty Friedan's *The Feminine Mystique* (London, Victor Gollancz, 1963), *For Her Own Good* (op.cit.) The increased time spent doing laundry is discussed by Joann Vanek, 'Time Spent in Housework', *Scientific American*, November 1974, quoted in *For Her Own Good*.

Hazel Kyrk's comments about labour-saving devices are quoted in *Objects of Desire*. The quotation from the *Journal of Domestic Appliances* appears in *From Mangle to Microwave*.

Chapter 10: BUYERS AND SELLERS

In *Soft Soap, Hard Sell: American Hygiene in an Age of Advertisement* (Iowa State University Press, 1992), Vincent Vinikas provides a wealth of information about the American way of cleanliness. I have drawn on this book for its detailed information about the work of the Cleanliness Institute, and for quotations from the Institute's publications. The comment from Henry Ward Beecher also comes from Vinikas. Forty, in *Objects of Desire*, is most helpful on the development of advertising in the soap trade. See also Joseph E. Dispenza, *Advertising the American Woman* (Dayton, Ohio, Pflaum Publishers, c. 1975).

Unless otherwise indicated, quotations from Christine Frederick in this chapter come from *The New Housekeeping* (1913) and from *Selling Mrs Consumer* (New York, The Business Bourse, 1929). Jennifer Scanlon's *Inarticulate Longings* (op. cit.) has been a valuable source for her comments on Frederick.

Lillian Gilbreth was married to efficiency expert Frank Gilbreth, best remembered for his book about raising eleven children, *Cheaper by the Dozen* (Chicago, Dramatic Publishing Co., 1950). Mrs Gilbreth's books include *The Homemaker and Her Job* (New York and London, D. Appleton & Co., 1927) and (with others) *Management in the Home: Happier Living Through Saving Time and Energy* (New York, Dodd Mead, 1955).

The 1959 *Sales Management* article is quoted in *For Her Own Good* (op. cit.).

Betty Friedan's *The Second Stage* and *The Feminine Mystique* (ops. cit.) are both quoted in this chapter. *The Second Stage* contains a memorable denunciation of Christine Frederick and Lillian Gilbreth. For me, Friedan's assessment of the role of the housewife in *Feminine Mystique* still radiates its original energy and anger and carries great conviction. Post-feminist scholars tend to be less convinced, see for example the collection of essays edited by Jo Anne Meyerowitz, *Not June Cleaver: Women and Gender in Postwar America 1945–1960* (Philadelphia, Temple University Press, 1994), especially Meyerowitz's own article 'Beyond the Feminine Mystique'.

Many assessments of the conditioning of housewives and the nature of their work have been made. See particularly *More Work for Mother, From Mangle to Microwave* (ops. cit.) and Meg Luxton, *More Than a Labour of Love: Three Generations of Women's Work in the Home* (Toronto, Women's Press, 1980).

Sources for advertisements quoted in this chapter are: 'A job you can do in your evening gown!', Gillett's Lye ad from *Canadian Home Journal*, September 1942; 'Is only *half* your lavatory clean?', Harpic ad from *Good Housekeeping*, March 1939; 'The Hoover takes the dirt you can't see', Hoover ad from *Good Housekeeping*, May 1939; 'I thought my frock was clean . . .', Persil ad from *Good Housekeeping*, September 1945; 'Mummy says I can't play at your house . . .', Harpic ad from *Good Housekeeping*, March 1956; 'Healthful Cleanliness', Old Dutch ad from the *Ladies'*

Home Journal, July 1928 (reproduced in *Objects of Desire* (op. cit.)).

Mrs Beecher's advice about dishcloths is quoted by Molly Harrison in *The Kitchen in History* (Reading, Osprey, 1972). 'The Virtues of a Damp Cloth' appears in the *American Kitchen Magazine*, May 1899.

Chapter 11: SEARCH AND DESTROY

In *Chasing Dirt*, Suellen Hoy cites the comment that 'a pin-point of dust' held three thousand organisms. The 1898 ad for the International Health Exposition appears in the *American Kitchen Magazine*, September 1898. The Victoria *Daily Times* is quoted in the *American Kitchen Magazine*, October 1899. The article on disinfection in *Good Housekeeping* mentioning picture frames is in the June 1932 edition, entitled 'Elementary Truths about Home Disinfection'.

The advice on disinfection from the *Good Housekeeping Housekeeping Book* (New York, Good Housekeeping Institute, 1947) and from Lydia Ray Balderston's *Housewifery: A Textbook of Practical Housekeeping* (Chicago, J.B. Lippincott Co., 1936) is entirely typical of books from the first half of the twentieth century. The theme of disinfection could not be stressed enough.

'It's a social blessing' Cromessol Fragrant Disinfectant ad is from *Good Housekeeping*, June 1932.

This chapter draws on interviews with independent consultant in food and environmental hygiene Elizabeth Scott; with Joe Rubino of Reckitt and Colman, Zig Vaitusis of the Environmental Protection Agency, Karen McCullagh of Health Canada, Dean Cliver of the University of California at Davis, Sally Bloomfield of King's College, University of London, Sayed Sattar of the University of Ottawa. My thanks to them all.

Any discussion of household bacteria opens up a highly technical field of research that I have only touched on lightly. Elizabeth Scott's unpublished PhD thesis, 'Bacterial Contamination in the Domestic Environment and its Control by Disinfectants' (University of London, 1981), has been helpful in this chapter. Also, the following articles: Dean O. Cliver, 'The Once and Future Cutting Board Study', *Food Research Institute Newsletter*, University of Wisconsin-Madison, September 1994; see also Dean Cliver's two articles on cutting boards in the *Journal of Food Protection*, 57, January 1994; J.G. Davis, 'A bacteriological investigation of towels', *Medical Officer*, 111, 1970; J.G. Davis, J.R. Blake and C.M. Woodall, 'A survey of the hygienic condition of domestic dish-cloths and tea-towels, *Medical Officer*, 120, 1968; C.P. Gerba, C. Wallis, and J.L. Melnick, 'Microbiological hazards of household toilets: Droplet production and the fate of residual organisms', *Applied Micro-*

biology, 30, 1975; Elizabeth Scott, S.F. Bloomfield and C.G. Barlow, 'A Bacterial survey of hygiene in the home' in *Disinfectants: Their Use and Evaluation of Effectiveness*, Collins, Allwood, Bloomfield and Fox (eds.), in *Soc. Appl. Bact. Technical Series* 16.141., 1981; Elizabeth Scott and S.F. Bloomfield, 'Investigations of the effectiveness of detergent washing, drying and chemical disinfection on contamination of cleaning cloths', *Journal of Applied Bacteriology*, 68, 1990; Elizabeth Scott and S.F. Bloomfield, 'The survival and transfer of microbial contamination via cloth, hands and utensils', *Journal of Applied Bacteriology*, 68, 1990. See also Mary Roach's article, 'What I learned from Dr Clean', in *Health*, July/August 1994.

Chapter 12: PURGE AND PURIFY

Hans Zinsser is quoted in *The History of Public Health* (op. cit.). Quotations and details about 'the bugg' are from *A Woman's Work is Never Done, Common Sense for Housemaids, The Housemaid, The House and Home* (ops. cit.). The comments of Jane Carlyle are cited by Caroline Davidson in *A Woman's Work is Never Done*.

Mary Ellen's Clean House by Ms Pinkham with Dale Burg (New York, Crown Publishers, 1993) provides an entertaining treasury of ideas for repelling various pests: boric acid for roaches; cucumber and cinnamon for ants; bay leaves, cayenne and mint-flavoured gum for beetles; fresh basil for fruit flies; a herb called Costmary or Alacost for book lice.

The use of DDT is often cheerfully recommended in advice books from the middle of the twentieth century. *The Good Housekeeping Housekeeping Book* of 1947 devotes several pages to the uses of this lethal chemical, with only mild warnings not to spray near food, and to keep this useful substance away from children.

Sources for advertisements quoted in this chapter are: 'A Fly in the Milk . . .', Nestlé's Baby Food, 'The War on Flies', Tanglefoot Fly Paper, 'Swat the Dirt', Gold Dust Washing Powder, are all from the *Ladies' Home Journal*, July 1913; 'Watch the Dust in a Beam of Sunlight', B-B Dustless Mop, *Ladies' Home Journal*, March 1913; 'Dust Germs Travel like Bad News!', Lifebuoy Soap ad, *Woman*, 5 June 1937; '. . . germ-laden, nap-wearing grit', Hoover ad, *Macleans'* magazine, 15 November 1921.

For more about the 'Swat the Fly' campaign, see Suellen Hoy's *Chasing Dirt* (op. cit.). The article 'How to Vanquish the Dust Enemy' is from the *American Kitchen Magazine* of March 1899.

The magazine *Equinox* contains a splendid article on dust mites in its April 1992 edition, pp. 34–39, 'Of Mites and Men: Life in the Wee Wild Kingdom' by Kevin Scanlon.

Chapter 13: CLEAN FREAKS AND CRAZIES

The testimony of the woman suffering from OCD comes from *Obsessive-Compulsive Disorder: The Facts* by Padmal de Silva and Stanley Rachman (Oxford, Oxford University Press, 1992).

Both Simon Schama's *The Embarrassment of Riches* (London, Harper Collins, 1987) and Witold Rybczynski's *Home: A Short History of an Idea* (op. cit.) are helpful in their exploration of the phenomenon of Dutch cleanliness. The quotation from Pieter van Godewijck is taken from Schama's book, as are the comments of Nugent and other travellers, and the passage from *The Stock Exchange of Women*.

Chapter 14: LOOKING FOR MR CLEAN

The poetic tale of Bob is told in Bill Richardson's 'Queen of all the Dustballs', in the anthology of the same name (Vancouver, Polestar Press, 1992).

The Vanier Institute report is quoted in *The Globe and Mail*, 15 June 1996. The indignant 1787 letter, from a woman pen-named 'Nitidia', comes from Ogden, *The Great American Housewife*, citing a reprint in *American Museum*, Vol. 1, No. 1.

Somebody Has to Do It: Whose Work is Housework? by Penny Kome (Toronto, McClelland and Stewart, 1982) has a characteristically hostile drawing on the front cover, man and woman glowering, back to back.

'His and Her Housework' by Wendy Whitfield was originally published in *Spare Rib* in April 1976 and reprinted in the Spare Rib *Reader* (op. cit.).

Among the many discussions in the press of shared housework, see *Utne Reader*'s special edition devoted to the subject, March/April 1990, entitled 'The Sexual Politics of Housework'. For a classic example of mock-comic reaction to the subject, see the *National Enquirer*'s article about the 'Fusspot Hubby of America' contest, 21 June 1994.

Chapter 15: PROS AND CONS

Louise Rafkin's eye-opening article entitled 'Dirty Laundry' is from *The New York Times Magazine* of 28 January 1996.

Don Aslett mentions the matter of status both in *Is There Life After Housework* (op. cit.) and in *Cleaning Up for a Living* (White Hall, Virginia, Betterway Publications, 1988).

Contemporary advice books alluded to or quoted in this chapter are: Don Aslett, *Is There Life After Housework*; Moyra Bremner, *Supertips to Make Life Easy* (London, Hodder and Stoughton, 1983); Shirley Conran, *Superwoman* (London, Penguin, 1977); Hilary Davies, *The Complete Household Hints* (London, Fontana, 1989); Astrid Derfler, *How to Clean Almost Everything!* (Globe Communications, Mini Mag

Series, 1995); Sandra Felton, *The Messies Manual* (New Jersey, Fleming H. Revell, 1981); Cassandra Kent, *Which? Way to Clean It* (London, *Which?* Consumer Guide, 1994); *Mary Ellen's Clean House* (op. cit.); Mary Rose Quigg, *Household Hints* (London, Sunburst Books, 1995); Deniece Schofield, *Confessions of an Organized Homemaker* (Cincinnati, Betterway Books, 1994); Jana Weingarten (ed.), *Clean It!* (New York, Nelson Doubleday, 1983); Pam Young and Peggy Jones (The Slob Sisters), *Get Your Act Together* (New York, HarperCollins, 1993).

For an introduction to Martha Stewart's world view, see: *Special Occasions: The Best of Martha Stewart* (New York, Crown, 1995); *The Martha Stewart Cookbook* (New York, Crown, 1995); *Martha Stewart's Gardening* (New York, Crown 1991), or any of the over two dozen books currently credited to her.

Chapter 16: FLAPPERS AND SCRUBBERS

Ellen Richards's desire for 'intelligent direction from within' is quoted in *The Great American Housewife* (op. cit.). In *The Cost of Cleanness*, Richards uses the phrase 'pizen clean', contrasting it to 'just above diphtheria level' of cleanliness.

'First aid to the housewife' and the 'Weapons for the spring assault upon Dirt' appear in *The Delineator*, April 1915. Sarah J. Macleod speaks of 'the daily battle against dirt' in *The Housekeeper's Handbook of Cleaning* (New York, Harper and Brothers, 1915). Such pugilistic phrases are common fare in most advice books. 'The Housewife's Lament' is in *Reprints from SING OUT!, The Folksong Magazine* (New York, Oak Publishing, 1962).

Alice Munro's comments are quoted in *The New Yorker*, combined edition of 26 June/3 July 1995.

Anti-vinegar article: Frances Litwin, *The Globe and Mail*, 11 October 1995.

Christine Frederick crying out 'Does your wife really have to work this way?' is described by Scanlon in *Inarticulate Longings*.

SELECT BIBLIOGRAPHY

This bibliography is presented in three sections. First, the general works, then household advice and home economics books, and finally the fiction and poetry used. For details of all journals, magazines, periodicals and newspapers cited in the book, see the Notes on Sources.

GENERAL WORKS

Andre, Rae, *Homemakers: The Forgotten Workers*, Chicago, University of Chicago Press, 1981.

Attar, Dena, *Wasting Girls' Time: The History and Politics of Home Economics*, London, Virago, 1990.

Beddoe, Deirdre, *Back to Home and Duty: Women Between the Wars, 1918–1939*, London, Pandora, 1989.

Beer, William R., *Househusbands: Men and Housework in American Families*, New York, Praeger, 1983.

Bourke, Joanna, *Husbandry to Housewifery: Women, Economic Change, and Housework in Ireland 1890–1914*, Oxford, Clarendon Press, 1993.

Brieger, Gert H. (ed.), *Medical America in the Nineteenth Century: Readings from the Literature*, Baltimore and London, Johns Hopkins Press, 1972.

Briggs, Asa, *Victorian Things*, London, Penguin, 1990.

Cahn, Susan, *Industry of Devotion: The Transformation of Women's Work in England, 1500–1660*, New York, Columbia University Press, 1987.

Chadwick, Edwin, *Report on the Sanitary Condition of the Labouring Population of Great Britain*, M.W. Flinn (ed.), reprinted Edinburgh, Edinburgh University Press, 1965 (first published 1842).

Citizens' Association of New York, *Sanitary Condition of the City*, New York, reprinted Arno Press, 1970 (first published 1866).

Cohen, Daniel, *The Last Hundred Years: Household Technology*, New York, M. Evans and Co., 1982.

Crawford, Christina, *Mommie Dearest*, New York, Berkley Books, 1981 (first published 1978).

Crisp, Quentin, *The Naked Civil Servant*, London, Flamingo, 1988 (first published 1968).

Dale, Rodney and Gray, Joan, *Edwardian Inventions*, London, W.H. Allen, 1979.

Davidson, Caroline, *A Woman's Work is Never Done: A History of Housework in the British Isles 1650–1950*, London, Chatto & Windus, 1982.

de Beauvoir, Simone, *The Second Sex*, trans. Parshley, H. M., New York, Vintage Books, 1974 (first published 1952).

de Silva, Padmal, and Rachman, Stanley, *Obsessive Compulsive Disorder: The Facts*, Oxford, Oxford University Press, 1992.

Dispenza, Joseph E., *Advertising the American Woman*, Dayton, Ohio, Pflaum Publishers, 1975.

Douglas, Mary, *Purity and Danger*, London, Pelican, 1970 (first published 1966).

Dudden, F.E., *Serving Women: Household Service in Nineteenth Century America*, Middletown, Connecticut, Wesleyan University Press, 1983.

DuVall, Nell, *Domestic Technology: A Chronology of Developments*, Boston, G.K. Hall and Co., 1988.

Ehrenreich, Barbara and English, Deirdre, *For Her Own Good: 150 Years of Experts' Advice to Women*, New York, Doubleday, 1978.

Ehrenreich, Barbara, *The Snarling Citizen: Essays*, New York, Farrar, Strauss & Giroux, 1995.

Fairbanks, Carol and Haakenson, Bergine, *Writings of Farm Women 1840–1940: An Anthology*, New York and London, Garland Publishing, Inc., 1990.

Foa, Edna B., *Stop Obsessing! How to Overcome Your Obsessions and Compulsions*, New York, Bantam, 1991.

Forty, Adrian, *Objects of Desire*, London, Thames & Hudson, 1986.

Frederick, Christine, *Selling Mrs Consumer*, New York, The Business Bourse, 1929.

Friedan, Betty, *The Feminine Mystique*, London, Victor Gollancz, 1963 and New York, W.W. Norton, 1963.

Friedan, Betty, *The Second Stage*, New York, Summit Books, 1981.

Gilbreth, Lillian, *The Homemaker and Her Job*, New York and London, D. Appleton and Co., 1927.

Gilbreth, Lillian (with others), *Management in the Home: Happier Living Through Saving Time and Energy*, New York, Dodd Mead, 1955.

Gilman, Charlotte Perkins, *Women and Economics: A Study of the Economic Relation Between Men and Women as a Factor in Social Evolution*, London, G.P. Putnam's Sons, 1905 (first published 1898).

Green, Harvey (with Mary Ellen Perry), *The Light of the Home*, New York, Pantheon, 1983.

Gwyn, Sandra, *The Private Capital: Ambition and Love in the Age of Macdonald and Laurier*, Toronto, McClelland and Stewart, 1984.

Hardyment, Christina, *From Mangle to Microwave*, Cambridge, Polity Press, 1988.

Hardyment, Christina, *Home Comfort: A History of Domestic Arrangements*, in association with the National Trust, Chicago, Academy Chicago Publishers, 1992.

Harrison, M., *The Kitchen in History*, Reading, Osprey, 1972.

Hayden, Dolores, *The Grand Domestic Revolution*, Cambridge and London, M.I.T. Press, 1982.

Hoy, Suellen, *Chasing Dirt: The American Pursuit of Cleanliness*, New York and Oxford, Oxford University Press, 1995.

Huggett, Frank E., *Life Below Stairs: Domestic Servants in England from Victorian Times*, London, John Murray, 1977.

Kome, Penny, *Somebody Has to Do It: Whose Work is Housework?*, Toronto, McClelland and Stewart, 1982.

Lewis, Jane (ed.), *Labour and Love: Women's Experience of Home and Family 1850–1940*, Oxford, Blackwell, 1986.

Luxton, Meg, *More Than a Labour of Love: Three Generations of Women's Work in the Home*, Toronto, The Women's Press, 1980.

Lynd, Robert S. and Lynd, Helen Merrill, *Middletown: A Study in Contemporary American Culture*, New York, Harcourt Brace, 1929.

Matthews, Glenna, *Just a Housewife: The Rise and Fall of Domesticity in America*, New York and Oxford, Oxford University Press, 1987.

Meyerowitz, Jo Anne, *Not June Cleaver: Women and Gender in Postwar America 1945–1960*, Philadelphia, Temple University Press, 1994.

Moodie, Susanna, *Roughing It in the Bush*, Toronto, McClelland and Stewart, 1962 (first published 1852).

Newsholme, Arthur, *Fifty Years in Public Health*, London, George Allen and Unwin, 1935.

Newsholme, Arthur, *The Last Thirty Years in Public Health*, London, George Allen and Unwin, 1936.

Nightingale, Florence, *Notes on Hospitals*, London, Longman, 3rd edition, 1863 (first published 1859).

Nightingale, Florence, *Notes on Nursing: What It is and What It is Not*,

Edinburgh, London and New York, Churchill Livingstone, 1980 (first published 1859).

Nightingale, Florence, compiled by Lucy Ridgely Seymer, *Selected Writings of Florence Nightingale*, New York, Macmillan, 1954.

Nightingale, Florence, introduction by Sir Harry Verney, *Florence Nightingale at Harley Street: Her Report to the Governors of Her Nursing Home 1853–1854*, London, J.M. Dent and Sons, 1970.

Oakley, Ann, *The Sociology of Housework*, New York, Pantheon, 1974.

Oakley, Ann, *Woman's Work: The Housewife Past and Present*, New York, Pantheon, 1974.

Ogden, Annegret S., *The Great American Housewife: From Helpmate to Wage Earner 1776–1986*, *Contributions in Women's Studies*, Number 61, Westport and London, Greenwood Press, 1986.

Palmer, Phyllis, *Domesticity and Dirt: Housewives and Domestic Servants in the United States 1920–1945*, Philadelphia, Temple University Press, 1989.

Prochaska, F.K., *Women and Philanthropy in Nineteenth Century England*, Oxford, Clarendon Press, 1980.

Rabuzzi, Kathryn Allen, *The Sacred and the Feminine: Towards a Theology of Housework*, New York, Seabury Press, 1982.

Rendall, Jane, *Women in an Industrializing Society: England 1750–1880*, Oxford, Blackwell, 1991.

Roberts, Elizabeth, *Women and Families: An Oral History 1940–1970*, Oxford UK and Cambridge USA, Blackwell, 1995.

Roberts, Elizabeth, *An Oral History of Working Class Women: 1890–1940*, Oxford and New York, Blackwell, 1984.

Rowe, Marsha (ed.), *Spare Rib Reader*, London, Penguin, 1982.

Rybczynski, Witold, *Home: A Short History of an Idea*, New York, Viking Penguin, 1986.

Rybczynski, Witold, *Looking Around: A Journey Through Architecture*, Toronto, HarperCollins, 1992.

Scanlon, Jennifer, *Inarticulate Longings: The* Ladies' Home Journal, *Gender, and the Promises of Consumer Culture*, New York and London, Routledge, 1995.

Schama, Simon, *The Embarrassment of Riches*, London, HarperCollins, 1987.

Schwartz Cowan, Ruth, *More Work for Mother: The Ironies of Household Technology from the Open Hearth to the Microwave*, New York, Basic Books, 1983.

Scott, Elizabeth, *Bacterial Contamination in the Domestic Environment and its Control by Disinfectants*, unpublished PhD thesis, University of London, May 1981.

Scott, Elizabeth, Bloomfield, S.F., and Barlow, C.G., 'A Bacterial survey of hygiene in the home', in *Disinfectants: Their Use and Evaluation of Effectiveness*, Collins, Allwood, Bloomfield and Fox, eds., in *Soc. Appl. Bact. Technical Series* 16.141., 1981.

Reprints from SING OUT!, *The Folksong Magazine*, New York, Oak Publishing, 1962.

Stanley, Liz (ed.), *The Diaries of Hannah Cullwick, Victorian Maid-servant*, London, Virago, 1984.

Strasser, Susan, *Never Done: History of American Housework*, New York, Pantheon, 1982.

Swinson, Arthur, *The History of Public Health*, Exeter, Wheaton of Exeter, 1965.

Sykes, Ella C., *A Home-Help in Canada*, London, Smith Elder, 1913.

Thomas, Bob, *Joan Crawford: A Biography*, New York, Bantam Books, with Simon and Schuster, 1978.

Vinikas, Vincent, *Soft Soap, Hard Sell: American Hygiene in an Age of Advertisement*, Ames, Iowa State University Press, 1992.

Wolf, Naomi, *The Beauty Myth*, London, Vintage, 1991.

Wright, Gwendolyn, *Building the Dream: A Social History of Housing in America*, New York, Pantheon, 1981.

Wright, Lawrence, *Clean and Decent*, London, Routledge and Kegan Paul, 1960.

HOUSEHOLD ADVICE BOOKS AND HOME ECONOMICS BOOKS

Abbott, Dr Lyman, Betts, L.W., and others, *The House and Home, A Practical Book*, New York, Charles Scribner's Sons, 1896.

'A Lady', *Common Sense for Housemaids*, London, T. Natchard, 2nd edition, 1853.

'An Experienced Housewife', *Washing, Cleaning, and Removing Stains*, London, Griffith Farran and Co., 1892.

Anon, *The Domestic World: A Practical Guide*, by the Author of 'Enquire Within', New York, George Routledge and Sons, 1872.

Anon, *The Housemaid: Her Duties and How to Perform Them*, London, Houlston and Sons, undated.

Anon, *A New System of Practical Domestic Economy*, London, Henry Colburn and Co., 1823.

Aslett, Don and Browning, Mark, *Cleaning Up for a Living: Everything You Need to Know to Become a Successful Building Service Contractor*, White Hall, Virginia, Betterway Publications, Inc., 1988.

Aslett, Don, *Is There Life After Housework?*, Cincinnati, Ohio, Writers' Digest Books, third revised and expanded edition 1992 (first published 1981).

Balderston, Lydia Ray, *Housewifery: A Textbook of Practical House-keeping*, Chicago, J.B. Lippincott Co., 1936.

Barnett, Mrs S.A., *The Making of the Home: A Reading-Book of Domestic Economy*, London, Cassell and Co., undated.

Beecher, Catharine and Stowe, Harriet Beecher, *The American Woman's Home*, New York, J.B. Ford and Co., 1869.

Beecher, Catharine, *Letters to the People on Health and Happiness*, New York, Harper, 1855.

Beeton, Isabella, *Mrs Beeton's Book of Household Management*, first published 1859–61 in supplements to *The Englishwoman's Domestic Magazine*, enlarged edition published Chancellor Press, 1982.

Bracken, Peg, *The I Hate to Housekeep Book*, New York, Harcourt, Brace and World, Inc., 1962.

Bremner, Moyra, *Supertips to Make Life Easy*, London, Hodder & Stoughton, 1983.

Campbell, Helen, *Household Economics: A Course of Lectures in the School of Economics of the University of Wisconsin*, New York and London, G.P. Putnam's Sons, 1896.

Campbell, Jeff and The Clean Team, *Spring Cleaning*, New York, Dell Publishing, 1989.

Child, Lydia Maria, *The Frugal Housewife*, Boston, Carter Hendee and Babcock, 1831 (6th edition).

Conran, Shirley, *Superwoman*, London, Penguin, 1977 (first published 1975).

Consumer Reports Books, *How to Clean Practically Anything*, New York, Consumers' Union, 1986.

Davies, Hilary, *The Complete Household Hints*, London, Fontana, 1989.

Derfler, Astrid, *How to Clean Almost Everything!*, Globe Communications, Mini Mag Series, 1995.

Felton, Sandra, *The Messies Manual: The Procrastinator's Guide to Good Housekeeping*, New Jersey, Fleming H. Revell, 1981.

Foods, Nutrition, and Home Management Manual, Home Economics Circular No. 1, Government of the Province of British Columbia, Department of Education, Victoria, B.C., 1950.

Frederick, Christine, *The New Housekeeping; Efficiency Studies in Home Management*, New York, Doubleday, Page & Co., 1913.

Frederick, Christine, *Household Engineering; Scientific Management in the Home*, Chicago, American School of Home Economics, 1920 (first published 1915).

Green, Joey, *Polish Your Furniture with Panty Hose*, New York, Hyperion, 1995.

Habeeb, Virginia, Ladies' Home Journal *Art of Housekeeping*, New York, Simon and Schuster, 1973.

Hale, Sarah Josepha, *The Good Housekeeper; or The Way to Live Well and to be Well While We Live*, Boston, Weeks, Jordan and Company, 1840.

Halpenny, J. and Ireland, Lillian B., *How to be Healthy*, Toronto and Winnipeg, Gage and Company, 1911.

Haweis, Mary Eliza, *The Art of Housekeeping*, London, Sampson and Low, 1889.

All New Hints from Heloise: A Household Guide for the 90s, New York, Perigree Books, 1989.

Howard, Mrs B.C., *Fifty Years in a Maryland Kitchen*, Baltimore, Turnbull Brothers, 1873.

Kendall, Helen W. (ed.), *The* Good Housekeeping *Housekeeping Book*, New York, Good Housekeeping Institute, 1947.

Kent, Cassandra, Which? *Way to Clean It*, London, *Which?* Consumer Guide, 1994.

Macleod, Sarah J., *The Housekeeper's Handbook of Cleaning*, New York, Harper and Brothers, 1915.

New York Herald Tribune Home Institute, *America's Housekeeping Book*, New York, 1956 (first published 1941).

Pattison, Mary, *Principles of Domestic Engineering; or the What, Why and How of a Home*, New York, The Trow Press, 1915.

Peel, Mrs C.S., *The Art of Modern Housekeeping*, London, Warne and Co., 1935.

Peel, Mrs C.S., *How to Keep House*, London, Constable, 1902.

Peet, Louise Jenison and Sater, Lenore E., *Household Equipment*, New York, J. Wiley and Sons and London, Chapman and Hall, 1940.

Phillips, Barty, *The Complete Book of Cleaning*, London, Piatkus, 1990.

Pinkham, Mary Ellen with Dale Burg, *Mary Ellen's Clean House*, New York, Crown Publishers, 1993.

Plunkett, Harriette Merrick (Mrs H.M.), *Women, Plumbers and Doctors; Or, Household Sanitation*, New York, D. Appleton and Co., 1885.

Quigg, Mary Rose, *Household Hints*, London, Sunburst Books, 1995.

Richards, Ellen, *The Cost of Cleanness*, New York, John Wiley and Sons, 1914.

Roberts, Robert, *Roberts' Guide for Butlers and Household Staff*, Cambridge, Applewood Books, 1988 (first published 1827).

The Sanitary Science Club of the Association of Collegiate Alumnae, *Home Sanitation: A Manual for Housekeepers*, Boston, Ticknor and Co., 1887.

Schofield, Deniece, *Confessions of an Organized Homemaker*, Cincinnati, Betterway Books, 1994.

Spon's Household Manual: A Treasury of Domestic Receipts and Guide for Home Management, London, E. and F. N. Spon, 1887.

Stanton, Florence, *The Practical Housekeeper and Cyclopedia of Domestic Economy*, Philadelphia, Keeler and Kirkpatrick, 1898.

Webster, Thomas with Mrs Parkes, *The Encyclopedia of Domestic Economy*, London, Longman, Brown, Green and Longmans, 1844.

Weingarten, Jana (ed.), *Clean It!*, New York, Nelson Doubleday, 1983.

Whatman, Susanna, Thomas Balston (ed.), *The Housekeeping Book of Susanna Whatman, 1776–1800*, London, G. Bles, 1956.

Youmans, Edward L., *The Handbook of Household Science: A Popular Account of Heat, Light, Air, Aliment and Cleansing*, New York, D. Appleton and Co., 1857.

Young, Pam and Jones, Peggy (The Slob Sisters), *Get Your Act Together*, New York, HarperCollins, 1993.

FICTION AND POETRY

Atwood, Margaret, *Cat's Eye*, Toronto, McClelland and Stewart, 1988.

Beaton, M.C., *Death of a Perfect Wife*, Ivy Books, 1989.

Bennett, Arnold, *Riceyman Steps*, London, Cassell, 1959 (first edition 1923).

Brelis, Nancy, *The Mother Market*, New York and London, Harper & Row, 1966.

Brontë, Charlotte, *Jane Eyre*, London, Penguin, 1966 (first published 1847).

Churchill, Jill, *Grime and Punishment*, New York, Avon Books, 1992.

Davies, Robertson, *Fifth Business*, Signet, 1971 (first published 1970).

Davies, Robertson, *The Rebel Angels*, London, Allen Lane, 1981.

Duras, Marguerite, *The Lover*, New York, Perennial Library, 1986.

Gaskell, Mrs Ruth, *Cranford*, Oxford, Oxford University Press, 1972 (first published 1853).

Gibbons, Stella, *Cold Comfort Farm*, London, Penguin, 1938.

Hoeg, Peter, trans. Barbara Haveland, *The History of Danish Dreams*, London, Harvill Press, 1995.

Irwin, Robert, *The Limits of Vision*, London, Viking in association with Dedalus, 1986.

Kaufman, Sue, *Diary of a Mad Housewife*, New York, Random House, 1967.

Montgomery, L.M., *Anne of Avonlea*, Toronto, McGraw Hill and Ryerson, 1969 (first published 1909).

Montgomery, L.M., *Rainbow Valley*, Toronto, McClelland and Stewart, 1923.

Munro, Alice, *Friend of My Youth*, Toronto, McClelland and Stewart, 1990.

Neely, Barbara, *Blanche on the Lam*, New York, Penguin, 1992.

Norton, Mary, *Bedknobs and Broomsticks*, London, J.M. Dent and Sons, 1962 (first published in two parts 1945 and 1947).

Porter, Eleanor H., *Pollyanna*, Boston, The Page Company Publishers, 1921 (first published 1912).

Richardson, Bill, *Bachelor Brothers' Bed and Breakfast Pillow Book*, Vancouver and Toronto, Douglas and MacIntyre, 1995.

Richardson, Bill, *Queen of All the Dustballs*, Vancouver, Polestar Press, 1992.

Silsbe, Brenda, *The Bears We Know*, Toronto, Annick Press, 1989.

Summers, Judith, *I, Gloria Gold*, London, Collins, 1988.

Tey, Josephine, *The Franchise Affair*, New York, Macmillan, 1948.

Wells, H.G., *Kipps*, London, Colins, 1952 (first published 1905).

INDEX

285